Global Finance

Global Finance

New Thinking on Regulating
Speculative Capital Markets

EDITED BY

Walden Bello

Nicola Bullard

Kamal Malhotra

The University Press
DHAKA

Zed Books
LONDON AND NEW YORK

in association with

Focus on the Global South
BANGKOK

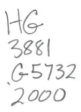

Global Finance: New Thinking on Regulating Speculative Capital Markets
was first published in 2000 by
Zed Books Ltd., 7 Cynthia Street, London N1 9JF, UK and
Room 400, 175 Fifth Avenue, New York, NY 10010, USA

in association with Focus on the Global South,
c/o CUSRI, Chulalongkorn University, Bangkok 10330, Thailand.

Published in Bangladesh, India and Pakistan by The University Press Ltd,
Red Crescent Building, 114 Motijheel C/A, PO Box 2611, Dhaka 1010, Bangladesh

Distributed in the USA exclusively by St Martin's Press, Inc.,
175 Fifth Avenue, New York, NY 10010, USA.

Cover design by Andrew Corbett
Designed and set in 10/12 pt Monotype Garamond
by Long House, Cumbria, UK
Printed and bound in Malaysia

ISBN   Hb 1 85649 791 7
       Pb 1 85649 792 5

Contents

Tables and Figures

Abbreviations and Acronyms

ACU	Asian Currency Units	HIPC	Highly Indebted Poor Countries
ADB	Asian Development Bank	IFC	International Finance Corporation
ACN	Africa Canada Network	IFI	International financial institutions
AMF	Asian Monetary Fund	IGGI	Intergovernmental Group on
APEC	Asia–Pacific Economic Cooperation		Indonesia
APMF	Asia Pacific Monetary Fund	IIA	International Investment Agreement
ASEAN	Association of Southeast Asian	ILO	International Labour Organization
	Nations	IMF	International Monetary Fund
ASEM	Asia–Europe Meeting	LBO	Leveraged buyout
ATTAC	Association pour la Taxation des	MAI	Multilateral Agreement on Investment
	Transactions financières pour l'Aide	MIB	Multinet International Bank
	aux Citoyens	MIT	Massachusetts Institute of Technology
BIBF	Bangkok International Banking	MITI	Ministry of International Trade and
	Facility		Industry (Japan)
BIS	Bank for International Settlements	MNC	Multinational corporation
CBI	Confederation of British Industry	NAFTA	North American Free Trade
CFD	Contract for differences (variety of		Agreement
	derivative foreign exchange instru-	NGO	Non-governmental organization
	ment)	NNGO	Northern NGO
CGI	Coordinating Group on Indonesia	ODA	Official Development Assistance
CHAPS	Clearing House Automated Payment	OECD	Organization for Economic
	System		Cooperation and Development
CLS	Continuous Linked Settlement	OPEC	Organization of Petroleum Exporting
CSC	Core Standards Commission		Countries
CSO	Civil society organization	OTC	Over-the-counter
CUTS	Consumer Unity and Trust Society	PVP	Payment-versus-payment settlement
DGAP	Development Group for Alternative	RMB	Renminbi (Chinese currency)
	Policies	RTGS	Real Time Gross Settlement
DVP	Delivery-versus-payment settlement	SANGOCO	South African Non-Governmental
ECHO	Exchange Clearing House		Organizations Coalition
	Organization	SAPRI	Structural Adjustment Participatory
ECOSOC	Econonomic and Social Committee		Review Initiative
	of the UN	SDR	Special Drawing Right
EFM	Efficient Market Hypothesis	SWIFT	Society for Worldwide Interbank
EMFM	Emerging Market Fund Manager		Financial Telecommunications
EMS	European Monetary System	UNCTAD	United Nations Conference on Trade
EMU	European Monetary Union		and Development
FAO	Food and Agriculture Organization	UNDP	United Nations Development
FDI	Foreign Direct Investment		Programme
FSF	Financial Stability Forum	US	United States
G7	Group of Seven Countries	USAID	United States Agency for
G8	Group of Eight Countries		International Development
G10	Group of Ten Countries	WDM	World Development Movement
G77	Group of 77 Countries	WFA	World Financial Authority
GATT	General Agreement on Tariffs and	WHO	World Health Organization
	Trade	WTO	World Trade Organization
GDP	Gross domestic product		

The Contributors

Walden Bello is Director of Focus on the Global South and heads its Global and Regional Paradigms programme. He is Professor of Sociology and Public Administration at the University of the Philippines in Manila and is the author of numerous books, including *The Siamese Tragedy: Development and Disintegration in Modern Thailand* (Zed Books, 1998), *Dragons in Distress* (Food First, 1990) and *Dark Victory: the United States, Structural Adjustment and Global Poverty* (Food First, 1994).

Manfred Bienefeld is an economist and currently a Professor at Canada's Carleton University's School of Public Administration. He has worked extensively in the field of international development, most recently focusing on the impact of globalization, and especially financial deregulation, on the ability of national societies to make economic, social and political policy choices.

Patrick Bond is Associate Professor at the University of the Witwatersrand Graduate School of Public and Development Management, and a research associate with the Alternative Information and Development Centre. He is the author of several books on Southern African political economy and works closely with social and labour movements in Johannesburg and Harare.

Robin Broad is Professor of International Development at the American University in Washington, DC. She is the co-author of *Plundering Paradise: the Struggle for the Environment in the Philippines* (University of California Press, 1993), and numerous articles on the global economy.

Nicola Bullard is Deputy Director of Focus on the Global South. She has worked extensively with non-government organisations and trade unions.

John Cavanagh is Director of the Washington-based Institute for Policy Studies. He is co-author of *A Field Guide to the Global Economy* (New Press, 2000) and nine other books on the global economy.

Zhiyuan Cui is Assistant Professor of Political Science at the Massachusetts Institute of Technology in the United States.

Sumangala Damodaran teaches at the Lady Shri Ram College for Women of the University of New Delhi, India.

Suzanne de Brunhoff is Honorary Research Director, Centre National de la Recherche Scientifique (CNRS), Paris, Member of the Scientific Committee of ATTAC, and author of many books and articles including *Marx and Money* (1976), *The State, Capital and Economic Policy* (1978), 'L'instabilité monétaire internationale' in F. Chesnais (ed.), *La Mondialisation financiaire* (1998).

Carlos Fortin is Deputy Secretary General of the United Nations Conference on Trade and Development. Before joining UNCTAD in 1990, he was Director of Programmes for the South Commission and a Fellow of the Institute of Development Studies, Sussex, 1974–88.

Susan George is an Associate Director of the Transnational Institute in Paris and currently President of l'Observatoire de le Mondialisation. Her numerous books include *Faith and Credit: the World Bank's Secular Empire* (with Fabrizio Sabelli, Penguin, 1994), *The Debt Boomerang* (Pluto, 1992) and, most recently, *The Lugano Report* (Pluto, 1999).

Bruno Jetin is Professor of Economics at the University of Paris Nord and a member of the scientific committee of ATTAC. He is the author of 'Controlling Capital Flows, It's Possible!' in *Against Market Dictatorship* (ATTAC) and 'The Tobin Tax: a First Step towards Capital Controls', in *Courrier de l'UNESCO.*

Martin Khor is Director of the Third World Network, based in Penang, Malaysia.

Richard Leaver teaches International Relations in the School of Political and International Studies at Flinders University, South Australia. He publishes widely within and between the fields of international political economy and strategic studies.

Kamal Malhotra was Co-Director of Focus on the Global South, 1994–9, and is currently a Senior Adviser in the Social Policy and Poverty Eradication Division of the United Nations Development Programme.

Marco Mezzera is a Research Associate with Focus on the Global South.

Rodney Schmidt is Programme Adviser to the International Development Research Centre (IDRC) economic and environment management project, based in Hanoi, Vietnam. He is also a Research Associate with the North–South Institute, Canada.

Leonard Seabrooke is researching a doctorate on financial internationalization in the late nineteenth and twentieth centuries in the School of Political and International Studies at Flinders University, South Australia. His book *The Victory of Dividends* will be published by Macmillan.

Jessica Woodroffe is Head of Campaigns at the World Development Movement, one of the UK's leading campaign groups on global economic issues. Prior to that she worked at Christian Aid and lectured in Development Studies at Manchester University.

Yu Yongding is Director of the Institute of World Economics and Politics at the Chinese Academy of Social Sciences, Beijing.

Introduction

> There is no limit to the damage that international finance can inflict on an economy.[1]

In July 1997 the Thai Government 'floated' the baht, setting in motion a series of international financial events which quickly become known as the Asian financial crisis. This crisis sent shock waves through the financial markets, which had become greedy for quick returns and high profits, lax in their risk assessment and increasingly blasé about the apparently unstoppable Asian tigers. When the bubble burst, this combination of greed and imprudence should have been fatal except that investors had an escape route. They bailed-out of the plunging market and scurried back to Wall Street and the City, safe in the knowledge that the International Monetary Fund's 'rescue package' would provide the Thai, Korean and Indonesian governments with enough liquidity to protect the investors from the 'discipline' of the market.

The crisis also sent shock waves through the international financial institutions, which had provided the ideological underpinning for the liberalization of the Asian 'tiger' economies. In the preceding decade, the IMF and the US preached the benefits of open capital accounts. The investors, in turn, insisted on the twin guarantees of unfettered financial mobility and pegged exchange rates, a policy combination designed to maximize benefits for capital while severely restricting national economic policy options. It was this policy combination, together with excessive speculative investment (creating asset bubbles) and poor quality investment decisions, that devastated the Asian economies. The cost, in terms of lost jobs and reduced working conditions, the collapse of local small and medium sized enterprises, increasing foreign domination of the financial and industrial sectors, and growing indebtedness, is still being counted.

The flow-on effect to Brazil and Russia also exposed the power of the financial markets to shape economic destinies. Both countries had aggressively pursued policies of financial liberalization, attracting billions in short-term investment. And both countries soon discovered that, once the markets started to get nervous, they had no way of stopping the currency speculators from attacking or of stemming the flow of billions of dollars back to the safe havens of the West. There were no capital controls, no standstill provisions and no penalties for investors: in short, there was no way of regulating and controlling capital.

But the Asian financial crisis also triggered a long-overdue debate in the media and in political and academic circles about the policies and functions of the International Monetary Fund, the effects of rapid financial liberalization, and the increasingly powerful and obscure world of international finance.

Proposals to review what became known as the 'international financial architecture' started to emerge, and were quickly taken up by the G7 who, for obvious reasons, wanted to control the terms of the debate. The G7 summit of 1998 in Birmingham launched a plan to review the 'international financial architecture' by establishing the G22 (comprising the G8, fourteen 'systemically significant' economies plus the BIS, the IMF, OECD and the World Bank). This, in turn, spun off a plethora of working groups which reported back to the G7, which then created the Financial Stability Forum (FSF) early in 1999, with a membership of national authorities from 'significant international financial centres' and international regulatory and supervisory authorities. The FSF is the most tangible result of the G7's concerns about the international financial architecture, yet its mandate is limited to 'promoting financial stability through enhanced information exchange and co-operation in financial supervision and surveillance.'

But even as the G7 tried to manage the international response in a conservative direction, the real world would not stand still. In Asia, reluctance by governments to continue to impose disastrous IMF programmes made the IMF tolerate policy u-turns that increased government spending. Malaysia, which defied the IMF, showed the wisdom of expansionary policy as a response to financial crisis as it embarked on a vigorous recovery.

Despite this, what started with a bang, threatens to end in a whimper. The 'international debate' has become 'privatized' and is little more than an in-house discussion between the G7, 'significant' financial centres, the finance industry and international institutions with the logical result that the 'reforms' of the international financial architecture have been designed primarily to discipline the debtors rather than the creditors.

At the national level, there have been some disparate efforts to review the international financial system, the most prominent so far being the US International Financial Institution Advisory Commission (producing the Meltzer Report). But overall, there has been no wide-ranging public debate and there is no international forum where all governments can meet on an equal footing to discuss how the international economy should be managed and by whom. Quite the opposite. The decisions are being made by the very people who caused the problems and who have not suffered the consequences: the banks and investors, the International Monetary Fund and the G7.

What's more, despite all this concerned talk, the fundamental cause of the financial crisis has not been addressed. Capital is still unencumbered and volatile, moving wherever and whenever its masters desire, whether in pursuit of maximum profits or fleeing to a safe harbour.

The debate about who manages the international economy, how it is managed, and in whose interests is far too important to be left to bankers, financiers and politicians. This is why we are publishing this book. It is the result of a ground-breaking conference held in Bangkok in March 1999 which brought together 340 activists and scholars from North and the South under the banner 'Economic Sovereignty in a Globalizing World: Creating People Centred Economics for the 21st Century.'

The views, ideas, analyses and proposals in this book are different from those coming out of the IMF and the BIS simply because their starting point is different. People-centred economics is profoundly different from profit-centred or market-centred or finance-centred economics. A people-centred approach seeks deliberately to consider how local, national and international economies can be managed in ways that would re-balance the growing (and dangerous) imbalances between capital and labour, between 'development' and the environment, and between the North and the South.

The authors have fascinatingly different approaches – technical, political, economic, sociological, legal, and in many cases a mix of all. What binds them together is an understanding that neo-liberal globalization is not a force of nature but a set of policies, or as Susan George puts it ' neoliberalism is not the natural human condition, it is not supernatural. It can be challenged and replaced because its own failures will require this.'[2] In different ways, each author is saying this, and going one step further by showing us that what has been made can be un-made, or made better.

The measures they propose, such as reform of the international financial institutions, national capital controls, financial transactions taxes and international bankruptcy procedures, are not an end in themselves. They are simply the first necessary steps to start shifting the balance in favour of people and nature.

We hope that this book will reinforce the urgency of the work to be done.

We would like to thank the hundreds of people who came to Bangkok from all over the world to create a memorable moment in March 1999, weaving a rich exchange of local and global, North and South, practical and theoretical. This book is merely a sample of that richness. In particular, we thank the authors who contributed their papers to this volume and who willingly helped finalize the texts, working closely with Geoff Keele who did a great job of copy-editing. The causes of international financial instability have not gone away, and we hope that this volume will contribute some new ideas to the critical debate about how and for whom the international economy is managed.

Walden Bello, Nicola Bullard and Kamal Malhotra

Notes

1   Akyuz, Yilmaz (2000) 'Causes and Sources of the Asian Financial Crisis,' paper presented at the Host Country Event: Symposium on Economic and Financial Recovery in Asia, UNCTAD X, Bangkok, 17 February 2000.'

2   George, Susan (2000) 'A Short History of Neoliberalism: 20 Years of Elite Economics and Emerging Opportunities for Structural Change,' in this volume, p. 27.

1

Notes on the Ascendancy and Regulation
Of Speculative Capital

WALDEN BELLO, KAMAL MALHOTRA,

NICOLA BULLARD AND MARCO MEZZERA

Since the outbreak of the Asian financial crisis in July 1997, people have been divided over the question of what was the fundamental cause of the debacle. To the powerful US Treasury Undersecretary Larry Summers, it was the witches' brew known as 'crony capitalism' that was 'at the heart of the crisis'.[1] Many of the policies that have been formulated to contain the crisis, in particular those of the International Monetary Fund (IMF) have stemmed from this line of thinking. As a result, the programmes for the troubled economies contain not only short-term monetary and fiscal measures but also stricter criteria for non-performing loans, more transparency in terms of ownership and accounting, tighter bankruptcy laws, prudential regulation, and the opening up of the financial sector to foreign investment.

Stanley Fischer, the American deputy director of the IMF, sums up the orthodoxy in this fashion: 'Making sure that the financial sector pursues sound lending policies, making sure that banks have strong and adequate capital and that lending is based on economic criteria and not political or other criteria – this is the key to resolving the crisis in Asian markets'.[2]

But another perspective, expressed very early on in the crisis, saw the focus on cleaning up domestic financial systems as flawed, stemming from a misdiagnosis of the problem.[3] One should be looking instead at the supply side of things, at the massive flow of foreign funds into these economies in the form of bank credit, speculative investment, and currency speculation. Indeed, the very same Stanley Fischer, in a statement at the World Bank-IMF Annual Meeting in Hong Kong in September 1997, appeared to put as much emphasis on the volatility of external capital as on the poor state of local financial regulation. '[M]arkets are not always right. Sometimes inflows are excessive, and sometimes they may be sustained too long. Markets tend to act fast, sometimes excessively.'[4] Another orthodox source, the *Economist*, had an equally surprising comment on the causes of the crisis:

The problem is that all financial markets, from currencies to shares, are subject to waves of excessive optimism followed by excessive pessimism. In theory, speculation should be stabilizing: to make money, investors need to buy when the price is low and sell when it is high. However, in a bubble it is profitable to buy even when the price of an asset is high, as long as it is expected to rise further – until the bubble bursts. An investor will lose money if he does not go with the crowd.[5]

From this perspective, 'the economic pain being imposed [by global capital markets] on the ex-tigers is out of all proportion to the policy errors of their governments'.[6]

With the crisis moving from East Asia to Russia and Brazil, the casino capitalism thesis became increasingly convincing. Even US Treasury Secretary Robert Rubin had to admit that part of the problem stemmed from volatile capital movements that were 'exacerbated by modern technology, which increases the size and speed of the mistakes people can make'.[7] At the IMF, Fischer was becoming even more critical of capital flows, saying that 'international capital flows are not only extremely volatile but also contagious, exhibiting the classic signs of financial panics'.[8] Thus, while international capital mobility 'is potentially beneficial for the world economy, including the emerging market and developing countries,' this potential 'can only be realized if the frequency and scale of capital account crises can be reduced'.[9] By early 1998, although the official posture at the US Federal Reserve, the Treasury and the Fund continued to be one of heaping the blame on Asian crony capitalism, the highest officials in these agencies could no longer avoid responding to demands for reforming the 'global financial architecture,' if only to preemptively kill expectations of substantive change.[10]

Finance Capital Unbound

For students of the global capitalist system, there is a world of difference between the international economy of the 1960s–1970s and that of the 1990s, and this largely lies in the way that, today, global finance 'drives' the world economy. Whether it was called the social democratic economy, the Keynesian economy, or state-assisted capitalism, the following features marked most key economies in both the North and the South during the 'Bretton Woods Era', which extended from 1945 to around the mid-1970s: a state-managed *modus vivendi* between labour and capital; limited capital flows; managed trade; dependence of corporations on retained earnings for investment; strong regulation of banks and the financial sector; fine-tuning of the economy through the use of monetary and fiscal mechanisms; and fixed exchange rates. Indeed, from today's perspective, the US economy under the Republican President Richard Nixon seems highly regulated.

In the financial sector, as a World Bank study noted, 'as recently as the early 1970s, few countries, whether industrial or developing, were without restrictions on capital movements'.[11] Capital controls were maintained in Europe well into the 1970s, with the IMF's Articles of Agreement (Article VI, Section 3) in fact allowing members 'to exercise such controls as are necessary to regulate international capital movements'.[12]

Several factors, however, led to the liberalization of financial flows. The first of these was the massive surplus dollars that found their way abroad in international transactions made by the US as it financed the war in Vietnam. These dollars formed the basis of the eurodollar or eurocurrency market centred in London, which the big commercial banks and other financial institutions tapped to expand their international and domestic activities – an option that freed them from their dependence on domestic retail banking.[13]

Second, eurocurrency liquidity was massively increased by the recycling of OPEC money following the oil price rises of the 1970s. Up to 1981, the Organization of Petroleum Exporting Countries piled up a total of $475 billion investable surplus, and $400 billion of this was placed in the industrial countries.[14] This was an enormous supply of funds seeking profitable investment, and pressure for greater global financial liberalization came from the big commercial banks, which sought to recycle a lot of these funds via cross-border lending. Much of this lending went into the Third World because of the relatively unattractive opportunities in the industrial North during that decade. This preference for offshore lending also contributed to greater domestic deregulation as governments 'started to make tax and other concessions to entice [capital] back onshore'.[15]

A third key factor was the rise to hegemony of the free-market, neoliberal ideology, which gathered steam with the increasing difficulties, including 'stagflation,' encountered by the Keynesian state. Liberalization of trade and liberalization of the capital account were the twin drives of neoliberalism's international programme. Capital account liberalization received a great boost upon Margaret Thatcher's assumption of power with her removal of foreign exchange controls in Britain. With London and Wall Street leading the way, the trinity of deregulation, globalization, and technological revolution combined to transform banking and finance.[16] 'Global bang' is what the *Financial Times* called the avalanche sweeping away geographic, institutional, and regulatory boundaries within the financial services industry. The technology of financial services has undergone an electronic revolution, and governments for reasons of necessity have scrapped, rewritten or ignored the rules that have controlled and compartmentalized the industry since the Depression of the 1930s. In most countries, banks, savings associations, insurance companies, and investment houses can now do what used to be each other's business. The lines of demarcation that distinguished the international eurocurrency markets from national, domestic financial markets have also become blurred or are disappearing altogether. Liberalization and globalization proceeded exponentially 'in a reflexive fashion', as Soros put it. 'Most regulations are national in scope, so the globalization of markets meant less regulation and vice versa.'[17]

Key Features of Finance Capitalism

The wave of liberalization in the 1980s exhibited several very important traits. First, having become overexposed in the Third World in the 1970s and early 1980s, the commercial banks pulled back from international lending. At the same time, other major players were emerging as key conduits for cross-border flows of capital. The most important of these were investment banks like Goldman Sachs and Merrill Lynch, mutual funds, pension funds, and hedge funds.

Related to this was a second development: the role of banks and conventional lending for raising funds was eclipsed by 'securitization', or the transfer of capital via the sale of stocks or bonds. Thus, while loans accounted for $59.4 billion of lending on international capital markets and securities for $36.2 billion in 1976–80, by 1993 the reverse was true, with securities accounting for $521.7 billion and loans for $136.7 billion.[18]

Third, there was an explosion of both old and new activities and instruments such as arbitrage and derivatives. Arbitrage is taking advantage of foreign exchange or interest-rate differentials to turn a profit, while trading in derivatives refers to buying and selling 'all the risk of an underlying asset without trading the asset itself'.[19] Derivatives are, as one description had it, 'very esoteric instruments, which are difficult to understand, monitor, or control'.[20] They include such instruments as futures, forward contracts, swaps, and options.

Fourth, a great many transactions, including those involving derivatives, were increasingly hard to monitor because they were made 'over the counter', that is, not via the floor of an exchange but among a few parties by telephone and computers. Monitoring was made all the more difficult by the fact that many of these transactions, such as forward contracts, were 'off-balance-sheet' or exchanges that were not reflected in the assets and liabilities statement, making the actual financial condition of many institutions very hard to ascertain.

Globalization's Volatile Engine

The globalization of finance meant that increasingly its dynamics serve as the engine of the global capitalist system. The increasingly unbalanced relationship of the financial sector to trade was captured in the fact, that by the mid-

1990s, the volume of transactions per day in foreign exchange markets came to over $1.2 trillion per day. This is equal to the value of world trade in goods and services in an entire quarter.[21]

With respect to production, the United Nations Conference on Trade and Development (UNCTAD) warned in its Trade and Development Report in 1991 of the 'ascendancy of finance over industry'.[22] One dimension of this was the increasing role of financial operators with access to large amounts of finance capital working with large stockholders in skewing the behaviour of corporations away from long-term growth, significant research-and-development spending, and limited returns on shares and towards short-term profitability and rising dividends. A spectacular manifestation of this trend was the LBO (leveraged buyout) phenomenon. Pioneered by Michael Milken of Drexel Burnham Lambert, firms with 'undervalued shares' were targeted for hostile takeovers, management was ousted, and firms were downsized and restructured for greater short-term profits and higher dividends.

While the LBO phenomenon has subsided, fund managers, especially those of increasingly assertive pension funds invested in key corporations, continue to greatly determine corporate performance. As the former chair of the US firm Contel saw it,

> In sum, we have a group of people with increasing control of the Fortune 500 who have no proven skills in management, no experience at selecting directors, no believable judgment in how much should be spent for research or marketing – in fact, no experience except that which they have accumulated controlling other people's money.[23]

Another dimension of the skewed finance–production relationship is perhaps even more worrying, and this is the fact that the ascendancy of finance may be related to the crisis of dwindling growth or even deflation which has increasingly overtaken the real sectors of the global economy. This crisis has its roots in over-capacity or under-consumption, which today marks global industries from automobiles to energy to capital goods.

One manifestation of this is the 40 per cent excess capacity of the manufacturing sector in China. Another is the 30 per cent over-capacity of the automobile industry worldwide,[24] which has been the spark behind the recent wave of mergers that saw, among other things, Chrysler hook up with Daimler Benz and Ford with Volvo. Another key measure indicating this trend is the so-called 'output gap' or the difference between actual output and output at full capacity. The estimated output gap of the European Union has been running, according to an estimate in the *Economist*, at 2 per cent of GDP for the last few years and is expected to widen. Japan's is a record 7 per cent. And the expected output gap globally is expected to be worse in 1999 than at any time since the Great Depression.[25]

Diminishing, if not vanishing, returns to key industries have led to capital being shifted from the real economy to squeezing 'value' out of the financial sector. The result is essentially a game of global arbitrage, where capital moves from one financial market to another seeking to turn a profit from the exploitation of the imperfections of globalized markets. This is done via arbitrage between interest-rate differentials, targeting gaps between nominal currency values and 'real' currency values, or short-selling in stocks, that is, borrowing shares to artificially inflate share values and then selling. Not surprisingly, volatility, being central to global finance, has become the driving force of the global capitalist system as a whole.

Since differences in exchange rates, interest rates and stock prices are much lower among the more integrated developed country markets, movements of capital from the North to the so-called 'Big Emerging Markets' of Asia, and other countries of the South, have been much more volatile. Thus while crises are endemic to the finance-driven global capitalist system, the crises of the last few years have been concentrated in the emerging markets.

The ascendancy of finance has been coupled with its almost absolute lack of regulation by the authorities. Deregulation at the national level has not been replaced by reregulation at the global level, so that, as Randall Kroszner has written,

> International financial transactions are carried out in a realm that is close to anarchy. Numerous committees and organizations attempt to coordinate domestic regulatory policies and negotiate international standards but they have no enforcement powers. The Cayman Islands and Bermuda offer not only beautiful beaches but also harbors that are safe from most financial regulation and international agreements.[26]

One of the reasons for this lack of regulation is finance capital's accumulation of tremendous political clout. Therefore, efforts to introduce even the minimum of regulation – such as the Tobin tax – have been opposed by a strong lobby in key Northern governments, especially in Washington. This lobby draws its power not only from interests but from the reigning free-market ideology, which it interprets (wrongly, according to free-trade proponent Jagdish Bhagwati) as applying not only to trade in goods but to capital mobility.[27]

Recently christened the 'Wall Street–Treasury Complex', the lobby has been personified by key people such as former Treasury Secretary Robert Rubin, who was one of the mainstays of the investment bank Goldman Sachs, and Federal Reserve Board Chairman Alan Greenspan, who ran a consulting firm in Wall Street for 30 years.[28] While finance capital was liberated from the straitjacket of the Keynesian economy by the Republican administrations of Ronald Reagan and George Bush, it has been under the Democratic administration of Bill Clinton that financial interests have become paramount in the foreign economic policy of the United States. As the *New York Times* put it, 'Clinton and Rubin ... took the American passion for free trade and carried it further to press for freer movement of capital. Along the way they pushed harder to win opportunities for American banks, brokerages, and insurance companies'.[29]

Finance Capital and the South

The integration of the South into global capital markets began, of course, in the nineteenth century, but the process was slowed down considerably by the Great Depression and the Second World War. Between the war and the 1970s the main conduits of capital flowing into the South were direct foreign investment and multilateral assistance provided by the World Bank, the IMF and the regional development banks. Integration speeded up, however, with the massive recycling of OPEC money to the South following the oil price hikes of the 1970s.

The changing pattern of capital flows was illustrated sharply in the case of Latin America. Official sources supplied 59.8 per cent of the average annual external resource inflow in 1961–5, then dropped to 40.4 per cent in 1966–70, 25.3 per cent in 1971–5, and to only 12.1 per cent in 1976–8. Foreign investment as a percentage of foreign capital inflow likewise dropped from 33.7 per cent in the second half of the 1960s to 15.9 per cent in the second half of the 1970s. On the other hand, the share of foreign bank and bond finance rose sharply from 7.2 per cent in the early 1960s to 46 per cent in the early 1970s, and to 64.6 per cent in the late 1970s.[30]

Just as 'irresponsible' Asian banks and companies are now scapegoated for the East Asian crisis, so were 'profligate' governments the whipping posts of the crisis that broke out in 1982, which led to Latin America losing a decade of growth. But then as now, the capital flow to the South was driven more by supply than demand. The hundreds of billions of dollars deposited in international commercial bank coffers by the OPEC countries was a massive amount seeking profitable investment, and the rationale for this movement of capital was provided by Citibank Chairman Walter Wriston, who formulated the famous principle of sovereign lending: 'countries don't go bankrupt'.[31]

The supply-driven dynamic of commercial bank lending is underlined by Lissakers in her comprehensive account of the process. Commercial bank lending to developing country governments had stopped, for all intents and purposes, during the Great Depression. But,

[a]wash in oil money, with credit demand depressed in the home market, commercial banks resumed large-scale lending to developing countries and their governments. For US banks, international borrowing and lending was transformed from a limited adjunct of domestic business to an activity that dominated the

balance sheet. While their domestic businesses languished, international activities exploded, accounting for 95 per cent of the earnings growth of the nation's ten largest banks during the first half of the decade and probably more than half their total earnings in the late 1970s.[32]

While long lines of New York bank senior managers trooped to the suites of developing country finance ministers during the annual World Bank–IMF meetings in Washington, their field representatives in those countries 'competed for the nod from the same cluster of state corporations and agencies'.[33]

On the eve of the Mexican default in 1982, some $400 billion in OPEC money had found its way to the coffers of Northern banks, and the bulk of it had been recycled to Third World and Eastern European governments, who by the alchemy of finance, collectively owed the banks some $500 billion.

The IMF and World Bank structural adjustment programmes that were supposed to discipline profligate governments paradoxically made the developing countries even more open to capital inflows from the Northern financial centres that had brought about the crash in the first place. For while tight fiscal and monetary policies were imposed on the state, foreign exchange controls were lifted and capital account liberalization was promoted with the objective of freeing the market from the straitjacket of state regulation. The upshot was a dramatically reduced role for the state as a mediator between the domestic private sector and foreign capital.

The continuing swift accumulation of finance capital and the limited absorptive capacity in the North continued to be a problem in the early 1980s, when US Federal Reserve Chairman Paul Volcker's anti-inflationary high-interest rate policy dampened economic activity, not only in the US, but in the rest of the now financially integrated Group of Seven economies as well. That the ravaged state of the real economies in the Third World was not perceived as a critical barrier to further capital flows by Northern financial interests emerged clearly when (after squeezing nearly $220 billion from the region in 1982–90) suddenly and in a spectacular fashion, to use Duncan Green's characterization, international capital markets started pouring money into Latin America. After years of net outflows, net capital inflow into the region came to $7 billion in 1991, then rose to $31 billion in 1992 and $32 billion in 1993. [34]

Mexico, in particular, was a star performer, attracting $4.5 billion in foreign investment in 1990, $15 billion in 1991, $18 billion in 1992, and $32 billion in 1993.[35] Yet, to show the lack of correlation between the state of the real economy and the attractiveness of the financial sector, GDP declined from 4.5 per cent in 1990 to 3.6 per cent in 1991, to 2.8 per cent in 1992, to 0.4 per cent in 1993. Indeed, when broken down into categories of foreign investment, the figures indicate the inverse relationship between the attractiveness of the financial sector and that of the real economy. As Timothy Kessler points out, 'The vast majority of foreign capital was invested in Mexico for the unambiguous purpose of extracting financial rents, while a decreasing proportion went to direct investment'.[36]

If Mexico and Latin America suddenly became the darlings of foreign investors in the early 1990s, the love match was made in no small part by the IMF and the World Bank. As noted above, both institutions pushed capital account liberalization, motivated by the desire to encourage the creation of other conduits of capital to replace the sovereign lending channel which had proved so dangerous. The Bank, in particular, came to the conclusion that portfolio investing might be a better way of channelling capital into the developing countries. This led to the public-relations transformation of Latin American countries from economies deep in debt into 'big emerging markets' – a phrase coined by a World Bank staffer.[37]

Beyond this, the Bank, via its private-investment arm, the International Finance Corporation (IFC), set up closed-end country funds in a selected number of countries, and then, in 1986, put up seed money, according to Justin Fox, for the first 'emerging markets' fund.[38] The Capital Group, a money management giant based in Los Angeles, ran this fund. The fund did 'exceptionally well', with total returns to investors of 24 per cent in 1987, 42 per cent in 1988, and 94 per cent in 1989. 'Those numbers,' according to Fox, 'drew in more and more money managers, which set the stage for the mad rush of 1993 ... '.[39]

When one realizes that in the advanced economies, 'a humdrum 15 per cent a year return is all one can realistically afford to achieve',[40] the mad rush was understandable. Or, as the Asian Development Bank put it, 'the declining returns in the stock markets of industrial countries and the low real interest rates compelled investors to seek higher returns on their capital elsewhere'.[41] In any event, 1993 saw a rush of foreign capital to the Third World more impetuous than any since the late 1970s (though instead of being loans to governments, the capital this time came in as credit to the private sector or as purchases of stocks and bonds). The dynamics of the lending bonanza of 1993–4 were brilliantly captured by Bernice Cohen in her 1997 book *The Edge of Chaos*:

> The herd instinct of the mighty US mutual fund managers came to the world's attention during the massive exodus of investment dollars that was poured into the emerging markets between 1993 and December 1994. This bubble was borne along a tidal wave of loose money, searching restlessly for a super-profitable home. A watershed was reached in September 1993 when some Morgan Stanley analysts visited China, with a group of fund managers, who collectively managed $400 billion of clients' funds. After this visit, the positive views of the world-renowned Barton Biggs, chief investment strategist at Morgan Stanley and

Company at that time sent Southeast Asian shares soaring. The Hong Kong Hang Seng index rose 20 per cent in five weeks. When Morgan Stanley had a change of heart shortly after this rise, these same markets were sent plunging, as investors *en masse*, rushed to respond to the updated advice. Quixotically, and in market-shaking quantities, they withdrew their cash. In 1993, almost $40 billion went into stock markets outside the industrialized world. Around $106 billion of emerging market shares were held by foreigners at the end of the year. During December 1993 and January 1994, net new sales of American mutual funds investing overseas totaled $11.5 billion. The proportion of money that found its way into Latin America during the second quarter of 1994 rose to 77 per cent, up from 14 per cent in the first three months of the year. Seven years earlier, the figure was only $2.4 billion. In five years, from 1988 to 1993, emerging market share prices had doubled. In 1992, the average return to investors was 67 per cent, compared to a pedestrian level of around 15 per cent from the funds held in the shares of the major industrial countries.[42]

Speculative Crisis: Two Case Studies

Crises are endemic to this system of global finance, and they have their root in the volatility of the movements of capital seeking to exploit evanescent differences in interest rates, currency values and stock prices. Since the early 1970s, there have been at least eight crises triggered by speculative capital movements, and these have been concentrated in the emerging markets: the Southern Cone financial crisis in the late 1970s; the Third World debt crisis of the early 1980s; the savings and loan debacle in the US in the late 1980s; the so-called ERM (Exchange Rate Mechanism of the European Monetary System) crisis in 1992; the Mexican crisis of 1994–5 and its follow-on crisis in Latin America (the so-called 'Tequila Effect'); the East Asian crisis of 1997; the Russian meltdown of 1998; and the collapse of the *real* in Brazil and its impact on the rest of Latin America.[43]

A close study of two cases, the Mexican and East Asian crises, reveals some common dynamics of what UNCTAD has called the 'Post-Bretton Woods Financial Crisis'.

Mexico: a Supply-Driven Crisis

There are two striking things about the Mexican example. First was the rapid and massive build-up in foreign capital inflows into the region, with the country receiving $91 billion in just four years, a figure that amounted to 20 per cent of all net capital inflows to developing countries.[44] Second, this surge was mainly a supply-driven phenomenon, with little basis in the actual prospects of the real economy, which experienced a decline in the GDP growth rate during the financial boom years, a continuing high unemployment rate that stood at around 40 per cent of the work force, and poverty that engulfed around half of the population – all of which were a legacy of the structural adjustment imposed on the economy after the debt debacle of the 1980s.[45] This lack of correlation between the sorry prospects for the real economy and the rosy view of investors was captured in the World Bank's observation that the 'rapidity and magnitude of the resurgence of private flows [to Mexico and other highly indebted countries] in the 1990s surprised many observers', demonstrating that 'the spate of commercial lending in the 1970s, however misguided, made the developing countries an object of continuing interest for international financiers'.[46]

But the process was not, of course, only supply-driven, since the country's technocrats formulated financial measures that would attract the money into the country, although it is hard to claim that these measures were purely domestic in inspiration. Interest rates were maintained at a much higher rate than in the Northern money centres, so that an investor borrowing in New York's money market 'could capture the spread between returns of five to six per cent in America and twelve to 14 per cent in Mexico'.[47] Informally fixing the rate of exchange between the dollar and the peso via government buying and selling in the currency market was a policy calculated to assure foreign investors that they would not be blindsided by devaluations that would reduce the value of their investments.

As Jeffrey Sachs has pointed out, the role of external actors in promoting this policy was not insignificant: financial authorities 'fell under the influence of money managers who championed the cause of pegged exchange rates' by arguing that 'only a stable exchange rate could underpin the confidence needed for large capital inflows'.[48] Finally, there was the policy of financial and capital account liberalization, and here again, the role of external institutions was central. The structural adjustment programmes imposed by the IMF and the World Bank in the 1980s targeted liberalization not only of the trade account but also of the capital account. It was the country's entry into the Organization for Economic Cooperation and Development (OECD) in 1993 that was decisive, however, for this required the full elimination of all restrictions on capital movements.[49]

These moves were especially significant, since a great deal of foreign investment was channelled into the purchase of government securities. Such sales had been restricted prior to 1990, but the IMF and OECD liberalization made them wide-open targets for foreign speculation.[50] *Cetes* were peso-denominated Federal Treasury Certificates and *Tesebonos* were dollar-denominated Treasury Bonds. On the eve of the financial crisis, *Cetes* issues totalled $7.5 billion and *Tesebonos* came to $17.8 billion.[51] In 1993 foreign investors possessed 60 per cent of short-term *Cetes*, 87 per cent of *Tesebonos*, and 57 per cent of inflation-indexed bonds or *ajustabonos*.[52] So popular were these government debt instruments that their purchase by foreigners grew by 756 per cent between 1991 and August 1994.[53]

The inflow of such a huge mass of foreign capital into the country caused a real appreciation of the currency, resulting in Mexico's exports becoming less competitive in world markets. It also resulted in a consumption boom that drove up the country's imports, since the deindustrialization that had occurred in the country as a consequence of structural adjustment ensured that much of domestic demand for light and durable consumer goods could no longer be met by domestic industry. The upshot was a current account deficit that stood at 8–8.5 per cent of GDP by 1994, a development that began to get foreign investors worried. This underlined the paradox of the situation brought about by capital inflows. As Ariel Buira notes,

> As inflows eventually translate into a growing current account deficit, the very same investors who were eager to bring in their capital will look at the size of the deficit and become nervous. Investors may overreact to any unfavorable develop-ment by withdrawing their funds and in this way may contribute to the emergence of a payments crisis. Thus, as capital inflows – a symbol of success – give rise to a current account deficit, ironically, they become the country's weakness.[54]

Worried about an unstable macroeconomic situation to which they them-selves had collectively contributed, individual investors began pulling out in 1994. The yawning current account gap served as another source of instability as currency speculators, local investors, and foreign investors, expecting or betting on a government 'correction' (that is, devaluation) that would reduce the deficit, subjected the peso to a massive assault that began in mid-November 1994 and subsided only when the peso was floated in late December and promptly lost half of its nominal value. This combined attack by speculators and panicky investors seeking to change their pesos for dollars and get the hell out before the expected devaluation was simply too strong for the government to repel. On 21 December, the Central Bank spent $4.5 billion of its already depleted reserves in a futile defence of the peso.[55] A massive devaluation was inevitable, and Mexico was plunged into its second financial crisis in 13 years.

Southeast Asia: Volatility Sinks a Development Model

In the case of Southeast Asia, the surge in the inflow of portfolio investment and short-term private bank credit in the early 1990s followed an earlier surge of foreign direct investment beginning in the mid-1980s. This sudden inflow of investment lifted the region clear of the recession of the mid-1980s and the effects of the pull-back of commercial bank lending to the Third World following the debt crisis of the early 1980s. A significant portion of these inflows came from Japan as a direct consequence of the Plaza Accord of 1985, which drastically revalued the yen relative to the dollar and other major currencies, forcing Japanese manufacturers to relocate a significant part of their labour-intensive operations out of Japan into Southeast Asia.

Between 1985 and 1990, some $15 billion worth of Japanese direct investment flowed into the region in one of the largest and swiftest movements of capital to the developing world in recent history.[56] Japanese direct investment brought with it billions of dollars more in Japanese bilateral aid and bank loans, and provoked an ancillary flow of billions of dollars in foreign direct investment from the first-generation newly industrializing economies of Taiwan, Hong Kong and South Korea.

It was this prosperity that attracted portfolio investors and banks. With the collapse of Mexico in 1995, fund managers, after a moment of uncertainty that saw them briefly cut their exposure in Asia, channelled the biggest chunk of their investments and loans for developing country markets to the East Asian region. The interests of speculative investors seeking better climes than the then low-yield capital markets of the North and the overly risky markets of Latin America coincided with the search of Asian technocrats for alternative sources of foreign capital to take up the slack caused by the levelling off of Japanese capital by the early 1990s.

With the advice of fund managers and the IMF, Thailand followed Mexico's example and formulated a three-pronged strategy: liberalizing the capital account and the financial sector as a whole; maintaining high domestic interest rates relative to interest rates in Northern money centres in order to suck in portfolio investment and bank capital; and fixing the local currency at a stable rate relative to the dollar in order to insure foreign investors against currency risk.

Portfolio flows to both equities and bonds rose, and so did credit from international banks to Thai financial institutions and enterprises, which sought to take advantage of the large differential between the relatively low rates at which they borrowed from Northern money-centre banks and the high rates at which they would relend the funds to local borrowers. The dynamics of this activity were described succinctly by one investment analyst:

> Since 1987 the Thai authorities have kept their currency locked to the US dollar in a band of [baht] 25–26 while maintaining domestic rates 500–600 points higher than US rates and keeping their borders open to capital flows. Thai borrowers naturally gravitated towards US dollar borrowings and the commercial banks accommodated them, with the result that the Thai banks have a foreign liability position equivalent to 20 per cent of GDP. The borrowers converted to baht with the Bank of Thailand the ultimate purchaser of their foreign currency. Fuelled by cheap easy money, the Thai economy grew rapidly, inflation rose, and the current account deficit ballooned.[57]

In the short term, however, the formula was wildly successful in attracting foreign capital. Net portfolio investment came to around $24 billion in the three years before the crisis broke in 1997, while at least another $50 billion entered in the form of loans to Thai banks and enterprises. These results encouraged finance ministries and central banks in Kuala Lumpur, Jakarta, and Manila to copy the Thai formula, with equally spectacular results. According to Washington's Institute of International Finance, net private capital flows to Indonesia, Malaysia, the Philippines, Thailand and Korea shot up from $37.9 billion in 1994 to $79.2 billion in 1995 to $97.1 billion in 1996.[58]

In retrospect, however, Thailand illustrated the fatal flaws of a development model based on huge and rapid infusions of foreign capital. First, just as in Mexico, there was a basic contradiction between encouraging foreign capital inflows and keeping an exchange rate that would make the country's exports competitive in world markets. The former demanded a currency pegged to the dollar at a stable order in order to draw in foreign investors. With the dollar appreciating in 1995 and 1996, so did the pegged Southeast Asian currencies – and so did the international prices of Southeast Asian exports. This process cut deeply into the competitiveness of economies that had staked their growth on ever-increasing exports.

The second problem was that the bulk of the funds coming in consisted of speculative capital seeking high and quick returns. With little regulation of its movements by governments that had bought into the IMF's *laissez-faire* ideology and had little experience in handling such massive inflows, foreign capital did not gravitate to the domestic manufacturing sector or to agriculture, for these were considered low-yield sectors that would, moreover, provide a decent rate of return only after a long gestation period of huge blocks of capital. The high-yield sectors with a quick turnaround time to which foreign investment and foreign credit inevitably gravitated to were the stock market, consumer financing and, in particular, real-estate development. In Bangkok, at the height of the real estate boom in the early 1990s, land values were higher than in urban California.

Not surprisingly, a glut in real estate developed quite rapidly, with Bangkok leading the way with $20 billion worth of new commercial and residential space unsold by 1996. Foreign banks had competed to push loans on to Thai banks, finance companies, and enterprises in the boom years of the early 1990s. In 1996, it began to sink in that their borrowers were loaded with non-performing loans.

At the same time, alarm bells began to be sounded by the flat export growth rates for 1996 (an astonishing zero growth in the case of both Malaysia and Thailand) and burgeoning current account deficits. Since a foreign exchange surplus gained through consistently rising exports of goods and services was the ultimate guarantee that the massive foreign debt contracted by the private sector would be repaid, this was a massive blow to investor confidence. What the investors failed to realize, however, was that the very policy of maintaining a strong currency that was calculated to draw them in was also the cause of the export collapse. And what many also failed to realize was that the upgrading of the quality of exports which could have counteracted the rise in export prices had been undermined by the easy flow of foreign money into the speculative sectors of the economy, as manufacturers chose to channel their investments there to realize quick profits, instead of pouring them into the hard slog of research and development and upgrading the skills of the work force.[59]

By 1997, it was time to get out and, because of the liberalization of the capital account, there were no mechanisms to slow down the exit of funds. With hundreds of billions of baht chasing a limited amount of dollars, the outflow of capital could be highly destabilizing. Many big institutional players and banks began to leave, but what converted a nervous departure into a catastrophic stampede was the speculative activity of the hedge funds and other arbitrageurs who, gambling on the authorities' eventual devaluation of the overvalued baht to contain the yawning current account deficit, in fact, accelerated it by unloading huge quantities of baht in search of dollars.

Hedge funds were particularly salient in the Thai debacle. These funds are essentially investment partnerships, which are limited to the very wealthy, are often based offshore, and are little regulated. They specialize in combining short and long positions in different currencies, bonds and stocks in order to net a profit. These funds had been attacking the Thai baht occasionally since 1995. But the most spectacular assault occurred on 10 May 1997, when in just one day hedge funds are said to have 'bet US\$10 billion against the baht in a global attack'.[60] Of the Bank of Thailand's \$28 billion forward book at the end of July 1997, approximately \$7 billion, according to an IMF report,

> is thought by market participants to represent transactions taken directly with hedge funds. Hedge funds may have also sold the baht forward through offshore counterparties, onshore foreign banks, and onshore domestic banks, which then off-loaded their positions to the central bank.[61]

Under such massive attacks, the Bank of Thailand went on to lose practically all of the \$38.7 billion of foreign exchange reserves it held at the end of 1996. On 2 July 1997 the decade-long peg of 25 baht to the dollar was abandoned, and the Thai currency went on to lose over 50 per cent of its value in a few months.

In Jakarta and Kuala Lumpur, there occurred the same conjunction of massive capital flow, property glut and a rise in the current account deficit. The same nervousness existed, but it was the baht collapse that triggered the panic among foreign investors. The deadly dynamics of capital flows liberated from capital and foreign exchange controls are captured in an account by Jeffrey Winters of the mass panic among a set of strategic actors in the portfolio investment scene, the so-called EMFMs ('Emerging Market Fund Managers'):

Suddenly, you receive disturbing news that Thailand is in serious trouble, and you must decide immediately what to do with your Malaysian investments. It is in this moment that the escape psychology and syndrome begins. First, you immediately wonder if the disturbing new information leaking out about Thailand applies to Malaysia as well. You think it does not, but you are not sure. Second, you must instantly begin to think strategically about how other EMFMs and independent investors are going to react, and of course they are thinking simultaneously about how you are going to react. And third, you are fully aware, as are all the other managers, that the first ones to sell as a market turns negative will be hurt the least, and the ones in the middle and at the end will lose the most value for their portfolio – and likely to be fired from their position as an EMFM as well. In a situation of low systemic transparency, the sensible reaction will be to sell and escape. Notice that even if you use your good connections in the Malaysian government and business community to receive highly reliable information that the country is healthy and not suffering from the same problems as Thailand, you will still sell and escape. Why? Because you cannot ignore the likely behavior of all the other investors. And since they do not have access to the reliable information you have, there is a high probability that their uncertainty will lead them to choose escape. If you hesitate while they rush to sell their shares, the market will drop rapidly, and the value of your portfolio will start to evaporate before your eyes.[62]

Winters comes to a radically different conclusion from Adam Smith, who believed that the invisible hand of the market is supposed to bring about the greatest good for the greatest number. Winters says, 'The chain reaction was set in motion by currency traders and managers of large pools of portfolio capital who operate under intense competitive pressures that cause them to behave in a manner that is objectively irrational and destructive for the whole system, especially for the countries involved, but subjectively both rational and necessary for any hope of individual survival'.[63]

The Three Schools of Global Financial Reform

In response to a thousand and one situations like the above, there are now a thousand and one proposals for world financial reform, ranging from suggestions for preemptive crisis mechanisms to recommendations for the reform of the International Monetary Fund, to several proposals for the establishment of a 'World Financial Authority'.[64] Rather than take them up one by one in technical fashion, let us instead go to the heart of the matter – the interests and ideologies served by the different proposals – and group the most important recommendations into three approaches or paradigms. Of course, some proposals resist being easily pigeonholed and some are eclectic in terms of their technical measures. However, it is the thrust of a set of recommendations that we are seeking to capture.

We will call the first 'It's the wiring, not the architecture' approach. The second might be termed the 'Back to Bretton Woods' school. And we might christen the third approach the 'It's the development model, stupid!' strategy.

'It's the Wiring, not the Architecture' [65]

One might say that this is basically the US position, although it is shared to some degree by many of the G7 members, with probably the notable exception of Japan. The basic idea is that the current architecture is sound, there is no need for major reforms, and that it's simply a question of improving the wiring of the system.

This school assigns primacy to 'reforming' the financial sectors of the crisis economies through increased transparency, tougher bankruptcy laws to eliminate moral hazard, prudential regulation using the 'Core Principles' drafted by the Basle Committee on Banking Supervision, and greater inflow of foreign capital not only to recapitalize shattered banks but also to 'stabilize' the local financial system by making foreign interests integral to it.

When it comes to the supply-side actors in the North, this perspective would leave them to comply voluntarily with the Basle Principles, although government intervention might be needed periodically to catch free-falling casino players whose collapse might bring down the whole global financial structure (as was the case in late 1998 when a consortium of New York banks – led by the Reserve Bank of New York – organized a rescue of the hedge fund Long Term Capital Management after the latter was unravelled by Russia's financial crisis).[66] The farthest the G7 has gone in terms of dealing with the controversial hedge fund question was to issue a declaration in October 1998 commenting on the need to examine 'the implications arising from the operations of leveraged international financial organizations including hedge funds and offshore institutions' and 'to encourage off-shore centres to comply with internationally agreed standards'.[67]

Finally, when it comes to the existing multilateral structure, this view supports the expansion of the powers of the IMF, proposing not only greater funding but also new credit lines, such as the 'contingency credit line' that would be made available to countries that are about to be subjected to speculative attack. Access to these funds would be dependent, however, on a country's track record in terms of observing good macroeconomic fundamentals, as traditionally stipulated by the Fund.

While much has been made of the conflict between the US and the other members of the G7 countries in the world press, in fact, the articulated differences appear to be marginal. France and Germany (at least before the resignation of Germany's Oskar Lafontaine as Finance Minister), with some support from Japan, have proposed the establishment of 'target zones' that would reduce the fluctuations among the yen, dollar, and euro. There are virtually no suggestions from the European Union on controlling capital flows on the supply side.

Japan has made additional proposals on the IMF, but these are variants of the position of either the US Government or some US think-tanks. The proposals include more IMF monitoring of hedge funds, getting the IMF to push private creditors and investors to participate in rescue programmes (or 'bailing them in' instead of bailing them out) and providing a 'certified' line of credit to countries that follow good economic policies which are under speculative attack, something similar to Clinton's contingency credit line.[68]

In sum, it seems fairly obvious that, especially given its priority of transforming developing country financial systems using Northern standards, one of the key objectives of this approach is to extend the reach and deepen the global hold of Northern finance capital in developing economies under the guise of reforming the global financial architecture and stabilizing global financial flows.

'Back to the Bretton Woods System'

The second school of thought would impose tougher controls at the global level, in the form of the Tobin tax or variants of it.[69] The Tobin tax is a transactions tax on capital inflows and outflows at all key points of the world economy that would 'throw sand in the wheels' of global capital movements. Controls at the international level may be supplemented by national-level controls on capital inflows or outflows. A model of such a measure was the Chilean inflow measure that required portfolio investors to deposit up to 30 per cent in an interest-free account at the Central Bank for a year, which was said to be successful in discouraging massive capital portfolio inflows.[70] Among some writers, there is an ill-concealed admiration for Prime Minister Mohamad Mahathir's tough set of outflow measures, which included the fixing of the exchange rate, the withdrawal of the local currency from international circulation, and a one-year lock-in period for capital already in the country.[71]

In addition to controls at the national and international level, proponents of this view also see regional controls as desirable and feasible. The Asian Monetary Fund is regarded as an attractive, workable proposal that must be revived. The AMF was proposed by Japan at the height of the Asian financial crisis to serve as a pool for the foreign exchange reserves of the reserve-rich Asian countries that would repel speculative attacks on Asian currencies. Not surprisingly, Washington vetoed it.

The thrust of these international, national, and regional controls is partly to prevent destabilizing waves of capital entry and exit and to move investment inflow from short-term portfolio investment and short-term loans to long-term direct investment and long-term loans. For some, capital controls are not simply stabilizing measures but are, like tariffs and quotas, strategic tools that may justifiably be employed to influence a country's degree and mode of integration into the global economy. In other words, capital and trade controls are legitimate instruments for the pursuit of trade and industrial policies aimed at national industrial development.

When it comes to the World Bank, the IMF, and the World Trade Organization, the thrust of this school is to reform these institutions along the lines of greater accountability, less doctrinal push for free trade and capital account liberalization, and greater voting power for developing countries. Like the G7, advocates of this approach view the IMF as a mechanism to infuse greater liquidity into economies in crisis, but, unlike the G7, they would have the Fund do this without the tight conditionalities that now accompany its emergency lending. Some people in this school recommend the establishment of a 'World Financial Authority' (WFA). The WFA's main task, in one formulation, would be to develop and impose regulations on global capital flows and serve as 'a forum within which the rules of international financial cooperation are developed and implemented ... by effective coordination of the activities of national monetary authorities'.[72]

In other words, the Fund, the World Bank, and the WTO continue to be seen as central institutions of a world regulatory regime, but they must be made to move away from imposing one common model of trade and investment on all countries. Instead, they must provide a framework for more discriminate global integration, that would allow greater trade and investment flows but also allow some space for national differences in the organization of global capitalism.

As formulated by Dani Rodrik, the current chief economic adviser to the G24 (a grouping of developing countries), the ideal multilateral system appears to be a throwback to the original Bretton Woods system devised by Keynes that reigned from 1945 to the mid-1970s, where 'rules left enough space for national development efforts to proceed along successful but divergent paths'.[73] In other words, a 'regime of peaceful coexistence among national capitalisms'.[74]

Not surprisingly, this 'Global Keynesian' perspective has resonated well with economists and technocrats from developing countries, the devastated Asian economies, and the UN system, which is well known as a refuge of Keynesians who fled the neoliberal revolution at the World Bank and academic institutions.

'It's the Development Model, Stupid!'

Let us proceed to the third perspective, the one that we call 'It's the Development Model, Stupid!' school. Those that we classify as belonging to this school regard the IMF and WTO, in particular, as Jurassic institutions that would be impossible to reform owing to both their deep neoliberal indoctrination and the hegemonic influence within them of the United States. Indeed, the world would be better off without them since they serve as the lynchpin of a hegemonic international system that systematically marginalizes the South.

The same scepticism marks this school's view on the possibility of imposing global capital controls or prudential regulations on hedge funds and other big casino players, again because of the strength of neoliberal ideology and financial interests. National capital controls are seen as much more promising, and the experiences of China and India in avoiding the financial crisis, of Chile in regulating capital flows, and of Malaysia in stabilizing its economy have convinced proponents of this view that this is the way to go. Like the Global Keynesians, this school would also see regional arrangements such as the Asian Monetary Fund as feasible and workable.

Where the proponents of this view differ from the Global Keynesians is the fact that their advocacy of capital controls is accompanied by a more fundamental and thorough critique of the process of globalization that goes beyond its blasting away legitimate differences among national capitalisms. Buffering an economy from the volatility of speculative capital is an important rationale for capital controls. Even more critical, however, is the consideration that such measures would be a *sine qua non* for a fundamental reorientation of an economy toward a more inner-directed pattern of growth that would entail, in many ways, a process of deglobalization.

The main problem, from this viewpoint, lies not in the volatility of speculative capital, but in the way that the export sector and foreign capital have been institutionalized as the engines of these economies. The problem is the indiscriminate integration of the developing economies into the global economy and the over-reliance on foreign investment, whether direct investment or portfolio investment, for development. It is not surprising, from this point of view, that Mexico and Thailand were the epicentres of the recent financial earthquakes, for these two economies are among that handful of developing economies that have gone furthest in terms of trade, investment and financial integration into the global capitalist economies.

Thus, while the current crisis is wreaking havoc on peoples' lives throughout the South, it also gives us the best opportunity in years to fundamentally revise our model and strategy of development. In this process it would, of course, be ideal to have a more congenial international financial architecture, but since that is not going to happen in the short and medium term, there are two overriding tasks in the area of international finance. The first is preventing the current efforts to reform the global financial architecture from becoming a project to more thoroughly subordinate, penetrate, and integrate the financial sectors of developing country economies within the global financial system controlled by the North. The second is to devise a set of effective capital controls, trade controls, and regional cooperative arrangements that would 'hold the ring', as it were, allowing a process of internal economic transformation to take place with minimal disruption from external forces.

Deglobalizing the Domestic Economy

What are some of the priorities of what we might call a model of limited deglobalization of the domestic economy? What makes it different not only from the neoliberal economy but also from the national capitalisms whose 'peaceful coexistence' would be ensured by Dani Rodrik's proposed Keynesian international architecture?

First, allow us to focus our observations on the East Asian region, the area with which we are most familiar. Now, comprehensive blueprints are few in our region today, and perhaps that is good. Nevertheless, there are some ideas or proposals being actively discussed throughout East Asia that are increasingly attractive to peoples in crisis. An inventory would place the following at the top:

1 While foreign investment of the right kind is important, growth must be financed principally from domestic savings and investment. This means progressive taxation systems. One of the key reasons for the reliance on foreign credit and foreign investment was that the élites of East Asia did not want to tax themselves to produce the needed investment capital to pursue their fast-track development strategies. Even in the depths of today's crisis, conspicuous consumption continues to mark the behavior of Asia's élites, who also send much of their wealth abroad to safe havens in Geneva, Tokyo, or New York. Regressive taxation systems are the norm in the region, where income taxpayers are but a handful, and indirect taxes that cut into the resources of lower-income groups are the principal source of government expenditures.

2 While export markets are important, they are too volatile to serve as reliable engines of growth. Development must be reoriented around the domestic market as the principal locomotive of growth. Along with the pitfalls of excessive reliance on foreign capital, the lessons of the crisis include the consequences of the tremendous dependence of the region's economies on export markets. This has led to extreme vulnerability to the vagaries of the global market and sparked the current self-defeating race to 'export one's way out of the crisis' through competitive devaluation of the currency. This move is but the latest and most desperate manifestation of the panacea of export-oriented development.

3 Making the domestic market the engine of development, to use a dis-
tinctly unfashionable but unavoidable term, brings up the linkage between
sustained growth and equity. For a 'Keynesian' strategy of enlarging the
local market to stimulate growth means increasing effective demand or
bringing more consumers (hopefully discriminating ones) into the market
via a comprehensive programme of asset and income distribution,
including land reform. There is in this, of course, the unfinished social
justice agenda of the progressive movement in Asia, an agenda that was
marginalized by the regnant ideology of growth during the 'miracle years'.
Vast numbers of people remain marginalized because of grinding poverty,
particularly in the countryside. Land and asset reform would simultaneously bring them into the market, empower them economically and
politically, and create the conditions for social and political stability.
Achieving economic sustainability based on a dynamic domestic market
can no longer be divorced from issues of equity.

4 Regionalism can become an invaluable adjunct to such a process of
domestic market-driven growth – but only if both processes are guided
not by a perspective of neoliberal integration but by a vision of regional
import-substitution and protected market integration that gives the
region's producers the first opportunity to serve the region's consumers.

5 While there are other elements in the thinking about alternative development now taking place in the region, one universal theme is 'sustainable
development'. The centrality of ecological sustainability is said to be one
of the hard lessons of the crisis. For the model of high-speed growth
fuelled by foreign capital for foreign markets is leaving behind little that
is of positive value. In the case of Thailand, 13 years of fast-track capitalism are leaving behind few traces except industrial plants that will be anti-
quated in a few years, hundreds of unoccupied high-rises, a horrendous
traffic problem that is only slightly mitigated by the repossession of
thousands of late-model cars from bankrupt owners, a rapid rundown of
the country's natural capital and an environment that has been irreversibly,
if not mortally, impaired, to the detriment of future generations.

In place of 8–10 per cent growth rates, many environmentalists are now
talking of rates of 3–4 per cent or even lower. This links the social agenda
with the environmental agenda, since one reason for the push for high
growth rates was so that the élites could corner a significant part of the
growth while still allowing some growth to trickle down to the lower classes
for the sake of social peace. The alternative – the redistribution of social
wealth – is clearly less acceptable to the ruling groups, but it is the key to a

pattern of development that will eventually combine economic growth, political stability and ecological sustainability.

These and similar ideas are already being discussed actively throughout the region. What is still unclear, though, is how these elements will hang together. The new political economy may be embedded in religious or secular discourse and language. And its ultimate coherence is likely to rest less on considerations of narrow efficiency than on a stated ethical priority given to community solidarity and security. Moreover, the new economic order is unlikely to be imposed from above in Keynesian technocratic style, but is likely to be forged in social and political struggles.

This fire down below, to borrow a line from William Golding, is one that is likely to upset the best-laid plans of the tiny global élite, which is currently seeking to salvage an increasingly unstable free-market order by extending its reach even further under the banner of 'global financial reform'.

If this project of limited deglobalization of national financial structures is one that we find desirable, then the relevant task for those of us who are grappling with issues of international financial reform is twofold. The first is a defensive one of repelling attempts to further subjugate and integrate domestic financial systems into the global system under the guise of improving the global financial architecture. The other is devising a set of capital and border trade controls at both the regional and national levels that would allow this process of domestic economic reorientation to take place with minimum disruption from the forces that will be always waiting in the wings to suffocate such a project.

Notes

1 Summers, Larry (1998) 'The Global Economic Situation and What It Means for the United States', remarks to the National Governors' Association, Milwaukee, Wisconsin, 4 August.

2 Quoted in Richard Mann (1998: 42) *Economic Crisis in Indonesia*, Gateway Books.

3 This view is most notably represented by Jeffrey Sachs. See, among others, Sachs, Jeffrey (1998) 'The IMF and the Asian Flu', in *American Prospect*, March/April.

4 Fischer, Stanley (1997) 'Capital Account Liberalization and the Role of the IMF', paper presented at the Asia and the IMF Seminar, Hong Kong, 19 September.

5 'Mahathir, Soros, and the Currency Markets', *Economist*, 27 September 1997, p. 93.

6 *Ibid.*

7 Ignatius, David, 'Policing Hedge Funds: Who's in Charge Here?,' *International Herald Tribune*, 22 February 1999.

8 Fischer, Stanley (1999) 'On the Need for an International Lender of Last Resort,' paper prepared for joint luncheon of the American Economic Association and the American Finance Association, New York, 3 January.

9 *Ibid.*

10 See, for instance, Robert Rubin (1998) 'Strengthening the Architecture of the International Financial System,' speech at the Brookings Institution, Washington, DC, 14 April.

11 World Bank (1996: 3) *Managing Capital Flows in East Asia*, World Bank, Washington, DC.

12 Henwood, Doug (1997: 107–8) *Wall Street*, Verso, New York.

13 Lissakers, Karin (1991: 254) *Bankers, Borrowers, and the Establishment*, Basic Books, New York.
14 *Ibid.*, p. 36.
15 Soros, George (1999: 108) *The Crisis of Global Capitalism*, New York: BBS.
16 Lissakers, p. 8.
17 Soros, p. 119
18 Hirst, Paul and Grahame Thompson (1996: 40) *Globalization in Question*, Polity Press, Cambridge.
19 Cooper, Ian (1998: 335) 'The World of Futures, Forwards, and Swaps', in *Mastering Finance*, Financial Times, London.
20 Hirst and Thompson, p. 41.
21 Buira, Ariel (1998: 68) 'Key Financial Issues in Capital Flows to Emerging Markets', in *International Finance in a Year of Crisis*, United Nations University, Tokyo.
22 Quoted in UNCTAD (1998: 1) *Trade and Development Report 1998*, UNCTAD, Geneva.
23 Quoted in Henwood, p. 292.
24 'Bavarians at the Gates', *Economist*, 13 February 1999, p. 22.
25 'Could It Happen Again?', *Economist*, 20–26 February 1999, pp. 19–23.
26 Kroszner, Randall (1998: 399) 'The Market as International Regulator', in *Mastering Finance*.
27 Bhagwati, Jagdish (1998: 7–12) 'The Capital Myth: The Difference Between Trade in Widgets and Dollars', in *Foreign Affairs*, Vol. 77, No. 3, May.
28 'The Three Marketeers', *Time*, 15 February 1999, p. 39; see also Bhagwati, p. 12.
29 'How US Wooed Asia to Let Cash Flow In', *New York Times*, 16 February 1999.
30 Lissakers, p. 59.
31 Quoted in Henwood, p. 224.
32 Lissakers, p. 45.
33 Lissakers, p. 104
34 Green, Duncan (1995: 70) *Silent Revolution: the Rise of Market Economics in Latin America*, Cassel, London.
35 Cameron, Maxwell and Vinoc Aggarwal (1996: 977) 'Mexican Meltdown: Markets and Post-NAFTA Financial Turmoil', *Third World Quarterly*, Vol. 17, No. 5.
36 Kessler, Timothy (1998: 57) 'Political Capital: Mexican Policy Under Salinas', *World Politics*, Vol. 51, October.
37 Fox, Justin (1998) 'The Great Emerging Markets Rip-Off', *Fortune*, 11 May (downloaded from the Internet.)
38 *Ibid.*
39 *Ibid.*
40 Cohen, Bernice (1997: 348) *The Edge of Chaos*, John Wiley, New York.
41 Tang, Min and James Villafuerte (1995: 10) *Capital Flows to Asian and Pacific Developing Countries: Recent Trends and Future Prospects*, Asian Development Bank, Manila.
42 Cohen, pp. 347–8.
43 This list is based on a number of sources, including UNCTAD (1998) *Trade and Development Report 1998*, UNCTAD, Geneva; and Eichengreen, Barry and Donald Mathieson (1998) *Hedge Funds and Financial Market Dynamics*, Occasional Paper 166, International Monetary Fund, Washington, DC.
44 Fanelli, Jose Maria (1998: 8) 'Financial Liberalization and Capital Account Regime: Notes on the Experience of Developing Countries', in *International Monetary and Financial Issues for the 1990s*, UNCTAD, Geneva.
45 For an account of this, see Bello, Walden (1994: 37–42) *Dark Victory*, Institute for Food and Development Policy, Oakland.
46 World Bank (1996: 5–6) *Managing Capital Flows in East Asia*, World Bank, Washington, DC.
47 Greider, William (1997: 260) *One World, Ready or Not: the Manic Logic of Global Capitalism*, New York: Simon and Schuster.
48 Sachs, Jeffrey, 'Personal View', *Financial Times*, 30 July 1997.

49 Buira, p. 7.
50 *Ibid.*
51 Cameron and Aggarwal, p. 977.
52 Kessler, p. 57.
53 *Ibid.*
54 *Ibid.*, p. 62.
55 Cameron and Aggarwal, pp. 977–8.
56 Japan Ministry of Finance figures.
57 HG Asia (1996) *Communique: Philippines,* Hong Kong: HG Asia (downloaded from the Internet.)
58 Institute of International Finance (1998: 3) *Capital Flows to Emerging Market Economies,* 30 April.
59 See HG Asia (1996) *Communique: Thailand,* 'Thailand – Worth a Nibble Perhaps but not a Bite', HG Asia, Hong Kong (downloaded from the Internet.)
60 Khantong, Thanong (1998) 'The Currency War Is the Information War', talk presented at the Seminar-Workshop on 'Improving the Flow of Information in a Time of Crisis: the Challenge to the Southeast Asian Media', Subic, Philippines, 29–31 October.
61 Eichengreen and Mathieson, p. 17.
62 Winters, Jeffrey (1998) 'The Financial Crisis in Southeast Asia', paper delivered at the Conference on the Asian Crisis, Murdoch University, Fremantle, Western Australia, August.
63 *Ibid.*
64 A list of the more significant proposals are found in Eichengreen, Barry (1999) *Toward a New Financial Architecture, Institute for International Economics,* Washington, DC.
65 Among the documents that broadly share this view are the following: Group of 22 (1998) 'Reports on the International Financial Architecture, Working Groups on Transparency and Accountability, Strengthening the Financial System, and International Financial Crises', October; Goldstein, Morris (1998) *The Asian Financial Crises: Causes, Cures, and Systemic Implications,* Institute for International Economics, Washington, DC; Rubin, Robert (1998) 'Strengthening the Architecture of the International Financial System', speech at the Brookings Institution, Washington, DC, 14 April (downloaded from the Internet); Fischer, Stanley (1999) 'On the Need for an International Lender of Last Resort', paper prepared for the joint luncheon of the American Economic Association and the American Finance Association, New York, 3 January; and Eichengreen, Barry (1999) *Toward a New International Financial Architecture,* Institute for International Economics, Washington, DC.
66 The Federal Reserve Chairman explicitly opposed regulation of hedge funds during hearings at the US Congress in October 1998, when the LTCM fiasco occurred. See David Ignatius, 'Policing Hedge Funds: Who's in Charge Here?', *International Herald Tribune,* 22 February 1999, p. 6.
67 Quoted in United Nations (1999) 'Towards a New Financial Architecture: a Report of the Task Force of the Executive Committee on Economic and Social Affairs of the United Nations', New York, United Nations, 21 January.
68 As summarized by David de Rosa, 'Miyazawa's Big Ideas on How to Run the IMF', Bloomberg News column, reproduced in *Manila Times,* 3 March, 1999, p.13.
69 Among the documents that might be said to broadly belong to this viewpoint are the following: United Nations (1999) 'Towards a New Financial Architecture: a Report of the Task Force of the Executive Committee on Economic and Social Affairs of the United Nations', New York, United Nations, 21 January; UNCTAD (1998: 83–110) 'The Management and Prevention of Financial Crises', *Trade and Development Report 1998,* UNCTAD, Geneva; Rodrik, Dani (1998) 'The Global Fix', in *New Republic,* 2 November (downloaded from the Internet); Eatwell, John and Lance Taylor, (1998) 'International Capital Markets and the Future of Economic Policy', CEPA Working Paper, No. 9, Centre for Economic Policy Analysis (CEPA), New School for Social Research, New York, September; Culpeper,

Roy (1999) 'New Economic Architecture: Getting the Right Specs', remarks at the Conference on 'The Asian Crisis and Beyond: Prospects for the 21st Century', Carleton University, Ottawa, 29 January.

70 The reserve requirement was brought down to zero per cent in October 1998, allegedly because speculative inflows had dropped considerably owing to the crisis.

71 See, for instance, Roy Culpeper.

72 Eatwell and Taylor, p. 14.

73 Dani Rodrik.

74 *Ibid.*

2

A Short History of Neoliberalism
Twenty Years of Élite Economics and Emerging Opportunities for Structural Change

SUSAN GEORGE

In 1945 or 1950, if you had seriously proposed any of the ideas and policies in today's standard neoliberal toolkit, you would have been laughed off the stage or sent off to the insane asylum. At least in Western countries, at that time, everyone was a Keynesian, a social democrat or a social-Christian democrat or some shade of Marxist. The idea that the market should be allowed to make major social and political decisions; the idea that the State should voluntarily reduce its role in the economy, or that corporations should be given total freedom; that trade unions should be curbed and citizens given much less rather than more social protection – such ideas were utterly foreign to the spirit of the time. Even if someone actually agreed with these ideas, he or she would have hesitated to take such a position in public, and would have had a hard time finding an audience.

However incredible it may sound today, the IMF and the World Bank were seen as progressive institutions. They were sometimes called Keynes's twins because they were the brainchildren of Keynes and Harry Dexter White, one of Franklin Roosevelt's closest advisers. When these institutions were created at Bretton Woods in 1944, their mandate was to help prevent future conflicts by lending for reconstruction and development, and by smoothing out temporary balance of payments problems. They had no control over individual governments' economic decisions, nor did their mandate include a licence to intervene in national policy.

In Western nations, the Welfare State and the New Deal had got under way in the 1930s but their spread had been interrupted by the war. The first order of business in the post-war world was to put them back in place. The other major item on the agenda was to get world trade moving: this was accomplished through the Marshall Plan, which established Europe once again as the major trading partner for the US, the most powerful economy in the world. And it was at this time that the strong winds of decolonization also began to blow, whether freedom was obtained by grant, as in India, or through armed struggle, as in Kenya, Vietnam and other nations.

On the whole, the world had signed on for an extremely progressive agenda. The great scholar Karl Polanyi published his masterwork, *The Great Transformation* in 1944, a fierce critique of nineteenth century industrial, market-based society. Over 50 years ago Polanyi made this amazingly prophetic and modern statement: 'To allow the market mechanism to be sole director of the fate of human beings and their natural environment ... would result in the demolition of society'.[1] Polanyi was convinced, however, that such a demolition could not happen in the post-war world because, as he said, 'Within the nations we are witnessing a development under which the economic system ceases to lay down the law to society and the primacy of society over that system is secured'.[2]

Alas, Polanyi's optimism was misplaced. The whole point of neoliberalism is that the market mechanism should be allowed to direct the fate of human beings. The economy should dictate its rules to society, not the other way around. And just as Polanyi foresaw, this doctrine is leading us directly towards the 'demolition of society'.

So what happened? Why have we reached this point half a century after the end of the Second World War? The short answer is, 'Because of the series of recent financial crises, especially in Asia'. But this begs the question, 'How did neoliberalism ever emerge from its ultra-minoritarian ghetto to become the dominant doctrine in the world today?' Why can the IMF and the World Bank intervene at will and force countries to participate in the world economy on basically unfavourable terms? Why is the welfare state under threat in all the countries where it was established? Why is the environment on the edge of collapse and why are there so many poor people in both the rich and the poor countries at a time when there is greater wealth than ever before? Those are the questions that need to be answered from an historical perspective.

As I've argued in detail in the US quarterly journal *Dissent*, one explanation for this triumph of neoliberalism and the economic, political, social and ecological disasters that go with it is that neoliberals have bought and paid for their own vicious and regressive 'Great Transformation'. They have understood, as progressives have not, that ideas have consequences. Starting from a tiny embryo at the University of Chicago with the philosopher-economist Friedrich von Hayek – and with students such as Milton Friedman at its nucleus – the neoliberals and their funders created a huge international network of foundations, institutes, research centres, publications, scholars, writers and public relations hacks to develop, package and push their ideas and doctrine relentlessly.

They have built this highly efficient ideological cadre because they under-stand what the Italian Marxist thinker Antonio Gramsci was talking about when he developed the concept of cultural hegemony. If you can occupy people's heads, their hearts and their hands will follow. We do not have the space to go into details here, but believe me, the ideological and promotional work of the right has been absolutely brilliant. They have spent hundreds of millions of dollars, but the result has been worth every penny to them because they have made neoliberalism seem as if it were the natural and normal condition of humankind. No matter how many disasters of all kinds the neoliberal system has visibly created, no matter what financial crises it may engender, no matter how many losers and outcasts it may create, it is still made to seem inevitable, like an act of God, the only possible economic and social order available to us.

Let me stress how important it is to understand that this vast neoliberal experiment we are all being forced to live under has been created by people with a purpose. Once you grasp this, once you understand that neoliberalism is not a force like gravity but a totally artificial construct, you can also understand that what some people have created, other people can change. But they cannot change it without recognizing the importance of ideas. I'm all for grassroots projects, but I also warn that these will collapse if the overall ideological climate is hostile to their goals.

So, from a small, unpopular sect with virtually no influence, neoliberalism has become the major world religion with its dogmatic doctrine, its priesthood, its law-giving institutions and perhaps most important of all, its hell for heathen and sinners who dare to contest the revealed truth. Oskar Lafontaine, the ex-German Finance Minister, was consigned to that hell because he dared to propose higher taxes on corporations and tax cuts for ordinary and less well-off families.

Having set the ideological stage and context, let me now fast-forward so that we are back within a twenty-year time frame. That means 1979, the year Margaret Thatcher came to power and undertook the neoliberal revolution in Britain. The Iron Lady was herself a disciple of Friedrich von Hayek; she was a social Darwinist and had no qualms about expressing her convictions. She was well known for justifying her programme with the single word TINA, short for There Is No Alternative. The central value of Thatcher's doctrine and of neoliberalism itself is the notion of competition – competition between nations, regions and firms, and of course between individuals. Competition is central because it separates the sheep from the goats, the men from the boys, the fit from the unfit. It is supposed to allocate all resources, whether physical, natural, human or financial with the greatest possible efficiency.

In sharp contrast, the great Chinese philosopher Lao Tzu ended his Tao-te Ching with these words: 'Above all, do not compete'. The only actors in the neoliberal world who seem to have taken his advice are the largest actors of all, the transnational corporations. The principle of competition scarcely applies to them; they prefer to practise what we could call alliance capitalism. It is no accident that, depending on the year, two-thirds to three-quarters of all the money labelled 'foreign direct investment' is not devoted to new, job-creating investment but to mergers and acquisitions which almost invariably result in job losses.

Because competition is always a virtue, its results cannot be bad. For the neoliberal, the market is so wise and so good that – like God – the 'invisible hand' can bring good out of apparent evil. Thus Thatcher once said in a speech, 'It is our job to glory in inequality and see that talents and abilities are given vent and expression for the benefit of us all'.[3] In other words, don't worry about those who might be left behind in the competitive struggle. People are unequal by nature, but this is good because the contributions of the well born, the best educated, the toughest, will eventually benefit everyone. Nothing in particular is owed to the weak, the poorly educated; what happens to them is their own fault, never the fault of society. If the competitive system is 'given vent', as Thatcher says, society will be the better for it. Unfortunately, the history of the past twenty years teaches us that exactly the opposite is the case.

In pre-Thatcher Britain, about one person in ten was classed as living below the poverty line, not a brilliant result but honourable as nations go and a lot better than in the pre-War period. Now one person in four and one child in three is officially poor. This is the meaning of survival of the fittest: people who cannot heat their houses in winter, who must put a coin in the meter before they can have electricity or water, who do not own a warm waterproof coat. I am taking these examples from the 1996 report of the British Child Poverty Action Group. I will illustrate the result of the Thatcher-Major 'tax reforms' with a single example: during the 1980s, 1 per cent of taxpayers received 29 per cent of all the tax reduction benefits, such that a single person earning half the average salary found his or her taxes had gone up by 7 per cent, whereas a single person earning ten times the average salary got a reduction of 21 per cent.

Another implication of competition as the central value of neoliberalism is that the public sector must be brutally downsized because it does not and cannot obey the basic law of competing for profits or for market share. Privatization is one of the major economic transformations of the past twenty years. The trend began in Britain and has spread throughout the world.

Let me start by asking why capitalist countries, particularly in Europe, had public services to begin with, and why many still do. In reality, nearly all public services constitute what economists call 'natural monopolies'. A natural monopoly exists when the minimum size to guarantee maximum economic efficiency is equal to the actual size of the market. In other words, a company has to be a certain size to realize economies of scale and thus provide the best possible service at the lowest possible cost to the consumer. Public services also require very large investment outlays at the beginning, like railroad tracks or power grids, which does not encourage competition either. That's why public monopolies were the obvious optimum solution. But neoliberals define anything public as *ipso facto* 'inefficient'.

So what happens when a natural monopoly is privatized? Quite normally and naturally, the new capitalist owners tend to impose monopoly prices on the public, while richly remunerating themselves. Classical economists call this outcome 'structural market failure' because prices are higher than they ought to be and service to the consumer is not necessarily good. In order to prevent structural market failures, up to the mid-1980s, the capitalist countries of Europe almost universally entrusted the post office, telecoms, electricity, gas, railways, metros, air transport and usually other services like water, rubbish collection, and so on to state-owned monopolies. The USA is the big exception, perhaps because it is too huge geographically to favour natural monopolies.

In any event, Margaret Thatcher set out to change all that. As an added bonus, she could also use privatization to break the power of the trade unions. By destroying the public sector where unions were strongest, she was able to weaken them drastically. Thus between 1979 and 1994, the number of jobs in the public sector in Britain was reduced from over seven million to five million, a drop of 29 per cent. Virtually all the jobs eliminated were unionized jobs. Since private sector employment was stagnant during those fifteen years, the overall reduction in the number of British jobs came to 1.7 million, a drop of seven per cent compared with 1979. To neoliberals, fewer workers is always better than more because workers impinge on shareholder value and competition pushes labour prices down.

As for other effects of privatization, they were predictable and predicted. The managers of the newly privatized enterprises, often exactly the same people as before, doubled or tripled their own salaries. The government used taxpayer money to wipe out debts and recapitalize firms before putting them on the market (for example, the water authority got five billion pounds of debt relief plus 1.6 billion pounds called the 'green dowry' to make the bride more attractive to prospective buyers). A lot of public relations fuss was made about how small stockholders would have a stake in these companies, and in fact nine million Brits did buy shares. However, half of them invested less than a thousand pounds and most of them sold their shares rather quickly, as soon as they could cash in on the instant profits.

From the results, one can easily see that the whole point of privatization was neither economic efficiency nor improved services to the consumer but simply to transfer wealth from the public purse, which could redistribute it to even out social inequalities, to private hands. In Britain and elsewhere, the overwhelming majority of privatized company shares are now in the hands of financial institutions and very large investors. For example, the employees of British Telecom bought only one per cent of the shares, those of British Aerospace 1.3 per cent. Prior to Thatcher's onslaught, a lot of the public sector in Britain was profitable. Consequently, in 1984, public companies contributed over seven billion pounds to the treasury. All that money is now going to private shareholders. Service in the privatized industries is now often disastrous – the *Financial Times*[4] reported an invasion of rats in the Yorkshire Water system and anyone who has survived taking Thames trains in Britain deserves a medal.

Exactly the same mechanisms have been at work throughout the world. In Britain, the Adam Smith Institute was the intellectual partner for creating the privatization ideology. USAID and the World Bank have also used Adam Smith experts and have pushed the privatization doctrine in the South. By 1991 the Bank had already made 114 loans to speed the process, and every year its Global Development Finance report lists hundreds of privatizations carried out in the Bank's borrowing countries.

I submit that we should stop talking about privatization and use words that tell the truth: we are talking about alienation and surrender of the product of decades of work by thousands of people to a tiny minority of large investors. This is one of the greatest hold-ups of ours or any generation.

Another structural feature of neoliberalism consists in remunerating capital to the detriment of labour and thus moving wealth from the bottom of society to the top. If you are, roughly, in the top 20 per cent of the income scale, you are likely to gain something from neoliberalism and the higher you are up the ladder, the more you gain. Conversely, the bottom 80 per cent all lose, and the lower they are to begin with the more they lose proportionally.

Lest you thought I had forgotten Ronald Reagan let me illustrate this point with the observations of Kevin Phillips, a Republican analyst and former aide to President Nixon, who published a book in 1990 called *The Politics of Rich and Poor*.[5] He charted the way Reagan's neoliberal doctrine and policies had changed American income distribution between 1977 and 1988. These policies were largely elaborated by the conservative Heritage Foundation, the principle think-tank of the Reagan administration and still an important force in American politics. Over the decade of the 1980s, the top 10 per cent of American families increased their average family income by 16 per cent. The top 5 per cent increased theirs by 23 per cent, but the extremely lucky top 1 per cent of American families could thank Reagan for a 50 per cent increase. Their revenues went from an affluent $270,000 to a heady $405,000 per annum. As for poorer Americans, the bottom 80 per cent all lost something; true to the rule, the lower they were on the scale, the more they lost. The bottom 10 per cent of Americans reached the nadir: according to Phillips's figures, they lost 15 per cent of their already meagre incomes: from an already rock bottom average of $4,113 annually, they dropped to an inhuman $3,504. In 1977, the top one per cent of American families had average incomes 65 times as great as those of the bottom 10 per cent. A decade later, the top 1 per cent was 115 times as well off as the bottom decile.

America is one of the most unequal societies on earth, but virtually all countries have seen inequalities increase over the past twenty years because of neoliberal policies. UNCTAD published some damning evidence to this effect in its 1997 Trade and Development Report, based on some 2,600 separate studies of income inequalities, impoverishment and the hollowing out of the middle classes. The UNCTAD team documents these trends in dozens of widely differing societies, including China, Russia and the other former socialist countries.

There is nothing mysterious about this trend towards greater inequality. Policies are specifically designed to give the already rich more disposable income, particularly through tax cuts and by pushing down wages. The theory and ideological justification for such measures is that higher incomes for the rich and higher profits will lead to more investment, better allocation of resources and therefore more jobs and welfare for everyone. In reality, as was perfectly predictable, moving money up the economic ladder has led to stock market bubbles, untold paper wealth for the few, and the kind of financial crises we have witnessed in Asia, Russia and Brazil. If income is redistributed towards the bottom 80 per cent of society, it will be used for consumption and consequently benefit employment. If wealth is redistributed towards the top, where people already have most of the things they need, it will go not into the local or national economy but to international stockmarkets.

The same policies have been carried out throughout the economic South and East under the guise of structural adjustment, which is merely another name for neoliberalism. I've used Thatcher and Reagan to illustrate the policies at the national level. At the international level, neoliberals have concentrated all their efforts on three fundamental points:

• free trade in goods and services;

• free circulation of capital;

• freedom of investment.

Over the past twenty years, the IMF has been strengthened enormously. Thanks to the debt crisis and the mechanism of conditionality, it has moved from balance of payments support to being quasi-universal dictator of so-called 'sound' economic policies, meaning of course neoliberal ones. The

WTO was finally established in January 1995 after long and laborious negotiations, often rammed through parliaments that had little idea what they were ratifying. Thankfully, the most recent effort to make binding and universal neoliberal rules, the Multilateral Agreement on Investment (MAI) has failed, at least temporarily. It would have given all rights to corporations, all obligations to governments and no rights at all to citizens.

The common denominator of these institutions is their lack of transparency and democratic accountability. This is the essence of neoliberalism. It claims that the economy should dictate its rules to society, not the other way around. Democracy is an encumbrance, neoliberalism is designed for winners, not for voters who necessarily encompass the categories of both winners and losers.

I'd like to conclude by asking you to take very seriously indeed the neoliberal definition of the loser, to whom nothing in particular is owed. Anyone can be ejected from the system at any time because of illness, age, pregnancy, perceived failure, or simply because economic circumstances and the relentless transfer of wealth from bottom to top demand it. Shareholder value is all. Recently the *International Herald Tribune* reported that foreign investors are 'snapping up' Thai and Korean companies and banks. Not surprisingly, these purchases are expected to result in 'heavy layoffs'.[6]

In other words, the result of years of work by thousands of Thais and Koreans is being transferred into foreign corporate hands. Many of those who laboured to create that wealth have already been, or soon will be, left on the pavement. Under the principles of competition and maximizing shareholder value, such behaviour is seen not as criminally unjust but as normal and indeed virtuous.

I submit that neoliberalism has changed the fundamental nature of politics. Politics used to be primarily about who ruled whom and who got what share of the pie. Aspects of both these central questions remain, of course, but the great new central question of politics is, in my view, 'Who has a right to live and who does not'. Radical exclusion is now the order of the day. However, I don't want to end on such a depressing and pessimistic note. A lot is already happening to counter these life-threatening trends and there is enormous scope for further action.

This book, and the conference which it has come out of, are going to help define much of that action, which I believe must include an ideological offensive. It's time we set the agenda instead of letting the Masters of the Universe set it at Davos. I hope funders may also understand that they should not be funding just projects but also ideas. We can't count on the neoliberals to do it, so we need to design workable and equitable international taxation systems, including a Tobin tax on all monetary and financial market transactions and taxes on transnational corporation sales on a *pro rata* basis. The proceeds of an international tax system should go to closing the North–South gap and redistributing to all the people who have been robbed over the past twenty years.

Let me repeat what I said earlier: neoliberalism is not the natural human condition; it is not supernatural. It can be challenged and replaced because its own failures will require this. We have to be ready with replacement policies, which restore power to communities and democratic states while working to institute democracy, the rule of law and fair distribution at the international level. Business and the market have their place, but this place cannot occupy the entire sphere of human existence.

Further good news is that there is plenty of money sloshing around out there and a tiny fraction – a ridiculous, infinitesimal proportion of it – would be enough to provide a decent life to every person on earth. There's enough to supply everyone with universal health and education, to clean up the environment and prevent further destruction to the planet and to close the North–South gap (at least according to the United Nations Development Programme, which calls for a paltry $40 billion a year). That, frankly, is peanuts.

Finally, please remember that neoliberalism may be insatiable but it is not invulnerable. A coalition of international activists obliged them to abandon, at least temporarily, their project to liberalize all investment through the MAI. The surprise victory of its opponents infuriated the supporters of corporate rule and demonstrates that well-organized network guerrillas can win battles. Now we have to regroup our forces and keep at them so that they cannot transfer the MAI to the WTO.

Look at it this way. We have the numbers on our side, because there are far more losers than winners in the neoliberal game. We have the ideas, whereas theirs are finally coming into question because of repeated crises. What we lack, so far, are the organization and the unity, which in this age of advanced technology we can overcome. The threat is clearly transnational so the response must also be transnational. Solidarity no longer means aid, or not just aid, but finding the hidden synergies in each other's struggles so that our numerical force and the power of our ideas become overwhelming.

Notes

1 Polanyi, Karl (1944: 73) *The Great Transformation*, New York.
2 *Ibid.*, p. 251.
3 'Poor Have Seen Incomes Fall 18% Since 1979', *Financial Times*, 17 April 1996.
4 'Rat Plague Blamed on Water Groups', *Financial Times*, 15 April 1996.
5 Phillips, K. (1990: 17) *The Politics of Rich and Poor*, Random House, New York.
6 Reuters, AFP and Bloomberg newswires, 5 January 1999.

3

Practical Proposals
The UN System and Financial Regulation
CARLOS FORTIN

This chapter looks at some of the ideas being discussed in the United Nations Secretariat on the question of the reform of the international financial architecture, with a view to better managing crises and, as far as possible, preventing them. The ideas that I will be presenting are those that command a consensus within the various parts of the Secretariat, and which furthermore appear to have some possibility of implementation. Therefore you may find that the proposals do not go far enough. But I believe we must not underestimate the difficulties in trying to reform the system. In the end it will be a question of who has the power to carry out reform. Unfortunately, the forces for reform are not necessarily the most powerful. So in the Secretariat we are trying to strike a balance: going as far as it is necessary to make reform meaningful, but not so far as to be thrown out of court and therefore lose any chance of an impact.

Let me start with a brief characterization of the crisis. We in the UN Secretariat feel that there are some features that need to be recognized before we go into the question of reform. The first one is that, contrary to what many people have said, crises are an expression of structural tendencies in the functioning of contemporary globalized capitalism and of the financial markets. The latter tend to operate through boom–bust cycles. This has always been the case, because of imperfect information and because of the fact that financial markets operate on the basis of expectations, which can change very rapidly. But it has been aggravated by liberalization and by floating exchange rates, by the emergence of new financial instruments, and by improvements in communications and information technology. So we now have a danger of continuing major crises of volatility which are structurally present and have to be dealt with as such, not simply as blips in what is otherwise a smooth path.

Second, the possibility of contagion has become much more serious today than in the past. The financial markets have shown themselves to be incapable of discriminating between different types of situations, and between financial indicators and the fundamentals of an economy. Therefore the idea that markets will separate out those economies that are in real, fundamental difficulty and those that are not, is an illusion. The reason for this is simple: because of the great mobility of capital you get a situation in which highly leveraged investors in one place, who are facing a crisis because of the poor quality of their assets there, respond by selling good assets elsewhere. So they create a crisis where there is no reason for it because they have to cover themselves.

Third, this crisis has shown that developing countries, and to some extent economies in transition too, are more vulnerable to the effects of the crisis than developed economies. That is essentially because of the premature liberalization of financial flows and capital movements that has taken place in those countries without appropriate regulation. It is also because the pool of potential development resources in those countries is limited and therefore, when they are siphoned off to face the crisis, the chances for development and growth are affected.

Fourth, it is clear that the social costs of the crisis and its management are borne by the poor. This is an extremely unfair situation, because the poor do not on the whole benefit from the boom part of the cycle; they are not the ones that reap the benefits when the economy is growing, but they are the ones who pay the cost when the economy is down.

The last point I would make is in fact a quote from the Director-General of the Thai Ministry of Foreign Affairs, Kobsak Chutikul, in an excellent article in the *Bangkok Post*:

> The recent crisis has demonstrated a fundamental problem in the global economy: the enormous discrepancy that exists between an increasingly sophisticated and dynamic international financial world with rapid globalization of financial portfolios, and the lack of a proper institutional framework to regulate it.[1]

In other words, we do need a thorough review and revision of the international architecture for finance. Anything short of that will simply not help. The question is, how far can we in the UN Secretariat go in trying to rethink and reshape the international financial architecture, while at the same time recognizing that it will be essentially the G7 countries and the Bretton Woods institutions that will have the last word in these matters? I believe we can go a significant way.

I will mention six areas in which we think meaningful changes are possible. They may sound modest, but we think they can make a difference. The first one has to do with *the management of macroeconomic policy at the global level*. An underlying cause of the crisis is the absence of coordination of macroeconomic policies among developed countries, and that furthermore those policies are still dominated by the concern with preventing inflationary processes. On the latter point there has been some change in thinking. A growing number of analysts believe that the exclusive preoccupation with inflation is misplaced, and that issues of growth and employment should take priority. In particular, Joseph Stiglitz, Chief Economist of the World Bank, is on record that his empirical econometric work has shown that levels of inflation of up to 40 per cent can be tolerated by economies without serious difficulties. I find that threshold a bit high, but Stiglitz does show convincingly that concentrating efforts to prevent relatively low levels of inflation is a mistake when the cost of it is to reduce employment and reduce output.[2]

Coordination of macroeconomic policy with a growth and employment orientation would call for some mechanism for surveillance. The IMF exercises surveillance over developing countries, but not over developed countries. Surveillance must be symmetrical, and must cover those countries particularly whose economic policies have a global impact. The IMF would be the obvious candidate to take up this function, but some object to that on the grounds that the IMF's decision-making processes are not democratic. Some have proposed the Economic and Social Committee of the UN General Assembly (ECOSOC), but that does not seem like a realistic possibility. On the other hand, some regional arrangements could be a possibility. I will come back to the regional issue, because we feel in the UN that a great deal of the surveillance process can be carried out more democratically and more efficiently by regional organizations rather than by global institutions.

An important point here is the question of the autonomy of the decision makers in the financial and monetary spheres. Here the tendency has been to give autonomy to central banks. We feel, however, that there should be some democratic accountability: money is too serious a matter to be left only to bankers, whether private or central bankers.

My second point is on *liquidity*. The problem here is that there are not enough resources that are continuously available to anticipate and prevent financial crises; resources are put together after the crisis has taken place for purposes of rescuing the situation. Rescuing means essentially that the public sector, national and international, is called upon to bail out private creditors and debtors who have entered voluntarily into commercial transactions without appropriate prudential safeguards and who subsequently have run into difficulties. Resources that could be used for development are thus diverted to support private failures of prudential judgement.

Rescue operations are also subject to conditionality. Certain forms of conditionality involving basic macroeconomic management can be acceptable, but the conditions imposed often go beyond that, and enter into areas which are outside the mandate of financial organizations and which tend to be counterproductive. Professor Jeffrey Sachs, of the Harvard School of

Economics, has gone as far as suggesting that IMF rescue packages are in a sense a cause of the crisis, because of the contractionary policies which form part of the conditions of the packages.[3]

What can be done about liquidity? There are several proposals on the table: increase the access of the IMF to official funds and allow it to borrow from financial markets; sales of gold; and the issuing of Special Drawing Rights (SDR). All of them might have to be considered if the question of adequacy of resources is to be addressed.

On the question of conditionality, the main points are, first, it should not involve contraction of the economy beyond what might be essential for macroeconomic balance; and, second, it should not cover structural or institutional aspects. It is rather odd that when a country is undergoing a crisis it is asked to change its economic structure. The reasonable thing to do is to first deal with the crisis and then look at institutional or structural change. A further point is that institutions and structures are usually the outcome of long and complex national political processes, which should not in principle be interfered with by outside forces.

Conditionality should moreover not include as a general prescription the convertibility of the capital account. This prescription might be appropriate in some cases, but we tend to think that more often than not complete convertibility is not the right policy for developing countries. Finally, conditionality should not involve any specific prescription for an exchange rate regime.

The third element of possible reform has to do with *surveillance, supervision, regulation and international codes of conduct, at the national and international levels.* Some progress has been made here. The Basle Committee has produced the Core Principles for Effective Banking Supervision, which includes some regulation of private agents in the financial markets. It is a start, and the G7 has in principle accepted that this is a way forward; but more is needed, particularly in the field of capital adequacy requirements.

An important issue here is the role of the rating agencies. On this the UN does not have a specific proposal, but it has a clear view that there is a problem. Private rating agencies behave on the whole in a pro-cyclical way and this, instead of reducing the level of volatility, tends to increase it. Sudden shifts in the rating of individual economies in a sense provoke volatility by exacerbating market sentiment shifts. Greater transparency and increasing the level of publicly available information about individual economies can be helpful. One should be aware however that it is not a panacea.

My fourth point is about *capital account management.* The history of the economic evolution of all developed countries shows that complete capital account convertibility and freedom of capital movements is the last stage of the process of opening up the economy; in fact, some developed countries are not there yet. History shows that various forms of capital control are needed until a certain level of development is reached, and it is not reasonable to suggest that developing countries should introduce capital account convertibility prematurely as compared with developed countries.

Controls, of course, do not need to be heavy and rigid. There are many flexible options: reserve requirements, taxes, and minimum stay or liquidity requirements. My own country, Chile, which is a model of liberalization, had until the recent crisis a well-functioning system for financial transactions of prior deposit of 30 per cent of the value of the transaction. When this was introduced during the military government, Chile was warned by many in the international financial community that this would frighten away foreign direct investment. In fact, Chile has had record levels of inflows of foreign direct investment, while the prior deposit system spared the economy the worst consequences of the crisis. Interestingly, Chile reduced the prior deposit required to zero per cent, because it needed additional short-term inflows. But the experience confirms that an intelligently devised system of capital controls can be a powerful instrument to make the process of opening and liberalization smooth.

My fifth point has to do with *standstill provisions and orderly workouts*. As I indicated before, rescue operations often mean that capital flight ends up being financed by the international community. It would make more sense for everybody to introduce a system of suspending the payment of the debt. In private economic life when a firm goes bankrupt it is regarded as reasonable that a suspension of payments should take place until a settlement is worked out. In the case of international debt this would take the form of 'bailing-in' operations: a standstill is introduced and discussions take place on ways in which the repayment of the debt can be resumed in a sustainable manner.

A UN document – prepared by the Economic Commission for Latin America and the Caribbean with the support of UNCTAD – suggests having the situation reviewed by a high-level independent panel, instead of by the creditors themselves as is the case at present. This would, again, be in line with what happens at the national level: in cases of bankruptcy, it is usually the courts, not the creditors, who assess the position and make decisions.

My sixth point concerns the issue of *regional and sub-regional interventions in crisis management*. We feel that progress can be made in terms of the introduction of international prudential supervisory and regulatory frameworks, and that an interesting avenue to pursue is to do that regionally: first, because the countries of the region are best placed to understand what happens and to help each other; second, because it is probably more feasible to introduce new schemes regionally than to try and create new global financial institutions.

A proposal has been made to create a new financial authority but it does not seem realistic at this stage. On the other hand, I have touched already on some of the problems involved in trying to use existing institutions. In that context, a regional approach appears as a promising alternative.

Finally, I would like to mention two issues, not to explore them here, but rather to flag their links with our discussion. The first is the general question of finance for development. Official development assistance (ODA) is going down, and the idea that it will be replaced by foreign direct investment (FDI) is made problematic by the fact that the FDI flows are concentrating in a few developing countries. So the question arises, who will be financing development, as distinct from bailing out creditors? And this links to my last point, which has to do with the issue of international debt, and in particular the questions related to the implementation of the Highly Indebted Poor Countries (HIPC) debt relief initiative of the IMF and the World Bank. Because of their lower level of access to, and integration in the international financial markets, the HIPC countries have not been affected by the financial crisis in the same way as more advanced developing countries, which are more fully integrated. The reform of the international financial architecture is less directly relevant to their immediate needs. Therefore we should keep those needs in mind when devising strategies aimed not only at stabilizing financial markets and flows but more generally at financing development.

Notes

1 Chutikul, Kobsak (1999) 'International Monetary System Also Cries Out for Reform', *Bangkok Post*, 24 March 1999.
2 Stiglitz, J.E. (1998) 'More Instruments and Broader Goals: Moving Towards the Post-Washington Consensus', 1998 WIDER Annual Lecture. World Institute for Development Economics Research, United Nations University, Helsinki.
3 Lacayo, R., 'IMF To The Rescue', *Time*, 8 December 1997.

4

Renewing the Governance
of the Global Economy

KAMAL MALHOTRA

Every cloud has a silver lining. The silver lining of the Asian-led global economic crisis lies in the opportunity it presents to rethink fundamentally the governance of the global economy, not just its financial aspects but also its broader economic and political aspects.

If we ever needed proof that the current dominant neoliberal economic and financial paradigm has disastrous implications for ordinary people and the sustainability of both short and long-term social policy and sustainable human development objectives, then the current economic crisis has provided it.

While for many long-time critics of the current economic growth paradigm, such a rethink is long overdue given the dramatic changes of the last 50 years, when our current system of global governance was designed, it is still not too late if we act quickly and seriously now. The fast-accelerating finance-led globalization process of the post-Cold War decade since 1989 has made this an urgent necessity, not an optional luxury.

Such a rethink should have many dimensions and it has to begin at the very beginning – that is, by rethinking objectives and strategies for sustainable human and social development.

Rethinking Sustainable Human and Social Development

We can no longer avoid what has been obvious to many people outside the halls of political and economic power: that our primary medium- and long-term objective should not be economic growth, but human development.

There are significant differences between the dominant neoliberal economic growth paradigm subscribed to by the World Bank and IMF (along with most of their G7 shareholders and Wall Street financial wizards) and the sustainable human development paradigm championed by people such as 1998 Nobel Economics Prize laureate Dr Amartya Sen and multilateral institutions such as the United Nations Development Programme (UNDP).

The first primarily focuses on shortages of income as the main indicator of poverty while the second adopts a much more comprehensive view of poverty.

The crisis should, at the very least, compel us to challenge the economic growth paradigm with an expanded understanding of the human development approach if we are seriously committed to achieving sustainable human and social development.

We need to ask questions such as: Growth for what – human or economic development? Growth in what – consumer luxuries, drugs, prostitution, child trafficking (all of which contribute to high GDP growth), or health, education, gender equity, environmental regeneration, meaningful participation and political empowerment (which may not contribute to high GDP growth, but do contribute to both the depth and breadth of human development)? These are the quality questions that the IMF, the World Bank, other multilateral development banks, Wall Street financiers and most G7 and developing country governments and their influential technocrats do not ask often enough.

If the aforementioned propositions are accepted, a primary challenge and objective for sustainable development over the medium-to-long term will be to subordinate macro and other economic policy making to human development and social policy goals. This might appear to be a radical proposal in the current neoliberal economic policy climate but – if you think about it, especially in the aftermath of the current global crisis – the proposal makes indisputably good sense.

Two additional crucial subordinations are recommended to enable this fundamental renewal of governance of the global economy at all levels. The first is the subordination of global level governance mechanisms to those at the local, national and regional levels, following the principle of subsidiarity. The second, which needs to happen at all four levels simultaneously, is the subordination of the financial 'bubble' economy to the real, productive economy.

The implications of subordinating economic to social policy and global-level governance structures to local, national and regional ones – together with the requirements and implications of broader political governance – constitute the main content of this chapter.

Before discussing these crucial issues, however, it is necessary to identify why it is so important to achieve the subordination of the financial to the real economy. The most important reason for this is that the fundamental objective of all financial policy is and should remain to ensure the best possible growth, redistribution and employment outcomes in the real economy (that is, the arena where useful goods and services are produced). In this context, the 'simplistic complaint that the financial sector produces nothing by itself contains an element of truth'.[1] In a similar vein, to quote Alan Greenspan,

Chair of the US Federal Reserve, 'a global financial system, of course, is not an end in itself. It is the institutional structure that has developed over the centuries to facilitate the production of goods and services'.[2]

Financial institutions and the broader system must, therefore, be judged by the contribution they make to growth, redistribution and employment in the real economy. As John Eatwell and Lance Taylor say, 'there is no point in having a financial sector that is in some senses efficient in its own terms if the result is a less efficient real economy'.[3] Yet this has been the case since, according to Eatwell and Taylor,[4] trend growth rates in every G7 economy in the 1980s and 1990s have slowed to around two-thirds of the equivalent rates in the 1960s. Similarly, in developing countries taken as a whole, the average rate of growth had also slowed to roughly the same extent. More importantly, four out of seven 'miracle economic growth' countries in East and Southeast Asia have exhibited the same characteristics in their trend growth rates *per capita* even prior to the current crisis.

It should be clear that, even if judged on purely economic criteria, the financial system has not been performing its functions very well in the past three decades. Indeed, it is useful to note that it was only after the breakdown of the Bretton Woods system of fixed exchange rates, which were accompanied by capital controls of varying types and effectiveness, that the era of deregulation, unregulated capital flows and financial liberalization began to flourish. It was from that point onwards that the financial system ceased to be just a means to achieve growth, redistribution and employment in the real economy and began taking on a life of its own unrelated to the real economy. Instead of being a means to an end, it began to be an end in itself – a trend that has become increasingly evident in the last decade. It is also not surprising, as a result, that the volatility of the world economic system and the frequency and magnitude of financial crashes have been amplified since the collapse of the Bretton Woods system in the early 1970s.

In the human development framework, however, it will not be enough merely to resubordinate the financial system to the real economy. Equally, if not more important, will be the identification of concrete strategies for subordinating macro and other economic policy making to social and human development policy objectives and strategies. In practical terms, such subordination will imply a very different form of economic and political governance, expressed in all structures and mechanisms (local, national, regional and global). These changes should also lead to significant shifts in the current balance of power towards the local, national and regional levels, and away from the global.

While all four levels of governance are necessary, and the importance of local level governance (for example, the role of local governments, small and medium business enterprises and community-based and other local civil society organizations) should not be underestimated, this paper gives pre-eminence to national level economic and political governance issues. These are viewed as particularly important in the context of currently dominant patterns and processes of globalization.

The National Level

Economic governance implications

What are the implications of such governance renewal at the national level? In terms of economic governance, such a renewal will necessitate the following, among other policy and strategy choices:

- *A monetary policy* that responds to the needs of small and medium-scale enterprises (instead of killing them) and to ordinary households in the real domestic economy, rather than to foreign investors, hedge funds, banks and speculators who dominate the financial 'bubble' economy.

- *A fiscal policy framework* which is based on a progressive direct taxation system instead of the largely minimalist and regressive tax regimes which hold sway in most industrialized and developing countries today. To become political and economic reality, such taxation systems will need to be supported by the political will, and the necessary institutional measures, to enforce tax collection.

  Only such a fiscal policy framework, together with significant reductions in both poverty and inequality among the general population, can provide the long-term domestic resources which are necessary for the range of public and social expenditures essential to sustain both comprehensive social policy and broader human development strategies.

  Avoiding this by substituting indiscriminate foreign financial flows as a soft political and economic option for progressive domestic taxation is neither a desirable objective nor a sustainable development strategy.

- *An economic policy* which is firmly rooted in both domestic savings and a domestic market through the expansion of the real purchasing power of the poor and marginalized, and is not as heavily dependent on external engines of growth (for example, foreign financial flows and exports) as is the current strategy of countries such as Thailand.

- *A discriminatory approach to foreign financial flows*. Indeed, a large contributor to the crisis has been an all too indiscriminate approach to attracting financial flows and a vast overrating of their real or potential contributions to people-centred economics and development.

We all know the problems of short-term flows so I will not dwell on these. But one has to be very discriminating about longer-term foreign direct investment as well. In a world where two-thirds of FDI comprises mergers and acquisitions, its potential or real contribution to increasing the production of useful goods and services in the real economy, genuinely adding to sustainable production capacity, increasing employment and creating new productive and useful assets is clearly very limited. In addition, given the liberal and competitive foreign investment regimes of most developing countries (for example, tax holidays, full repatriation of profit), the impact of FDI on the balance of payments, especially over the long-term, is frequently negative. Effective technology transfer through FDI flows is also the exception rather than the rule.

National-level capital controls – over which there has been a lot of controversy recently, and a large amount of ideological debate and hype in the aftermath of Malaysia's imposition of them in September 1998 – should be put in perspective and context. Rather than being viewed separately and given inflated prominence as they have been, such controls need to be viewed merely as one essential element of an economic governance framework which is a potentially viable alternative to today's neoliberal market fundamentalism.

Within such a framework, and particularly in the absence of an appropriate global multilateral regulatory framework for financial flows, national-level capital controls, selectively and wisely applied, will remain essential. The case for this is argued convincingly by many globally eminent economists, most notably Yilmaz Akyuz, UNCTAD's Chief Macroeconomist, John Eatwell of the University of Cambridge, Lance Taylor of the Centre for Economic Policy Analysis of New York's New School for Social Research and, on a more selective basis, even by Joseph Stiglitz, Senior Vice President and Chief Economist at the World Bank, who was previously Chair of President Clinton's Council of Economic Advisers.

Such national capital controls will be needed to ensure a discriminatory approach not merely to short-term financial flows but also to longer-term foreign direct investment, to make sure that a country is able to ensure that its foreign exchange outflows are not exceeded by or grossly mismatched with its foreign exchange earnings and, overall, to allow all countries a significant measure of economic and, therefore, political sovereignty in this era of accelerating and borderless globalization.

Political governance implications

It has already been argued that economic and political governance issues need to be viewed as indivisible. This is clearly one of the key lessons of the current global crisis: good economic governance depends as much or more on good political governance as it does on sound macroeconomic and other 'fundamentals'.

While this paper is particularly concerned with governance of the global economy, this crucial interdependency and indivisibility necessitate a few comments on national-level political governance issues as well. With some modifications, these comments apply equally to the regional and global levels, especially in terms of the potential and appropriate roles and responsibilities of organizations of civil society.

The demands of better and more sustainable political governance pose at least two immediate challenges. The first is that of moving beyond electoral to more substantive and popular forms of transparent and accountable democracy; the second is a much more serious consideration of process and participation issues than has been undertaken in the past. A crucial dimension of both challenges is the need to institutionalize civil society input at all levels of political, economic and social policy making. This remains a formidable but essential task, which has hardly begun.

The implications of popular forms of transparent and accountable political governance will require the inclusion of a vibrant civil society whose independent societal watchdog roles and responsibilities need to be viewed as crucial to any reasonable practice of economic and political governance at this point in world history.

The respective governance roles and responsibilities of the state and civil society

The definition and elaboration of appropriate governance roles for organizations of civil society *vis-à-vis* states and their governments should be considered against a context wherein the core social, economic, political and cultural responsibilities and commitments of governments to their citizens, especially those who are already poor and vulnerable, are increasingly difficult to meet in the current dominant global framework of economic neoliberalism.

While this is not a good rationale to justify civil society organizations (CSOs) becoming substitutes for the state in service delivery in areas where the latter has a primary and legitimate responsibility (health, education, water, power, roads, and other public infrastructure), it has been both ideologically convenient and expedient from a practical standpoint in an era of economic neoliberalism to transfer such roles to certain types of civil society organizations.

Empirical evidence suggests that this is wishful thinking. CSO strengths do not lie in large-scale service delivery. Only governments and inter-governmental multilateral institutions are equipped to operate on the scale that is necessary if poverty eradication, full employment and social integration are to be achieved in a sustainable manner.

Indeed, there is no empirically proven substitute for the state in the provision of public goods: market failure in this area has been even greater than state failure, while civil society organizations, given their fragmented and relatively small-scale nature, are not up to such a task, nor is this an area of comparative advantage for most of them. This is borne out both by the historical experience of the industrialized countries and the present experience of developing countries. The assignment by proponents of the neoliberal economic paradigm of such roles to certain types of CSOs instead of to states, governments and intergovernmental organizations whose main responsibility this should be is, therefore, both an indication of inappropriate and poor governance, and counterproductive from the viewpoint of achieving social and human development, especially in the long run.

As David Rieff argued in a recent issue of *The Nation*,

> In fairness, the perception of the weakening of the nation [state] and of the impotence of international organizations has not been mistaken. What has been misplaced is that a network of [civil society] associations could accomplish what states could not.[5]

This depressing situation has major implications for the governance roles and responsibilities of both states and intergovernmental organizations, given the character of our global economy. Rieff goes on to argue powerfully that,

> The suggestion that civil society can cope where nations have failed is, in fact, a counsel of despair… Without a treasury, without a legislature or an army at its disposal, civil society is less equipped to confront the challenges of globalization than nations are, and more likely to be wracked by divisions based on region and self-interest of the single-issue groups that form the nucleus of the civil society movement.[6]

Indeed, as Rieff says,

> Why should fragmented groups of like-minded individuals be more effective in, say, resisting the depredations of environmental despoilers than a national government?… One can admire the efforts and sacrifices of activists in the poor world without losing sight of the fact that their countries would be better off with honest and effective governments and legal systems, and with militaries that stay in the barracks, than with denser networks of local associations [as a substitute], which may stand for good values or hideous ones.[7]

To agree with David Rieff is not to deny that CSOs have important, indeed crucial roles to play in political and economic governance. Such (more appropriate) CSO roles, however, are primarily in the areas of monitoring, advocacy and influencing policy to ensure that states and intergovernmental organizations create and sustain an enabling environment for the achievement of social and human development objectives and poverty elimination.

This implies that if CSOs are to contribute usefully to effective governance of our global economy (by playing appropriate roles in which they have a comparative advantage over states and governments), they will need to direct their limited resources and energies to campaigning, advocacy and other policy-influencing strategies aimed at ensuring that states fulfil their core responsibilities and nationally and internationally agreed commitments. Such roles also imply a CSO commitment to and capacity for monitoring the performance of governments and intergovernmental organizations and pioneering process or content alternatives to the dominant mainstream policies of the international financial institutions (IFIs).

Sadly, however, this complementary governance potential of CSOs is far from being realized because the state has often been a CSO disabler. Moreover, development and humanitarian non-governmental organizations (NGOs), an important and visible sub-set of CSOs, have not played the governance roles discussed in the previous paragraphs. They have operated instead primarily within a North–South resource transfer paradigm which has not been significantly different from the framework of the much larger bilateral and multilateral donors in this respect. Funding, for example – not monitoring, advocacy and other forms of policy influencing – has been the key resource in the relationship between Northern NGOs (NNGOs) and their Southern 'partners' and counterparts.

While the traditional resource transfer paradigm has remained the over-arching framework for North–South NGO relationships in the five development decades after the Second World War, most NGO roles have shifted from purely financial transfers to surrogate service provision in the past fifteen years. NGOs (from both North and South) in much larger numbers and on a much larger scale than in previous decades have often been all too willing to play inappropriate roles in social service and welfare provision that traditionally have been part of the economic and political governance functions and responsibility of states (health, education, disability).

This has happened both because of the abdication of the state's traditional governance roles to the 'magic hand of the market' (as a result of the fast globalizing neoliberal market economy and the concomitant shrinking state) and due to the active commission of many NGOs by both bilateral and multilateral donors and governments to fill the increasing gaps in social policy created by the latter's increasing failures in this area.

NGOs have been favoured for these roles at least partly because this has kept the lid on simmering public discontent and social explosion. This lid would be much more likely to blow off if the gaps created by state and ODA omission had been left totally unfilled by NGO service provision.

The unsustainable social safety net programmes that are attempting inadequately to deal with the growing gaps in the social policy and human development areas can be seen as constituting the 'global soup kitchen', with NGOs being described by one astute commentator as 'ordained to be ladles in the global soup kitchen'[8] of this new world order.

*Key future governance challenges and dilemmas for the
state–civil society relationship*

Empirical experience from around the world suggests that there are important governance roles for both the state and civil society, which cannot easily
be substituted or transferred from one to the other. To ensure that both
states and governments realize their best governance potential, additional
roles that more CSOs need to be willing to take up in the future include:

- Effectively challenging the authoritarian roles and tendencies of governments, while simultaneously attempting to identify and strengthen the
enabling and activist role that the state has also played in a number of
cases, for example, in the erstwhile 'economic miracle' and aspiring
miracle countries of East and Southeast Asia.

  Indeed, is it possible for the state to have one role without the other
or are they inseparable, like Siamese twins – in effect two sides of the
same coin? While it is clearly a formidable challenge and dilemma, it has
to be our endeavour to separate the enabling from the disabling role of
the state and support the former while discarding the latter. This is
because neither NGOs, nor civil society more broadly, nor the market are
viable or even desirable substitutes in the performance of the economic
or political governance roles that correctly belong with the socially activist
and enabling state.

  Challenging the authoritarian roles and tendencies of governments is
particularly important in non-democratic states where it is hard to see
how CSOs can work in partnership or collaboration with their governments for sustainable human development. Putting continuous pressure
on such governments for change in appropriate ways may be the primary
governance role (that is, creating an enabling environment) that CSOs
should prioritize and play in such situations, if they realistically can.

- Helping build transparent and accountable states and governments with
the political will, capacity and ability to guard, strongly regulate and
enforce legislation and other appropriate action against the excesses of
both an unregulated market and civil society on behalf of and in favour
of vulnerable and marginalized people all over the world.

  This is an increasingly urgent but challenging task in the current
neoliberal environment, which is nevertheless essential for the achievement of the core responsibilities and commitments of states and for
sustainable human development.

- Devising an appropriate and effective response to the major and
increasing service delivery gaps being created by the dominance of neoliberalism, which is simultaneously causing the roll-back of the state and

the growing asymmetrical power of the market, especially transnational corporate and finance capital, over both governments and civil society.

It is crucial that CSOs find ways of doing this without themselves becoming mere 'ladles in the global soup kitchen'. While this does not imply that they should never be involved in direct poverty alleviation or employment expansion programmes, it does imply that their state substitution roles in scaled-up direct service delivery should be limited to situations of short-term crisis and humanitarian response as far as possible.

Their major governance role at the local community level, in addition to demonstrating innovative approaches of service delivery for replication by government, should be to strengthen the capacity of powerless and marginalized communities and population groups to make legitimate social demands and claims on the state and governments in power. These demands, if met, will directly contribute to the achievement of sustainable human and social development. This once again implies prioritizing awareness building, organizing and analytical capacity building functions over direct service delivery ones.

- Finally, in this era of fast-accelerating globalization, there is a need to support state capacity and ability. This will constrain and regulate the power and reach of global international financial and trade institutions and transnational corporate conglomerates; in turn, this will redirect the flow of power to both local communities and a reformed, more activist and enabling national state. Sustainable development will be impossible to achieve without such a change in the balance of power.

The Asian economic crisis has also highlighted a number of other issues with major implications for sustainable human and social development and the future economic and political governance roles of states and governments if they wish to support such objectives.

1 The need to design and implement comprehensive social security policies and systems. This is partly because it is already clear that even the best designed social safety net programmes and investment funds will be grossly inadequate in dealing with the structural unemployment and other social policy issues emerging with the crisis – issues which are fundamentally inimical to the achievement of sustainable human development. Only states and governments, through the exercise of their legitimate governance functions, can design and implement such social security policies on a scale sufficient to make a difference.

2 The challenge not just of universalizing primary education but, for most developing countries, simultaneously investing in primary, secondary and tertiary education, especially in this era of globalization when the defini-

tion of basic education is in urgent need of redefinition to include at least secondary education. Again, only states and governments can ensure this, and priority attention to such policies is one of the hallmarks of good public policy and governance.

3 The crucial role of institutions, both in designing crisis response programmes and in avoiding future crises. Building local institutional capacity in financial, economic, political and social governance should be a major medium- and long-term governance objective if we are to move in the direction of sustainable development. Further financial liberalization of the type sought by the IMF as a solution in the immediate aftermath of the crisis (despite the clear evidence that premature and unregulated financial liberalization was such a big factor in the crisis) is an indicator of bad governance; it is also likely to detract from rather than enable the pursuit of sustainable development. Again, only states and governments can ensure that such institutional strengthening takes place and that no further financial liberalization occurs until affected countries are able to absorb financial flows effectively and usefully in the real economy.

Good governance has always implied that core responsibilities for the provision of basic social services and other public goods must rest with states and governments. In the current context of the shrinking state, such roles urgently need to be returned to the state if we are to have any chance of good governance. This will require, among other things, a retreat from the current minimalist definition of public goods that the IFIs and most governments appear to have embraced. It cannot be overemphasized that regulation, however effective and comprehensive, cannot be considered either a substitute for the performance of such roles or the only or even the main governance function of states and governments in the current globalizing world economy.

The Regional Level

This chapter has emphasized the preeminence of the national level in any renewed governance of the global economy. This is despite, and indeed, because of, the current dominant patterns and processes of finance-led globalization.

Notwithstanding this, appropriate, enabling and supportive (to national measures) regional governance and consultation bodies and mechanisms are likely to take on added significance in the context of accelerating globalization and the increasing number of official intergovernmental regional economic groupings and blocs, such as the Asia–Pacific Economic Cooperation forum (APEC) or the North American Free Trade Agreement (NAFTA).

While there is little doubt that this context requires an enhanced role for regional organizations and consultation mechanisms in both the inter-governmental and civil society arenas, the regional level in the global govern-ance chain is still by far the weakest. Indeed, in many cases it is even weaker than our dismal national and international institutions and mechanisms.

Intergovernmental regional institutions and mechanisms

At the intergovernmental level, various scholars and policy makers have emphasized the successes of regional groupings such as the Association of Southeast Asian Nations (ASEAN), Mercosur and the European Union, including the recent creation of the euro and European Monetary Union (EMU). While these and perhaps other regional groupings clearly have success stories to tell, such tales are limited in number and in their inspira-tion. More crucially, the record of intergovernmental regional bodies and mechanisms as intermediary, mediating or countervailing layers of economic and political governance which are supportive of the national and local levels against the global level is far from satisfactory. Instead, more often than not, there have been successful or unsuccessful attempts either to make them handmaidens of global multilateral mechanisms and institutions (such as APEC and NAFTA for the WTO) or to kill them before they are born (for example, Japan's proposed Asian Monetary Fund, stillborn because of opposition from the IMF and the US Treasury).

This poor track record may be changing slowly in the aftermath of the Asian crisis and with the creation of the EMU and euro. The latter has the potential to be a counterbalance to the US dollar as a currency of inter-national reserves and transactions. In the Asian region, likewise, the crisis has catalyzed talk about both the creation of an 'Asian currency system' based on a trade-weighted basket of currencies that includes not only the US dollar but also the Japanese yen and the euro.[9] Furthermore, the Japanese proposal for an Asian Monetary Fund, which was actively resisted when it was first mooted (the Japanese unfortunately meekly retreated under the attack), re-emerged as the Miyazawa Initiative when the crisis deepened. Even though this is a watered-down and much more poorly resourced version of the original proposal, it does indicate that the momentum for economic govern-ance alternatives at a regional level may be growing.

There is little doubt that the governance of the global economy would greatly benefit from the creation at the regional level of an appropriate monetary fund or facility, even if the type of mechanism proposed by the Japanese at the outset of the Asian crisis may not be the most appropriate one from a people-centred economics perspective. It is critical, however, that such a mechanism, whatever form it takes, should contribute to pluralism and provide much needed competition in our current hegemonic global monetary system.

Regional civil society initiatives

Civil society initiatives at the regional level have so far been largely reactive to intergovernmental initiatives, rather than strategic and proactive, and this remains the weakest link in civil society activism and action. Nevertheless, noteworthy civil society regional initiatives have included the *Common Frontiers/ Common Fronteras* project of Canadian-Mexican-US networks, supported by the continental free trade policy research and analysis project of Action Canada Network (ACN); the series of annual mobilizations around the Asia Pacific Economic Cooperation (APEC) forum; and a similar but parallel mobilization in Asia and Europe around the Asia-Europe Summit (ASEM).

These campaigns are elaborated in detail in various documents[10] and will not be covered, therefore, in this chapter. Nevertheless, it is important to emphasize that if these campaigns are to be useful and contribute to the governance of the global economy, they will need to move beyond critique to the articulation of workable, substantive and sustainable process and content alternatives to the existing structures of global economic and political governance. While some civil society proposals are attempting to do this, they are still few and far between and often lack the coherence and comprehensiveness that they will need if they are to be influential.

The Global Level

Finally, there are crucial issues to deal with at the global level and in relation to the future global financial, economic and social architecture if sustainable human development is to be pursued seriously. Once again, as in the case of regional mechanisms and bodies, the fundamental principle that should underlie the creation of mechanisms and institutions of global governance is that they should be enabling and supportive of national (especially) and regional efforts and should not attempt to dominate or supplant them.

Yet, in the context of a highly globalized economy and financial system, merely resorting to national- or even regional-level regulatory and other measures will, of itself, be inadequate. This is because international financial liberalization results in major increases in risk to both the national and international real economy of each country; as a result, an effective policy towards capital markets will need to be global in nature. The debate on capital controls illustrates this vividly, since national-level controls, however desirable, are likely to be ineffective in dealing with both the source and magnitude of the problem, and can be easily subverted by neighbouring countries pursuing contrary (for example, financial liberalization) policies to attract finance capital.

Accountability of the Bretton Woods institutions to a reformed UN system

At a broader level than just financial flows, if it is accepted that economic policy should exist primarily to serve medium- and long-term human and social policy goals, then it follows that regional and global financial institutions such as the IMF, World Bank, African Development Bank (ADB) and WTO should be more accountable to human and social policy. Even more importantly, they should play subordinate roles to regional and global multilateral institutions that are primarily concerned with human and social policy issues (for example, UNDP and some of the specialized agencies of the United Nations).

While this is far from today's reality, and such a major global governance change will be neither credible nor feasible without substantial progressive reform of the entire UN system, it is a prerequisite for renewing the governance of the global economy. Indeed, such a restoration of the balance of power intended when the United Nations system was created in San Francisco in 1945 — while it may be threatening to and resisted by the Bretton Woods twins, as well as by financial institutions such as the Bank for International Settlements (BIS) — should not be a clear, non-negotiable aim. The current dispensation is threatening people's livelihoods and right to development, not just in the developing world but increasingly in industrial-ized countries. It is precisely for this reason that the centre of gravity of global economic governance needs to be shifted away from the current institutions such as the IMF, BIS and the World Bank — with a narrow financial and economic orientation — to more democratic institutions which place the emphasis on social and human development, such as those in the non-Bretton Woods United Nations system.

Despite the serious shortcomings and relative impotence of the latter, there is no need to create new global multilateral institutions (with perhaps one exception, a democratically constituted World Financial Authority, accountable to the United Nations, to be described later in this chapter) until the more fundamental issues of economic and political governance dealt with in previous sections are first addressed. This is because without addressing the underlying skewed power balances and policies that currently shape our dysfunctional global governance, the creation of new institutions will merely multiply existing skews and imbalances, adding to the problem rather than contributing to the solution.

Shutting down the IMF and World Bank, as many have demanded over the years, will not resolve the underlying problems of global governance that we currently face: the Bretton Woods institutions today are a symptom, not a cause, of the malaise that has set in, particularly after the demise of the Bretton Woods system in the early 1970s. Moreover, their shutdown would merely lead to the creation of 'new' but identical institutions to perform the specialized tasks that they were originally established to accomplish. These tasks are even more necessary in our current globalized world economy – but other tasks have arisen, too. This is why some form of World Financial Authority (WFA), constituted as a UN multilateral global finance regulatory body with executive powers and armed with mandatory sanctions (similar in terms of its executive powers and authority to the WTO) needs to be established in a democratically accountable manner at the same time that the IMF and World Bank are reformed. The WFA should be viewed as a body which has overall regulatory oversight and other governance functions over the global financial system and its institutions, including the Bretton Woods twins. It is not being proposed to replace them.

The creation of a World Financial Authority

A key principle underlying the creation of such a new global multilateral institution is that, given the magnitude and rapidity of international capital movements today, such a mechanism can only work if there is a high degree of mutually reinforcing cooperation between national monetary and financial authorities. In a useful article Eric Helleiner argues that both Keynes and Harry Dexter White, the key UK and US negotiators at the Bretton Woods conference in 1944, foresaw the need for this, and that the world's leading powers (G7) have led an international cooperation effort to target international financial flows associated with money laundering to curtail such financial movements since the late 1980s.[11] Both Australia and the United States, as part of this effort, have started monitoring cross-border capital flows related to money laundering and 'in the past decade many governments have criminalized money laundering, signed mutual legal assistance treaties and required financial institutions in their territories to introduce "know your customer" rules and report all suspicious transactions. Even some offshore financial centres have agreed not to let bank secrecy laws interfere with international cooperation'[12] in this area.

Helleiner goes on to argue that international efforts to combat money laundering raise the interesting question of whether the new regulations and surveillance procedures can be used to track and control other forms of financial flows. It appears clear from this example that the real issue is not whether states are able or even willing to regulate financial flows but rather, which financial flows the international community deems undesirable.[13] For example, as has often been suggested, can capital flight be treated as part of an expanded definition of money laundering,[14] and can certain speculative activities such as hedge funds and other unregulated financial institutions be treated as undesirable financial flows by the international community?

The proposal for a World Financial Authority was made in late 1998 by John Eatwell and Lance Taylor in the context of this set of rationales and principles. The WFA's main objectives, if it were created, would be to ensure that the operations of global financial markets remain consistent with, and indeed promote, growth, redistribution and employment in the real economy. To enable this, its central tasks would be to minimize systemic risk arising from the operations of securities and futures markets, and to develop policies to manage such systemic risk and avoid the creation of moral hazard.

To fulfil these responsibilities, the WFA would need to develop rules that would ensure that current 'externalities' are internalized (so that moral hazard is reduced) and that a credible and effective lender of last resort function is created, implemented and enforced. In addition to its regulatory functions, the WFA is also envisaged as a forum in which the rules of international financial cooperation are developed and implemented through effective mutual cooperation and coordination between countries, something that rarely happens at present. The proposal also envisages that the WFA would be given the responsibility of ensuring transparency and accountability of the IFIs such as the World Bank and the IMF, whose activities are currently not evaluated systematically by an external body with authority of the type envisaged for the WFA. Making a reformed set of Bretton Woods institutions accountable to the WFA should also help improve their relevance and performance. Besides, such a body could also monitor and regulate the activities of international banks, currency traders and fund managers.

The WFA would also support national government efforts, in both developing and industrialized countries, aimed at improving regulatory and control functions over their entire national financial system (for example, through the imposition of capital and/or reserve requirements on all major financial institutions such as banks, mutual funds, insurance and pension funds for all off-shore and on-shore operations, whether on or off the balance sheet), despite the difficulties associated with doing this.

Crucial to the proposal is that national governments, in consultation with the WFA, would be able to impose restrictions on external capital movements (for example, through taxation of cross-border financial flows). The WFA would also have the authority to ensure that the controls of one country are not subverted by the policies of other countries – instead, all countries should be enabled to help one another's efforts at implementing national policies in this area.

Given what is proposed, the WFA would need to be given executive authority with surveillance and mandatory enforcement capabilities, such as the WTO has, but within a much more democratic governance framework. The fact that the WTO has been created with this authority shows that if the political will to regulate global financial flows exists among the G7,-as it already does for trade liberalization, then a WFA of the type described is feasible and viable.

British Prime Minister Tony Blair has spoken out in support of such an institution, while India's Finance Minister Yashwant Sinha has said that 'sooner or later, the international community will have to devise the norms and set up the authority to deal with the system'.[15] Political support for such an institution is generally weak, however, and hostility towards such a proposal has been strong from the IMF and fund managers.

A reformed IMF

Apart from being made more transparent and accountable to the WFA, a reformed IMF should be confined to its original narrow mandate, consistent with its original charter. As Martin Feldstein – former Chair of the Council of Economic Advisers under conservative Republican US governments – correctly pointed out in the context of the Asian crisis and the IMF 'bail-out rescue' packages that followed, '[the IMF] should not use the opportunity to impose other economic changes that, however helpful they may be, are not necessary to deal with the balance of payments problem and are the proper responsibility of the country's own political system'.

In this context, further attempts to rewrite the IMF's Articles of Agreement to enable it to require full capital account convertibility and financial market liberalization from its client borrowers should also be rejected. As Eatwell and Taylor indicate, such proposals 'are without sound intellectual foundation'.[16]

The IMF, under the authority and scrutiny of the WFA, should develop procedures to deal with rescue and 'bail-in' (as opposed to 'bail-out') packages in liquidity crises, drawing private creditors into these 'bail-ins' rather than bailing them out. This will require very different policies and responses from those made thus far by the IMF. It should also minimize the moral hazard problem which has been such a dominant feature of the systemic financial crises that the world economy has witnessed since the early 1970s, with increasing frequency and devastation.

Civil society action at the global level

Civil society campaigns and proposals for global governance are much more plentiful and wide-ranging than at the regional or even national level. They cover issues such as political reform of the UN Security Council and the creation of a global people's assembly as part of the UN General Assembly, as well as much more specific efforts such as the successful Campaign to Ban Land Mines, the campaign against the OECD's Multilateral Agreement on Investment (MAI), the Structural Adjustment Participatory Review Initiative (SAPRI) and Social Watch. Various documents and proposals describe these campaigns and their critiques and proposals.[17] As in the case of regional civil society campaigns, the challenge will be in the articulation of more cohesive and comprehensive alternatives for global economic and political governance and their effective use around the various millennium events planned at and around the United Nations during the next three to five years.

Who's Wagging Whom?

To conclude, I believe that in many areas today, the tail is wagging the dog. This situation must be turned around if we are seriously interested in good economic and political governance of the global economy. This is the only way in which we will achieve sustainable human development. There is no better place to start than by promoting the three subordinations mentioned at the very beginning of this chapter – the resubordination of the financial system to the real economy, the subordination of macro and other economic policy to social policy and human development objectives and strategies, and the subordination of the global level of governance to the local, national and regional levels – but especially the national.

Notes

1 Eatwell, John and Lance Taylor (1998) *International Capital Markets and the Future of Economic Policy*, Centre for Economic Policy Analysis (CEPA) Working Paper Series III, Working Paper No. 9, New School for Social Research, New York, September.
2 *Ibid.*
3 *Ibid.*
4 *Ibid.*
5 Rieff, David (1999) 'The False Dawn of Civil Society', *The Nation*, New York, 22 February, pp. 11–16.
6 *Ibid.*
7 *Ibid.*
8 Fowler, Alan (1994: 18–24) 'Capacity Building and NGOs: a Case of Strengthening Ladles for the Global Soup Kitchen?', *Institutional Development*, Vol. 1, No. 1, PRIA, New Delhi.
9 APEC Business Summit, *Smart Partnerships in Key Economic Sectors: Reform of the International Monetary System*, Kuala Lumpur, Malaysia, 16 November 1998.
10 For the Common Fronteras campaign against NAFTA see, for example, Foster, J. W. (1993) 'Redefining Governance: the Transnationalization of Civic Participation in North America', mimeo, Ottawa; and Thorup, C. (1991: 12–26) ' The Politics of Free Trade and the Dynamics of Cross Border Coalitions in US–Mexico Relations', *Columbia Journal of World Business*, Vol. 26, No. 2. For the civil society mobilization around APEC see, for example, (eds) Bello, W. and J. Chavez-Malauan (1996) 'APEC: Four Adjectives in Search of a Noun', Manila People's Forum on APEC, Focus on the Global South and Institute of Popular Democracy, Manila, November; and Bello, W. (1995) 'Challenging the Mainstream: APEC and the Asia Pacific Development Debate', ARENA, Asia Alliance of YMCAs, CCA, DAGA, Hong Kong, October. For civil society contributions around ASEM, see (eds) Brennan, B., Heijmans, E. and P. Vervest (1997) 'ASEM Trading New Silk Routes: Beyond Geo-Politics and Geo-Economics, Towards a New Relationship Between Asia and Europe', Transnational Institute, Netherlands and Focus on the Global South, Amsterdam, February.
11 Helleiner, E. (1998) 'The Myth of the All-Powerful Financial Markets', *Perspectives on*

International Financial Liberalization, Discussion Paper Series 15, Office of Development Studies, Bureau of Development Policy, UNDP, New York.

12 *Ibid.*

13 *Ibid.*

14 See, for example, Lissakers, K. (1991) *Banks, Borrowers and the Establishment,* Basic Books, New York; and Helleiner, E. (1985: 81–110) 'Handling "Hot Money": US Policy towards Latin American Capital Flight in Historical Perspective', *Alternatives,* 20.

15 'Ministry to Hold Talks with Vigilance Panel', *Business Line,* India, 16 September 1998 cited in Singh, K. (1998) 'Capital Controls, State Intervention and Public Action in the Era of Financial Globalization', Occasional Paper 4, Public Interest Research Group (PIRG), Delhi.

16 Eatwell, John and Lance Taylor (1998) *International Capital Markets and the Future of Economic Policy,* Centre for Economic Policy Analysis (CEPA) Working Paper Series III, Working Paper No. 9, New School for Social Research, New York, revised September.

17 For example, for detailed information on SAPRI and its global network SAPRIN, contact its secretariat at The Development Group for Alternative Policies (D-GAP) in Washington, DC, USA at e-mail address dgap@igc.org and for similar information on Social Watch, contact its secretariat at the Instituto del Tercer Mundo, Montevideo, Uruguay at e-mail address item@chasque.apc.org or read its latest publication *Social Watch* No. 3, 1999.

5

Their Reforms and Ours
Balance of Forces and Economic Analysis in a New Global Financial Architecture

PATRICK BOND

In 1999 Washington claimed that the dangers of financial meltdown and deflation, which had plagued the global economy for two years, had been averted and finally extinguished through a combination of policy measures and good fortune.[1] But, looking ahead, how convincing and durable were the multiple reassertions of financial power?

At a time of uneasy US geopolitical hegemony and awesome overhangs in the US economy (trade and debt imbalances, consumer borrowing, stock market overvaluation, etc.), scepticism should be the appropriate response to Washington's regularly expressed confidence in capitalism's flexible capacity to resolve perpetual crisis tendencies. In this context, then, what socio-economic forces are now in play, both systemically and anti-systemically, and what is the likelihood of their success? Given the particularly virulent ways in which the crises erupted – Mexico (early 1995), South Africa (early 1996 and mid-1998), Southeast Asia (1997–8), South Korea (early 1998), Russia (periodic but especially since mid-1998), Brazil and Ecuador (early 1999) – are these semi-peripheral sites good examples of national-scale contradictions, contemporary social struggles and potential resolutions?

This chapter addresses these issues. During the years 1997–9, varying positions emerged about the global economic crisis, representing different material interests and economic ideologies. Although fluidity is the only constant, as of mid-1999 five broad tendencies appear to have firmed up, representing systematic reactions to the global financial crisis: (1) the 'Washington Consensus'; (2) the 'Old World Order'; (3) the 'Post-Washington Consensus'; (4) 'Third World Nationalism'; and (5) 'New Social Movements' (see accompanying table on page 72). Once we glance over the array of forces, a few strategic conclusions about 'scale politics' may emerge.

The Array of Forces Contesting Global Finance

The Washington Consensus

Let's first consider the most powerful tendency: the *status quo*. The Washing-ton Consensus continues dogmatically to promote free trade, financial liberalization, foreign investment incentives, business deregulation, low taxes, fiscal austerity, privatization, high real interest rates, and flexible labour markets.[2] According to the Consensus, if there are problems outstanding in the world economy, they are merely temporary. Any problems can be overcome by more IMF bail-outs (embarrassingly generous to New York bankers though they were), intensified application of 'sound' macroeconomic policies, augmented by greater transparency, a touch more financial sector supervision and regulation, and less Asian cronyism. (An early 1999 IMF attempt to go a bit further, and establish a Washington Consensus 'lender of last resort', was initially discredited, for it was seen as a naked power play.)

Providing the political cover for the *status quo* at the end of the century were Bill Clinton and Tony Blair. Providing operational support were then US Treasury Secretary Robert Rubin, his deputy (and 1999 replacement) Lawrence Summers, US Federal Reserve chair Alan Greenspan, and IMF Managing Director Camdessus. Those offering periodic intellectual justification were IMF Deputy MD Stanley Fischer and Summers in another role. A variety of bank and corporate-sponsored Washington think-tanks echoed the party line, while outside the Washington Beltway allies were found in the WTO, the BIS, the OECD and numerous university economics departments. At its core, the Washington Consensus is under-girded by a 'Wall Street–Treasury Complex,' in the words of Columbia University's Jagdish Bhagwati; and indeed, as another world-famous conservative economist, Rudiger Dornbusch, conceded in 1998, 'The IMF is a toy of the United States to pursue its economic policy offshore'.[3]

The Old World Order

Amongst those scornful of the Consensus were conservatives, largely based in reactionary pockets of the United States. But it was a mistake to discount US politicians like Jesse Helms, Trent Lott, Pat Buchanan and their ilk as mere populist rednecks. Their critique of public bail-outs for New York bankers was backed by think-tanks like the stalwart-conservative Heritage Foundation and the libertarian but surprisingly influential Cato Institute in Washington. Their critique was closely paralleled by élite conservative concerns – notably Henry Kissinger and George Shultz, geopoliticians who lost dear friends like Suharto in the 1997–8 financial turmoil. Together, this led to a formidable attack on IMF policies as unworkable and to opposition towards the US Treasury Department's request for $18 billion in further IMF funding.[4] ~

This has also led to the interesting problem of deciphering the occasional tactical alliance between a Pat Buchanan, say, and left-populist movements such as the Ralph Nader networks and Friends of the Earth.[5] Political strategies that unite right and left, as inter-war Germany showed, do most damage to the left, a point to which we will return.

While the right-wing challenge appears formidable at times, it is also subject to cooption, as occurred in October 1998 when Bill Clinton bought off Republican opposition by doing a deal which will make IMF conditionlity even more fierce, since it shortens repayment periods and raises interest rates on future bailout loans. Xenophobia and isolationism are logical political threats from this position, and economically it wouldn't be hard to envisage latter-day Smoot-Hawley-style protective tariffs kicking off a downward spiral of trade degeneration reminiscent of the early 1930s, if Old World Order advocates had their way.

The Post-Washington Consensus

There appears to be an emerging reform position, although it is one that often takes one step forward and two steps back. We can term this the 'Post-Washington Consensus' in honour of World Bank chief economist Joseph Stiglitz.[6] Aimed at perfecting the capitalist system's 'imperfect markets', Stiglitz cites organic problems like asymmetric information in market transactions (especially finance) and anti-competitive firm behaviour as key contributors to the present instability. Likewise, speculator George Soros has attributed financial volatility to the herd instincts of bankers.[7] However, even though they advocate somewhat more substantive national regulatory interventions (tougher anti-trust measures, and even 'speed bumps' or dual exchange rates to slow down hot money) and more attention to social development and employment, Stiglitz and Soros are still reluctant to tamper with the underlying dynamics of the market. This is especially so when you look at Soros, whose call for a global banking insurance fund looks suspiciously self-interested (particularly coming at a time, in August 1998, when he lost several billion dollars of his Russian investments due to Boris Yeltsin's default on state debt).[8]

Others from a neoliberal economic background who are jumping the Washington Consensus ship include Massachusetts Institute of Technology economist Paul Krugman, who claims both a temporary fondness for capital controls and responsibility for Mohamad Mahathir's September 1998 restrictions on trading the Malaysian ringgit.[9] Likewise, Jeffrey Sachs, Director of the Harvard Institute for International Development, offers critiques of IMF austerity economics so vociferous as almost to disguise his own previous advocacy of deregulatory shock therapy from Latin America to Eastern Europe.[10]

More durable than the growing chorus of reform-oriented neoliberals are the institutions which have an actual material stake in promoting human welfare, such as several key United Nations agencies (whether they succeed or not is another matter).[11] More confusing than any of the other reformers is the World Bank, whose President James Wolfensohn allows Stiglitz space to attack the IMF but whose own unoriginal contribution to the debate – a January 1999 paper on the Bank's 'new paradigm' reminiscent of modernization theory – describes his institution's function as the opposite side of the same coin of the IMF, one performing macroeconomic 'stabilization', the other 'development'.[12] Potentially more significant than any of the above are the shifting political sands of social-democratic (and Green or otherwise left-leaning) party politics in Germany, France, Italy and Japan. However, the March 1999 departure of Oskar Lafontaine represents a profound setback for this current, which realigns Germany away from France (at least Jospin's wing of Socialism) and towards Britain. This matches the failure of the Japanese (led by Miyazawa) to establish an Asian Monetary Fund as a result of a Rubin/Summers veto.[13]

More and more, the presence of Keynesian-oriented officials from Tokyo and Paris would benefit from the mid-1999 realization that state fiscal stimulation actually produced some results in Japan. Moreover, especially given its importance to the South African debate, the Stiglitz 'information-theoretic' approach to economics (and the role of Stiglitz himself) should be revisited again a bit later.

Third World nationalism

The equivalent group in the Third World nationalist camp cannot claim to share traditions in any respect. While China and India are forthrightly resisting financial liberalization and Russia formally defaulted in August 1998, it is in rather different nationalist regimes in Asia, Africa and Latin America that we can identify more radical discourses of opposition to the Washington Consensus. From Malaysia (Mahathir) to Zimbabwe (Robert Mugabe) to Venezuela (Hugo Chavez), IMF-bashing is back in style, even if the rhetorical flourishes have different origins (one Muslim, one self-described socialist, one simply populist). Yet the trajectory chosen in these three cases amounts, at best, to attempting to join the system, playing by its rules and, having discovered that the game isn't fair, adjusting the rules somewhat in the Third World's favour.[14] More typical of a tamed nationalism was the offhand remark by Nelson Mandela at the July 1998 Mercosur meetings of South American nations, that 'Globalization is a phenomenon that we cannot deny. All we can do is accept it'.[15]

Not even reflective of the 1970s call for a New International Economic Order, this strain faded badly over the subsequent two decades. Most leaders and political parties of Second and Third World societies who at one point (at least momentarily) carried the aspirations of a mass popular electorate[16] rapidly reversed allegiance, imposing ineffectual and terribly unpopular structural adjustment programmes. In the cases of Mahathir, Mugabe and others, 'talking left' also entailed repression of public interest groups and trade unions (and women and gay rights movements).

Not just a problem of Third World nationalism, selling out the poor and working classes on behalf of international finance was also the general fate of so many labour and social democratic parties in Western Europe, Canada and Australia. Even where once-revolutionary parties remained in control of the nation state – China, Vietnam, Angola, and Mozambique, for instance – ideologies wandered over to hard, raw capitalism. And yet, the very universality of financial crisis would necessarily allow counter-hegemonic voices to emerge.[17]

New Social Movements

Which brings us to the very broadly defined New Social Movements (a phrase chosen for convenience, not to imply a particular political-intellectual tilt), whose goal typically was to promote the globalization of people and halt or at minimum radically modify the globalization of capital.[18] These movements have spanned Old Left forces (many labour movements, and some ex-Stalinist Communist Parties),[19] newer political parties,[20] progressive churches, human rights and disarmament movements, democracy activists, urban or rural community and indigenous peoples' movements, organizations of women, youth and the elderly, HIV and health activists, disability rights lobbyists, consumer advocates, and environmentalists who work at both the local and the global scales.

Naturally, these movements are all extremely diverse in all aspects of their existence. Are there any discourses that can combine the mass-based movements and the NGOs, the proletarian (or often lumpen) activists and petit-bourgeois intellectuals, the women and the men, the environmentalists and the workers? In both strategic and tactical respects, achieving a synthesis of 'militant particularist' struggles (to borrow Raymond Williams's evocative term) is always difficult, not least in the simple matter of movement leaders and activists finding common and mutually supportive discourses.[21] Nevertheless, by the turn of the century virtually all countries provided evidence of coalitions and networks of anti-globalization activists, many of which were fairly well grounded in mass democratic organizations that acted locally but thought globally.[22]

Some localized efforts were already having inspiring results by the turn of the century, such as anti-dam struggles in parts of South Asia and the unveiling of Chile's repressive legacy as part of an international campaign to bring General Pinochet to justice. But it was always vital to question whether these sorts of organizations could forge links. In other words, not only to think globally and act locally, but to act globally as well.[23] The most successful of these groups during the late 1990s tackled three global issues: landmines (nearly victorious were it not for the United States), the Multilateral Agreement on Investment (where several stunning stalemates were won mainly in European settings) and Third World debt. Indeed it was possible to locate within the 'Jubilee 2000' debt cancellation movement (particularly its Asian, African and Latin American components) an extremely effective campaigning spirit that not only attracted the likes of celebrities such as Muhammad Ali and U-2 singer Bono, but also drew tens of thousands of activists to protest at G8 meetings in Birmingham in 1998 and Cologne in 1999.[24]

Social movements showed that they could shake ruling-class confidence in major neoliberal initiatives (NAFTA and US support for GATT were threatened more by radical US farmer and labour activists than by right-wing Republican populists). They have also claimed quite substantial resources for future struggles, including effective advocacy networks[25] and a few progressive nerve centres in sites of power, particularly Washington, DC.[26] In addition, there were several radical economic think-tanks associated with the social movements,[27] as well as university allies,[28] a handful of accessible international activist-oriented periodicals[29] and publishing houses,[30] not to mention world-class spokespeople and luminaries from the new movements who easily outwit conservative debating partners.[31]

The global balance of forces is very clearly weighted against Third World Nationalists and New Social Movements, and there is no apparent basis for any forms of alliance between the two, given the former's penchant for authoritarianism and patriarchy. There are also a variety of other important organized social forces (such as Muslim fundamentalist oppositionists, Andean guerrillas or still-stodgy US trade unionists) which don't neatly fit into any camp as yet but may influence matters to some degree. In addition, the global crisis resurrected platforms for well-meaning economist-technocrat reformers who do not easily fit into any of the camps noted above.[32]

Amongst the New Social Movements there are two fault-lines. One is a terribly dangerous tendency amongst the more conservative (and often 'inside-the-Beltway') NGOs and environmental groups – some even derisively called Co-opted NGOs or 'Co-NGOs' – to cut pragmatic yet ultimately absurd and untenable deals with the establishment (endorsements of the US–Africa 'Growth and Opportunity' free trade deal, or numerous negotiations over the environment).[33] The other is an ongoing debate over whether energy should be invested in helping Post-Washington Consensus reforms constitute a global state regulatory capacity – expanding upon embryos like the IMF and World Bank, WTO, United Nations and BIS – or whether in contrast the immediate task should be defunding and denuding the legitimacy of the current sites of potential international regulation so as to reconstitute progressive politics at the national scale. This latter problem we can now address briefly.

Scales of Political Reform

In June 1999, John Kenneth Galbraith advised an audience at the London School of Economics, 'When you hear it being said that we've entered a new era of permanent prosperity with prices of financial instruments reflecting that happy fact, you should take cover. Let us not assume that the age of slump, recession, depression is past'.[34] But, as noted at the outset of this essay, many do just that, supported by emollient proclamations from sites of international financial power. After a year of sweating through discrete but severe hazards (the Russian default, hiccups on Wall Street, Malaysian capital controls, Long Term Capital Management's bankruptcy, Brazilian and Ecuadorean currency meltdowns), G7 leaders who met in Cologne were cocky about the restoration of global economic stability and growth. If they are right, the steady construction of a world state can continue apace without opponents' legitimate recourse to the 1997–9 critique shared by forces as diverse as mass-popular movements and George Soros: global financial architects (who in fact aim not to build anything anew, but to redecorate) are incompetent.

It is therefore worth beginning a discussion of scale politics by defending the assertion that the reforms proposed by the Washington Consensus and the Post-Washington Consensus are inadequate. Because together they identify the global crisis as emanating from lack of information and account-ability, or from corruption or ill-regulated financial markets, the policy recommendations of both Washington and Post-Washington will continue simply to shift deck chairs on the financial *Titanic*.

This is not just a matter for technical debates amongst economists.[35] A great many public relations dollars have been invested in the idea that, for example, a new group at the World Bank (Wolfensohn and Stiglitz) will sort out the maniacs across the road at the IMF. South Africa's premier newspaper, the *Mail and Guardian*, reported after a high-profile January 1999 trip to South Africa, that 'Reflecting the changing face of the World Bank, Joseph Stiglitz is a hero in some left-wing circles.... His intention is noble: to free the poor from the powerlessness that is such a feature of poverty'.[36]

Stiglitz claimed, however dubiously, that by late 1998, 75–80 per cent of his senior Bank colleagues agreed with him, so his information-theoretic analytical innovations should be seen in an institutional context. Brown

University political economist Robert Wade attributed the Bank's new open-mindedness to an acknowledgement of internal intellectual sclerosis, Japan's increasing donor role (and its own self-interest in expansionary not contractionary policies for countries in which its firms invested), and self-reflective case study, including the counter-intuitive East Asian miracle.[37]

Indeed, the disjuncture between the *status quo*-oriented Camdessus-Summers-Greenspan-Fischer bloc and reformers centred on Stiglitz boiled down to an élite fight between hostile brothers. To illustrate precisely the institutional role Stiglitz had to continue playing – defending a key Washington Consensus institution, the World Bank – soon led to his South African delegitimization. In January 1999, his World Bank Pretoria-based colleagues set up a formal meeting with 50 members of the South African NGO Coalition (SANGOCO). Stiglitz went on to reverse tack on the larger economic issues, once some embarrassing questions about 'moral hazard' were put to him (including his Helsinki-speech consent to allowing inflation rates to rise to 40 per cent, which he reduced to 8 per cent). As recounted by SANGOCO Vice-President Mercia Andrews and Campaign Against Neoliberalism in South Africa coordinator George Dor,

> We asked him for his views on the contradiction between his speech in Helsinki and the World Bank contribution to the [homegrown structural adjustment] *Gear* strategy. He told us he didn't know much about South Africa.... We put it to him that perhaps the Bank should take action against its staff members on the *Gear* team who got the employment predictions so horribly wrong by suggesting that *Gear* would generate hundreds of thousands of jobs each year when, in reality, hundreds of thousands are being lost. Everything in his tortuous reply suggested that he was not particularly concerned whether Bank staff members produce work of poor quality and that staff members can get away with shoddy work that has a profound impact on people's chances of finding employment....
>
> Our engagement with him highlights a significant retreat from his Helsinki position. There are a number of possible reasons. His Helsinki speech may have been a deliberate strategy to create the impression of change. The World Bank may have reined him in after Helsinki. Perhaps he felt restrained in Johannesburg by the need to talk the language of his entourage. He portrays the confidence that he has the ear of the institution but insider talk suggests that he is a maverick who is not to be taken too seriously. Whatever the reason for his retreat, his hero's halo has now vanished.[38]

But even if the Washington Consensus/Post-Washington Consensus are as capricious and shallow as Stiglitz indicated to the Johannesburg NGOs, and as the June 1999 Cologne G7 meeting confirmed to all other observers, we must broach the larger question of what kind of political strategy leads to what kinds of change. Given the character of the (over-accumulation) crisis, it would indeed be logical to move from a Marxian analysis to a revolutionary socialist strategy. But there is so little organization aiming in this direction that it would be futile.

Instead, given the contradictory opportunities for alliance amongst the various social forces arrayed against Washington, the project of thorough-going change (for those who analyze the problems as being structural) calls up the need for non-reformist reform strategies rather than the kinds of ameliorative or delaying tactics that we have come to expect from most of the other players. However, quite unlike the defenders of Washington-consensus orthodoxy, a less dogmatic tradition of economists and policy-makers have occasionally had to view their task more honestly: to save the system from its own worst self-destructive tendencies. Therefore, it may be worth revisiting Keynes's ideas to identify what, at the very minimum, that intelligent and farsighted defender of capitalist economics understood as the appropriate institutional arrangements for financial markets.

In 1936, Keynes devised a philosophically grounded analysis – based on the disjuncture between savings and investment that recurs periodically under capitalism – and a remedy to Depression-ridden capitalism that, from the early 1940s, revolutionized economic thinking for a period of more than three, relatively high-growth and less unequal decades. That remedy is famously considered to lie in fiscal populism. But just as crucial, for Keynes, was controlling financial capital that otherwise flowed merrily around the world in the twinkling of an eye, doing enormous damage. For Keynes, a footloose flow of capital

> assumes that it is right and desirable to have an equalization of interest rates in all parts of the world. In my view the whole management of the domestic economy depends upon being free to have the appropriate interest rate without reference to the rates prevailing in the rest of the world. Capital controls is a corollary to this.[39]

Thanks largely to Keynes's arguments in 1944 against the American negotiating team at Bretton Woods, the IMF Articles of Agreement still allow member countries to 'exercise such controls as are necessary to regulate international capital movements'. However, the IMF has attempted (so far unsuccessfully) to undo such a significant concession. As recently as 1990, 35 countries retained formidable capital controls, although the details (especially the technical policing capacity) are important to study. If indeed capital controls are potentially a common denominator of alliance activity amongst and between New Social Movements, they probably should be understood as a 'necessary but insufficient' strategic priority for lobbying national élites and for opening up sufficient manoeuvring space globally. Their merit lies not merely in the potential technical resolution of problems, but in limiting the damage done by the Washington Consensus in other spheres of economic and social policy engineering. To put the case simply, there is less need for an IMF seal of approval if fewer hot-money brokers are interested in a particular country.

There are related areas of nation-state intervention, such as prohibiting certain kinds of deregulated financial market activity, which should also be promoted. Indeed, a gathering at the Institute for Policy Studies in Washington in December 1998 established a variety of other approaches. These included regional crisis funds (belonging to a manageable set of countries with similar norms, values and practices) and domestic redirection of locally raised monies (hence 'soft currency' in many cases, intermediated by worker-influenced pension funds or mutual funds) along with progressive national taxation.

Is the nation state the right scale at which to pursue reforms, however, or has the world so changed since Keynes's time that it is now crucial to construct global rather than local regulatory processes? A debate continues over the potential for reforms to existing global institutions.[40] The strongest possible case in favour of a 'world state' was a book published in 1992 by Warren Wagar[41] positing a global social democratic political party taking control of world government midway through the twenty-first century. World-systems sociologists Terry Boswell and Chris Chase-Dunn make the argument forthrightly:

> A world polity of global institutions, for the first time ever in world history, is becoming capable of directing the processes of the modern world-system.... 'Global governance' has increased geometrically in the period following World War II as the strength of a globally oriented world bourgeoisie has increased vis-à-vis the nationally oriented fractions of capital. These processes, like market integration, are driven by the falling costs of communications and transportation and the increasing size of business enterprises. They are also driven by the interaction between the logic of capitalist accumulation and the organizational efforts by people to control and to protect themselves from market forces.
>
> The formation of a global polity opens the possibility of alternate paths to hegemony and even of a transformation of the system to include a world government. Of course, it is also possible, and perhaps, probable, that these changes are temporary, and that the cycle of hegemonic rivalry and war will again repeat in devastating fashion. But the possibilities for fundamentally changing the system are greater now than in the previous century.[42]

The practical implication for a country like South Africa would be to continue positioning itself the way it currently is, attempting to attain leadership positions (including Thabo Mbeki's goal of taking a permanent African seat on the UN Security Council) and making major reforms to the international institutions it presently influences. Others view organizations like the Non-Aligned Movement or G77 as the appropriate vehicles for making such demands. In some cases there are extremely sharp conflicts over how to reform the embryonic global state institutions.[43]

But even if NGOs and environmentalists continue lobbying the Bretton Woods institutions for change, or if some of the more outspoken South governments continue to demand better terms and accuse the IMF of heavy-handedness, this is a long way from a coherent strategy of 'democratizing' the embryonic world state. How sensible such a strategy is depends largely upon whether any real progress is being made given the global balance of forces discussed above. That balance of forces has been extremely unfavourable for many years, and it is no accident that 'New International Economic Order' demands have long been off the international agenda.

Perhaps because of this, the noted philosopher Iris Marion Young makes a case that although the New Social Movements have 'affected both the discourse and policies of international financial institutions' (which normally 'do not even pretend to be inclusive and democratic'), the 'reasonable goal' for these movements remains reform of the United Nations, 'the best existing starting point for building global democratic institutions'. 'Why focus on the UN?' asks Young. 'As members of the General Assembly, nearly all the world's peoples today are represented at the UN.' Moreover, the UN is a site where imperial powers 'seek legitimacy for some of their international actions' and where states 'at least appear to be cooperative and interested in justice'. Likewise, civil society organisations have mobilized around UN events and issues. But Young also concedes the challenges associated with such a strategy: 'The world's economic powers often seek to bypass UN economic institutions altogether'. UN humanitarian interventions 'will remain a cynical joke as long as actions with that name are organized and led by the US primarily with hardware and personnel under its national command'; 'the entire staff of the allegedly bloated UN bureaucracies numbers about that of the State of Wyoming'; and the UN has perpetual financial problems (hence, Young argues, 'Any social movement for strengthening global democracy and inclusion must work to shame states like the United States, who refuses to pay the dues it owes to the United Nations at the same time that it exercises its Security Council power').[44]

Not surprisingly, an entirely different strategic orientation to global government has emerged from a section of the world-systems scholar-activist community, resulting in entirely different tactical advice. As Arrighi, Hopkins and Wallerstein argue in their 1989 book *Anti-Systemic Movements*, the most serious challenge to the capitalist mode of production occurs when 'popular movements join forces across borders (and continents) to have their respective state officials abrogate those relations of the interstate system through which the [neoliberal] pressure is conveyed'.[45] I interpret this line of argument as saying uneven development is being exacerbated by globaliza-tion, hence the class-forming process – by which a global proletariat is created – is being perpetually disrupted by the destruction of working-class

Table 5.1 Five Reactions to the Global Crisis

	New Social Movements	Third World Nationalism	Post-Washington Consensus	Washington Consensus	Old World Order
Main argument	Resist globalization of *capital* (in contrast to globalization of *people*), so as one day to establish popular democracy	Join the system, but on much fairer terms	Reform 'imperfect markets' plus more 'development'	Slightly adjust the *status quo* (transparency, supervision & regulation)	Restore US hegemony – and penalize NY bankers' mistakes
Key institutions	Global activist networks; think-tanks; regional coalitions; academic sites; key social/labour movements (Jubilee 2000, Third World Network, Mexico's Zapatistas, Brazil's Movement of the Landless and Workers' Party, South Africa's COSATU and other civil society groups, India's National Alliance of People's Movements, South Korean workers, Burkina Faso's National Federation of Peasant Organizations, Greenpeace, Friends of the Earth, etc.)	Key nation-states (Malaysia, China, India, South Africa?)	Many United Nations agencies, World Bank(?), governments of France, Germany and Japan?	Official agencies (US Treasury Department, International Monetary Fund, World Bank(?), US Federal Reserve, White House, 10 Downing St, World Trade Organization); various Washington, DC think-tanks; University of Chicago (and others) Department of Economics	US Republican Party, Hoover Institute, Cato Institute
Key proponents	Marcos, Lula, Castro, Menchu, Bendana, Bello, Amin, George, Patkar, Khor, Shiva, Nader, Said, Pollitt, Chomsky	Mahathir, Mugabe, Chavez	Stiglitz, Soros, Sachs, Krugman, Wolfensohn, Jospin	Clinton, Blair, Summers, Camdessus, Greenspan, Fischer	Kissinger, Shultz, Buchanan, Helms

power. I endorse this point of view, partly for technical economic reasons similar to those Keynes considered.

The most urgent practical implication of this latter view would probably be to campaign against the current character of most nation states' international economic relations (especially financial). Jubilee 2000 is the most advanced of the movements working on this front. Jubilee 2000 is deeply split over strategies and tactics, however, with some of the Northern groups (particularly more moderate components of the US affiliate) ready to accept extremely weak changes to the Highly Indebted Poor Countries (HIPC) initiative. Many of the Southern groups are now taking an increasingly principled stand against HIPC itself. This kind of conflict may well be unavoidable, given the different positions.

A similar wedge issue for the international progressive movement during the 1990s has been the effort of some NGOs and trade unions to reform the WTO and other bilateral trade arrangements through social, labour and ecological clauses associated with trade. This strategy had two problems, namely its close association with Northern protectionist tendencies and the failure by most Northern unions and environmentalists to consult with affected Southern unions and people's movements. Consequently, quite powerful South voices (like the Third World Network) spoke out very critically against Northern progressive reformers.

In general, the various good-faith efforts of New Social Movement allies, in Washington and other settings, to establish reforms of the World Bank along green, gender, transparency and participation lines, or via the very uneven Structural Adjustment Participatory Review Initiative, suffer from their reification of the embryonic global state.[46] In the field of international finance, for example, establishing a global regulatory body will not be easy, in any event; nor, if the WTO is anything to go by, would the social movement perspective initially be given any credence whatsoever. Working with international lenders to establish bankruptcy arrangements has similar dangers, yet the need for so many of our sovereign states to find a way to go bankrupt formally is not in question. Furthermore, as noted, debt relief (especially with HIPC-style conditions), if pursued along the lines Clinton and even the Post-Washington Consensus forces recommend, may do more harm than good.[47]

What is required to resolve this cross-purpose activity is growing political maturity and sophistication by social movement strategists who attempt to reflect upon, if not speak in the name of, the popular struggles occurring in each national setting. Those struggles have common roots, and we have common enemies coming out of the woodwork of the decaying international financial (and broader economic) architecture. The implications of this analysis are that some of the creakiest parts of the current framework may have to be allowed to crash. More IMF bail-outs for New York investment banks – with or without a coming Wall Street crash – simply reproduce the moral and economic hazard that the Washington Consensus and international financiers will continue the *status quo*. The bail-outs should be resisted, first and foremost, including the IMF's regular calls for more taxpayer funding to replenish its bail-out funds.

But what we in the social movements need to do far more rigorously than we have is to establish whether our core tasks should be to think globally and act globally, or perhaps, more strategically, think globally, act globally, but redefine the economic and financial systems at the scale of the nation state, for a less uneven form of capitalist development.

◆ ◆ ◆

Postscript

(November 1999)

If the global economy rebounded slightly, nevertheless some momentous social events and personal journeys during 1999 amplified the five dynamics outlined above. Starting from the left of the spectrum this time, I noted in February the growing debate between those in New Social Movements supportive of reforming the embryonic global state, alongside the Post-Washington Consensus, and those who saw the immediate task as defunding and denuding the legitimacy of the current sites of international regulation. In November, two processes confirmed this strategic conflict. A diverse collection of New Social Movements gathered to protest the WTO in Seattle. Most pleaded for a seat at the table, led by the ever-stodgy US labour aristocracy and major Washington CoNGOs. Yet a significant fraction of workers moved from the stage-managed AFL-CIO rally (endorsed in retrospect by President Clinton as part of a divide-and-rule triangulation firmly aimed at Third World governments), to join a Direct Action Network of greens, anarchists, indigenous and Third World representatives and other radicals who did succeed, at least for a day, in disrupting the WTO opening through inspired civil disobedience. (The lack of resolution on social, labour and ecological clauses, however, remained an important barrier for future work linking First World and Third World radicals.) The latter more militant spirit was also invoked at the Jubilee South Summit in Johannesburg, where the main Third World anti-debt movements rebuffed several major northern CoNGOs' endorsement of the September 1999 HIPC expansion and IMF poverty reduction, by committing to work towards the shutdown of the World Bank and IMF, in part through pressuring local élites to establish a Third World debtors' cartel.

Third World nationalists, meanwhile, were heartened by élite acknowledgements in September 1999 that the previous year's Malaysian currency controls were effective, but several efforts by Mahathir to gather likeminded world leaders both at home and, by invitation of Mugabe, at Victoria Falls, had no apparent impact in expanding the nationalist current. Chavez continued Venezuela's political reform without apparent threat to international financial interests, although Ecuador managed a controlled default on foreign bonds with backing from nationalists and New Social Movements. South Africa proved particularly resistant to nationalist boat-rocking during its 1999 leadership of various fora (including the 1999–2000 chair of the governing board of the IMF and World Bank).

Within the World Bank, the Post-Washington Consensus forces waned when in November 1999 Stiglitz was dismissed – as Bhagwati put it in the *Financial Times* – 'with a fig leaf, a sorry episode'. Wolfensohn first censured and then censored Stiglitz in October, weakly rebutting his critique of the IMF's disastrous role in Russia and then apparently prohibiting him from press comment (according to the *Washington Post*). Yet in a twenty-first-century role as Washington think-tanker and Stanford academic, Stiglitz was expected to raise his critical voice, and his disciplinary credentials were endorsed in the *New York Times* by Nobel laureate Kenneth Arrow (Summers's father-in-law): 'The Stiglitz group represents one of the most important innovations in economics in the last 100 years.'

So too did Camdessus's resignation reflect institutional failure. The Washington Consensus remained, nevertheless, in hegemonic position. Minor reforms to global financial market regulation announced at the Cologne G8 meeting and 1999 IMF/World Bank annual meetings were not, by virtually all accounts, sufficient to prevent a future wave of financial panics. A further complication was ongoing pressure against international agency funding and free-trade deals from conservative members of the US Congress and from right-wing populists everywhere – who also enviously realised that when it came to mass mobilisation around international financial and trade matters, the Right had nothing like the capacity shown by the Left in Seattle, Cologne, Birmingham and even the dramatic 18 June anti-capitalist riots in London.

And looming still, as potentially a dénouement to financial power and in turn the creator of space required to reestablish national economic sovereignty, is the likelihood of a further global financial 'correction'. Next time, all observers either feared or hoped, it would be more directly the function of the US economy, whose capacity to suck in foreign goods on credit gave the appearance of superficial strength, while economic fundamentals were in fact rotting. The United States trade deficit, foreign debt, domestic corporate and consumer debt and asset inflation all stood at unprecedented levels at year-end 1999. The previous quarter-century build-up of financial stress in the global economy – and the power balances that accommodated these – cannot be sustained forever. It now becomes a matter of shifting the alliances and mobilising more activists to confront the extraordinary combination of financial power and vulnerability.

Notes

1 Among these were a slightly looser Federal Reserve monetary policy adopted in September 1998, in the immediate wake of the successful public-private bailout of the Long Term Capital Management hedge fund; a new $90 billion IMF insurance scheme announced the following month; the convening of key countries in a Forum on Financial Stability; the lack of financial contagion (contrary to expectations) in the wake of Brazil's January 1999 currency meltdown; the long-awaited revival (however infirm) of the Japanese economy; new plans for somewhat more transparent budgetary and exchange rate systems in emerging markets; and a decision at the G8 Cologne meeting in June 1999 to sell 10 per cent of the IMF's gold to fund partial debt relief to the poorest Third World countries.

Indeed many observers were surprised at IMF Managing Director Michel Camdessus's success at turning the debt relief strategy into a vehicle for tougher 'Enhanced Structural Adjustment Facility' conditions, just months after the IMF was criticized to the point of ridicule for its East Asian, Russian and Brazilian mishaps (effectively, granting $200 billion in bad loans over 15 months, in exchange for the application of inappropriate austerity measures). To add insult to injury, an IMF plan to unite foreign bankers so as to avoid fracturing their power in forthcoming bankruptcy negotiations with sovereign states was unveiled to a select group on 1 March 1999, when Camdessus spoke – behind the scenes to an Institute of International Bankers meeting in Washington – of the parallel need for 'creditor councils' which discipline 'individual "dissident" creditors' who catalyse 'panic-stricken asset-destructive episodes' through too-zealous foreclosure actions (Camdessus, Michel (1999: 9) 'Capital Flows, Crises and the Private Sector', remarks to the Institute of International Bankers, Washington, DC, 1 March).

2 In an important overview of the debate on global financial reform, Walden Bello, Kamal Malhotra, Nicola Bullard and Marco Mezzera (see Chapter 1 of this volume) argue that there are three approaches to global financial reform: 'It's the wiring, not the architecture' (Washington Consensus plus G22), 'Back to Bretton Woods' (a strong version of Post-Washington Consensus), and 'It's the development model, stupid!' (New Social Movements) – ignoring the far-right critique and collapsing nationalists and Post-Washington Consensus economists into the second category.

The term 'Washington Consensus' comes from Williamson, John (1990) 'The Progress of Policy Reform in Latin America', Policy Analyses in International Economics, Washington, DC: Institute for International Economics (see Chapter 6 by Broad and Cavanagh in this volume). As one minor personal indication of the awesome power invested in Washington Consensus leaders, *Time* magazine, 15 February 1999, anointed Rubin, Summers and Greenspan the 'Three Marketeers' who could save the world from depression.

The arrogance of Consensus-think was evident in Camdessus's description of the Asian crisis as a 'blessing in disguise' (*Wall Street Journal*, 24 September 1998). Illustrative of crisis-era justifications are articles and speeches by Robert Rubin, 'Strengthening the Architecture of the International Financial System', remarks to the Brookings Institution, Washington, DC, 14 April 1998; Laurence Summers, 'The Global Economic Situation and What it Means for the United States', remarks to the National Governors' Association, Milwaukee, Wisconsin, 4 August 1998; Stanley Fischer, 'IMF – The Right Stuff', *Financial Times*, 17 December 1997, 'In Defence of the IMF: Specialised Tools for a Specialised Task', *Foreign*

Affairs, July–August 1998, and 'On the Need for an International Lender of Last Resort', IMF mimeo, Washington, DC, 3 January 1999; and Michel Camdessus, 'The IMF and its Programs in Asia', remarks to the Council on Foreign Relations, New York, 6 February 1998 (see also OECD (1998), Report of the Working Group on International Financial Crises, OECD, Paris).

3 See Bhagwati, Jagdish (1998) 'The Capital Myth: the Difference between Trade in Widgets and Trade in Dollars', *Foreign Affairs*, 3, May/June. Dornbush cited in Doug Henwood, 'Marxing up the Millennium', paper presented to the 'Marx at the Millennium' Conference, University of Florida, 19 March 1999.

4 For a good description, see Richard Leaver and Leonard Seabrooke, 'Can the IMF Be Reformed?', Chapter 7 in this volume. For their own words, see Cato Institute, <http://www.cato.org/research/glob-st.html>; Henry Kissinger, 'IMF no Longer Able to Deal with Economic Crises', *Los Angeles Times*, 4 October 1998; George Shultz, William Simon and Walter Wriston, 'Who Needs the IMF?', *Wall Street Journal*, 3 February 1998.

5 G. Franke-Ruta, 'The IMF Gets a Left and a Right', *The National Journal*, Vol. 30, No. 3, 1998.

6 Stiglitz, Joseph (1998) 'More Instruments and Broader Goals: Moving Toward a Post-Washington Consensus', WIDER Annual Lecture, UN University, Helsinki, 7 January. See also his 'Towards a New Paradigm for Development: Strategies, Policies, and Processes', Prebisch Lecture, UN Conference on Trade and Development, Geneva, 19 October 1998. Illustrative of Stiglitz's attack on conventional wisdom – including self-corrective financial markets (for which his two decades of work will no doubt soon be rewarded with a Nobel Prize) – are the following lines from the Helsinki paper: 'The policies advanced by the Washington Consensus are hardly complete and sometimes misguided ... the advocates of privatization overestimated the benefits of privatization and underestimated the costs ... [below 40 per cent per year] there is no evidence that inflation is costly ... The focus on freeing up markets, in the case of financial market liberalization, may actually have had a perverse effect, contributing to macroinstability through weakening of the financial sector.'

7 In *The Crisis of Global Capitalism: the Open Society Endangered* (New York, Public Affairs, 1998), Soros asserts, 'To put the matter simply, market forces, if they are given complete authority even in the purely economic and financial arena, produce chaos and could ultimately lead to the downfall of the global capitalist system.' In another article – 'Avoiding a Global Breakdown', *Financial Times*, 31 December 1997 – he specifies what is wrong with financial market forces: 'The private sector is ill-suited to allocate international credit. It provides either too little or too much. It does not have the information with which to form a balanced judgment. Moreover, it is not concerned with maintaining macroeconomic balance in the borrowing countries. Its goals are to maximize profit and minimize risk. This makes it move in a herd-like fashion in both directions. The excess always begins with over-expansion, and the correction is always associated with pain.'

8 In a perceptive review of the 1998 book, Doug Henwood ('Let George Do It', *Left Business Observer* Vol. 88, February 1999) argues that Soros has lifted from post-Keynesian economist Paul Davidson unattributed arguments about financial market disequilibrium ('nonergodicity'), and that his analysis is far less convincing in these matters than Keynes, Joan Robinson, Karl Polanyi and Hyman Minsky – who pioneered theories of imperfect financial markets long before Stiglitz.

Most tellingly, Soros's solutions wilt when it comes to national exchange controls, at a time when honest economists were reviewing this once widely practised technique as part of the solution to financial market turbulence – and at a time when Stiglitz (who was initially worried that the September 1998 Malaysian exchange controls represented 'too much of a backlash') was prepared to endorse Malaysia's controls. After all, Stiglitz conceded in mid-1999, 'There was no adverse effect on direct foreign investment ... there may even have been a slight upsurge at some point' (*Agence France Press*, 23 June 1999). Soros, whose famous tiff with an evidently anti-semitic Mohamad Mahathir in 1997–8 may have influenced matters (*Economist,* 27 September 1997), shied well away from exchange controls, for if widespread, these would end his speculating days. And as Henwood concludes of Soros's insurance proposal, 'Making creditors bear the risk of lending beyond sanctioned limits might not do all that much to cool down hot money flows in any event.'

9   Paul Krugman, 'Saving Asia: It's Time to get RADICAL', *Fortune,* 7 September 1998.

10 Jeffrey Sachs, 'The IMF Is a Power unto Itself', *Financial Times,* 11 December 1997; 'The IMF and the Asian Flu', *The American Prospect,* March–April 1998.

11 See especially the work of UNCTAD economist (and post-Keynesian) Yilmaz Akyuz, 'Taming International Finance', in Michie, J. and J.G.Smith (eds) (1995) *Managing the Global Economy,* Oxford, Oxford University Press, Oxford; and 'The East Asian Financial Crisis: Back to the Future', in Jomo K.S. (ed.) *Tigers in Trouble* (1998), Zed Books, London.

12 James Wolfensohn, 'A Proposal for a Comprehensive Development Framework (a Discussion Draft)', Washington, DC, World Bank, 29 January 1999.

13 Hirakawa Hitoshi, 'The Asian Monetary Fund and the Miyazawa Initiative', paper presented to conference on 'Economic Sovereignty in a Globalising World', Bangkok, 24 March 1999; Oskar Lafontaine and Christa Mueller, *Keine Angst vor der Globalisierung: Worhlstand und Arbeit fuer Alle,* Bonn, Dietz Verlag, 1998.

14 Mohamad Mahathir, 'The Future of Asia in a Globalised and Deregulated World', speech to the conference 'The Future of Asia', Tokyo, 4 June 1998. In a spirit mirroring Mahathir's, other rulers of two formerly free-market Asian countries defended themselves from speculators in September 1998: the Hong Kong state prohibited the short-selling of local stock market shares and also bought $14 billion in shares to prop up the Hang Seng index, and Taiwan outlawed what were described as illegal funds – trades by Soros hedge funds.

15 Mandela's televised comment is cited in my 'Global Financial Crisis: Why We Should Care, What We Should Do', *Indicator SA,* Vol. 15, No. 3, 1998. This was not atypical. Jonathan Michie and Vishnu Padayachee are right to conclude that 'In the South African context, globalization has become a synonym for inaction, even paralysis, in domestic economic policy formulation and implementation' (Jonathan Michie and Vishnu Padayachee, 'The South African Policy Debate Resumes' in J.Michie and V.Padayachee, eds (1997: 229) *The Political Economy of South Africa's Transition,* The Dryden Press, London).

16 Very different circumstances prevailed, amidst very different ideologies, but this fate befell, amongst others, Aquino (Philippines), Arafat (Palestine), Aristide (Haiti), Bhutto (Pakistan), Chiluba (Zambia), Dae Jung (South Korea), Havel (Czech Republic), Mandela (South Africa), Manley (Jamaica), Museveni (Uganda), Mugabe (Zimbabwe), Nujoma (Namibia), Ortega (Nicaragua), Perez (Venezuela), Rawlings (Ghana), Walensa (Poland) and Yeltsin (Russia). In 1999, Megawati (Indonesia) was preparing to follow the pattern, with Chavez (Venezuela) wavering.

17 Thus there was talk within South Africa's ruling African National Congress of potential interlocking interests of major Southern Hemisphere nations, which would potentially reflect renewed muscle in the Non-Aligned Movement, Group of 77 and various other fora of revived nationalisms. Such cooperation is not without foundation – for example, an October 1998 ANC–Alliance document ('The Global Economic Crisis', discussion document, Johannesburg, p.5.) explicitly asked, 'Can we forge a Brasilia-Pretoria-Delhi-Beijing Consensus in the absence of any Washington Consensus?' (though cynics would retort that if the global establishment looked fragmented at that point, so too did Brazil's crisis-ridden liberal-corporate regime, the ANC's neoliberal proto-Africanism, Hindu nationalism and Chinese bureaucratic-Communism-cum-rampant-capitalism). That the South African government, during 1998–9, occupied a host of crucial positions – head of the Non-Aligned Movement, president of UNCTAD, head of the Commonwealth, head of the Organization of African Unity, host of the Southern African Development Community, UN Security Council member, holder of a director position at the IMF and World Bank – meant that

while ANC economic policy was without question still loyal to the Washington Consensus, nevertheless the kinds of questions raised by South African political leaders were potentially very important for change in the wider world.

18 In this regard, what many such movements are saying is a striking echo of John Maynard Keynes's position (in a 1933 *Yale Review* article): 'I sympathise with those who would minimise, rather than with those who would maximise, economic entanglement among nations. Ideas, knowledge, science, hospitality, travel – these are the things which should of their nature be international. But let goods be homespun whenever it is reasonably and conveniently possible and, above all, let finance be primarily national' (Keynes, J.M. (1933: 769), 'National Self-Sufficiency', *Yale Review*, Vol. 22, No. 4). Add political solidarity to his list of what should be globalized, and Keynes would fit nicely into this current.

19 Like those of the Philippines, South Africa, parts of Eastern Europe and Cuba.

20 From the Brazilian Workers Party, Sandinistas and their São Paulo Forum allies in Latin America, to the emergent new workers' party – the Movement for Democratic Change – in Zimbabwe.

21 One of the best works on such contending discourses, as applied to debates between the orthodox 'ecological modernisation' approach and radical 'environment justice', is Harvey, David (1996) *Justice, Nature and the Geography of Difference*, Basil Blackwell, Oxford.

22 To cite only a few such mass movements which apparently worked well with other local and global anti-neoliberal initiatives – simply so as to give a flavour of this current – consider Mexico's Zapatistas (both the retreating army and the emerging peasant and worker civil society organizations), Brazil's Movement of the Landless, India's National Alliance of People's Movements, Thailand's Forum of the Poor, the Korean Confederation of Trade Unions, and Burkina Faso's National Federation of Peasant Organizations. At a regional scale, an interesting example is the São Paulo Forum of Latin American leftists.

23 Again, by way of example, local struggles to make housing and food social entitlements – expanding the sphere of human rights discourse beyond 'first generation' liberal political rights into more radical socio-economic spheres – were aggregated into the Habitat International Coalition and Food First International Action Network. Other international networks had successes in banning the dumping and incineration of toxic waste (Health Care without Harm). The Zapatista 'Intergalactic Encounters for Humanity, Against Neoliberalism' planted more visionary seeds, as have growing anarchist-inspired networking and activism – epitomised by the civil disobedience of the impressive network known as 'Peoples' Global Action' – in London, Paris, Geneva, Davos, San Francisco and other sites of Northern power.

24 Admittedly, classic South versus North sentiments arose not only in J2000 critiques of the Washington Consensus and the highly conditional debt relief schemes on offer from Washington, but also in J2000 South critiques of their northern advocacy counterparts, who often appeared extremely pliant to Northern politicians' gambits. For an excellent article on this topic, see Dot Keet, 'The International Anti-Debt Campaign: an Activist's View from the South, to Activists in the North', AIDC discussion document <http://aidc.org.za>.

25 Again a handful of examples will suffice: the Third World Network based in Penang and Accra, the Third World Forum in Senegal, the International Rivers Network in Berkeley.

26 Worth citing are the Nader organizations, Alliance for Global Justice, and the Centre for International Environmental Law.

27 For example, Focus on the Global South in Bangkok, the Preamble Centre and Institute for Policy Studies in Washington, Amsterdam's Transnational Institute and International Institute for Research and Education.

28 Critical masses of political economists had amassed at London's School of Oriental and African Studies, the University of Massachusetts/Amherst, and American University in Washington.

29 In English, these included *The Ecologist, Green-Left Weekly, International Socialism, International*

Viewpoint, Left Business Observer, Links, Monthly Review, Multinational Monitor, New Internationalist, Red Pepper, Third World Resurgence, and *Z*.

30 These included Pluto, Zed, Monthly Review and Verso, amongst just the English-language presses. It may be useful to list several of the radical (or 'critical') English-language books – not to mention seminal articles and papers, for the list is vast – about global capitalism (and resistance) just prior to the turn of the century (here 1997 is an arbitrary cut off because in 1996 important books were produced by Alexander, Berger and Dore, Boyer and Drache, Clarke, Helleiner, Hirst and Thompson, Hopkins and Wallerstein, Mander and Goldsmith, Michie and Grieve Smith, Robinson, and others, and in 1995 the list was as long): Amin, Samir (1997) *Capitalism in the Age of Globalization,* Zed Books, London; Blecker, Robert (1999) *Taming Global Finance,* Economic Policy Institute, Washington, DC; Brenner, Robert (1999) *Turbulence in the World Economy,* Verso, London; Caufield, Catherine (1997) *Masters of Illusion,* Macmillan, London; Chossudovsky, Michel (1997) *The Globalization of Poverty,* Zed Books, London; Greider, William (1998) *One World Ready or Not,* Penguin, London; Hahnel, Robin (1999) *Panic Rules!,* South End, Boston; Henwood, Doug (1997) *Wall Street,* Verso, London; Hoogvelt, Ankie (1997) *Globalization and the Postcolonial World,* Macmillan, London; Karliner, Joshua (1997) *The Corporate Planet,* Sierra Club, San Francisco; Jomo K.S. ed. (1998), *Tigers in Trouble,* Zed Books, London; Martin, Hans-Peter and Harald Schumann (1997) *The Global Trap,* Zed Books, London; Moody, Kim (1997) *Workers in a Lean World,* Verso, London; Shutt, Harry (1999) *The Trouble with Capitalism,* Zed Books, London; Sinha, Mrinalini, Donna Guy and Angela Woollacott, eds (1999) *Feminisms and Internationalism,* Blackwell, Oxford; Wade, Robert (1999) *The Gift of Capital,* Verso, London; Waterman, Peter (1998) *Globalization, Social Movements and the New Internationalisms,* Cassell, London; and Weiss, Linda (1998) *The Myth of the Powerless State,* Polity, Cambridge.

31 In the same illustrative spirit, some of the leading anti-neoliberal spokespeople, activist leaders and leftist luminaries of the late 1990s deserve mention: Subcomandante Marcos of the Zapatistas, Lula (Luis Ignacio da Silva) of the Brazilian Workers Party, Cuban premier Fidel Castro, Guatemalan Nobel laureate Rigoberta Menchu, Alejandro Bendana of Nicaragua, Samir Amin of the World Forum for Alternatives in Dakar, Kenyan environ-mentalist Wangari Maathai, South African poet Dennis Brutus of the debt cancellation movement, Indian anti-dams and social movement campaigner Medha Patkar, Martin Khor of Third World Network, Indian writer Arundhati Roy, feminist-scientist-environmentalist Vandana Shiva, Walden Bello of Focus on the Global South, Australian journalist John Pilger, Russian intellectual Boris Kagarlitsky, Susan George of the Transnational Institute, French intellectual Pierre Bourdieu, US consumer activist Ralph Nader, *Monthly Review* co-editor Ellen Meiksins Wood, Irish journalist Alexander Cockburn, Palestinian literary critic Edward Said, and US intellectual Noam Chomsky.

32 For instance, James Tobin, author of the international 0.05 per cent cross-border financial transaction tax proposal which bears his name; John Eatwell and Lance Taylor, who argued for a World Financial Authority; futurist Hazel Henderson, who suggests means to prevent currency 'bear raids' by focusing on electronic funds transfers (and a transparent transaction reporting system); or post-Keynesian Paul Davidson, who wanted an international clearing union providing for capital controls. See Tobin, James (1978) 'A Proposal for International Monetary Reform', *The Eastern Economic Journal,* July/October; Eatwell, John and Lance Taylor (1998) 'International Capital Markets and the Future of Economic Policy', CEPA Working Paper Series III, Working Paper 9, New School for Social Research, New York, September; Henderson, Hazel (1996) *Building a Win-Win World,* Berrett-Koehler, San Francisco and 'The Global Financial Casino: a View Beyond Textbook Economics', paper presented to conference on 'Economic Sovereignty in a Globalising World', Bangkok, 24 March 1999; Davidson, Paul (1997) 'Are Grains of Sand in the Wheels of International Finance Sufficient to Do the Job when Boulders are often Required?', *The Economic Journal,* 107, and 'The Case for Regulating International Capital Flows', paper presented at the Social

Market Foundation Seminar on Regulation of Capital Movements, 17 November 1998. The most progressive variants of these arguments for a global financial regulatory authority can be found at the website of the Financial Markets Centre in Washington, a populist-inspired think-tank whose intellectual allies include Jane D'Arista, James Galbraith, William Darity, William Greider and Dean Baker: <http://www.fmcenter.org>.

Interestingly, a few Washington Consensus and post-Washington Consensus economists once engaged these issues with a degree of intellectual rigour that is surprising in retrospect, given their present reluctance to offend financial markets in substantive ways. Most notably, Lawrence Summers co-authored an article with practical implications he would distance himself from in later years: 'When Financial Markets Work Too Well: A Cautious Case for a Securities Transactions Tax', *Journal of Financial Services*, 3, 1989. Likewise, one of the most fanatical mid- and late-1990s financial liberalizers, Stanley Fischer, argued as recently as 1991 that 'domestic firms should not be given unrestricted access to foreign borrowing, particularly non-equity financing' (in his book *Issues in International Economic Integration*, Bangkok, 1991, p. 20). And Stiglitz once offered a tax-based approach in the article, 'Using Tax Policy to Curb Speculative Short-Term Trading', *Journal of Financial Services*, 3, 1989 (which Davidson has ridiculed as a 'noise-trader-as-fool argument').

33 For a description of CoNGOism from a pro-IMF angle, see Jan Aarts Scholte, 'The IMF Meets Civil Society', *Finance and Development*, Vol. 35, No. 3, 1998, and 'Civil Society and a Democratisation of the International Monetary Fund', in Yeros, P and S. Owen, eds (1999) *Poverty in World Politics: Whose Global Era?*, Macmillan, London. More generally, see Fowler, Alan (1994) 'Capacity Building and NGOs: A Case of Strengthening Ladles for the Global Soup Kitchen?', *Institutional Development*, Vol. 1, No.1.

34 *Associated Press*, 29 June 1999.

35 The post-Washington Consensus critique of Washington is reviewed above. For a critique of the post-Washington Consensus, see especially the work of Ben Fine, including 'Industrial Policy Revisited', *Indicator SA*, Vol. 15, No. 4, 1998; a forthcoming edited collection drawing upon the School for Oriental and African Studies 1998–9 economics seminar; and 'The Developmental State is Dead – Long Live Social Capital?' *Development and Change*, Vol. 30, No. 1, 1999.

36 *Mail and Guardian*, 8 January 1999.

37 Wade, Robert (1998) 'The Gathering World Slump and the Battle over Capital Controls', *New Left Review*, 231, September–October and 'From "Miracle" to "Cronyism": Explaining the Great Asian Slump', *Cambridge Journal of Economics*, Vol. 22, No. 6, November 1998.

38 *International Viewpoint*, 310, April 1999; for an official SANGOCO report on the meeting in the same spirit, see also their newsletter *NGO Matters*, January 1999.

39 See Moggeridge, D., ed. (no date) *The Collected Works of J. M. Keynes*, Vol. 25, Macmillan, London, p. 149.

40 See, for example, Malhotra, Kamal 'Renewing the Governance of the Global Economy', Chapter 4 in this volume.

41 Wagar, Warren (1992) *A Short History of the Future*, University of Chicago Press, Chicago. See also reactions in *Journal of World Systems Research*, 2, 1996 (including Patrick Bond and Mzwanele Mayekiso, 'Towards the Integration of Urban Social Movements at the World Scale').

42 Boswell, Terry and Chris Chase-Dunn (forthcoming) *The Spiral of Capitalism and Socialism*, Lynne Reiner, Westview. Boswell and Chase-Dunn immediately confront potential criticism that the dominant institutions today will be difficult to influence:

> While the idea of a world state may be a frightening spectre to some, we are optimistic about it for several reasons. First a world state is probably the most direct and stable way to prevent world war, which must be at the top of everyone's list. Secondly, the creation of a global state that can peacefully adjudicate disputes among nations will transform the existing interstate system. The interstate system is the political structure that stands

behind the manoeuverability of capital and its ability to escape organized workers and other social constraints on profitable accumulation. While a world state may at first be largely controlled by capitalists, the very existence of such a state will provide a single focus for struggles to socially regulate investment decisions and to create a more balanced, egalitarian, and ecologically sound form of production and distribution.

43 In 1998–9, for example, major Southern governments (especially India and Brazil) argued forcefully against stronger powers for the key reforming agency within the World Bank (the 'Inspection Panel', often used by development and environment NGOs to protest damaging Bank projects) – and indeed the Southern government representatives severely weakened the scope for reforming the Bank in ways which would make its loans more subject to citizen accountability.

44 Young, Iris Marion (1997) *Inclusion and Democracy*, Oxford University Press, Oxford. In Chapter 7 Young draws upon the work of Erskine Childers, Brian Urquhart and Chadwick Alger. A similarly strong group of proponents for the utilisation of the UN as a potential liberated zone are those involved in human rights work and in the UN Non-Governmental Liaison Service.

45 Arrighi, Giovanni, Terence Hopkins and Immanuel Wallerstein (1989: 74) *Anti-Systemic Movements,* Verso, London.

46 There is an interesting debate amongst progressive economists over one potential exception: the 'Tobin tax' campaign that is being waged in Canada, the US and France to establish a penalty for international financial transactions as a disincentive to speculation, which can effectively be accomplished by the G7 countries acting in concert. As formidable a Marxist economist as Suzanne de Brunhoff has signed on to this campaign (http://www.attac.org) (also see Chapter 14 in this volume) although others (such as Leo Panitch and Gerard Greenfield of the *Socialist Register*) insist that national capital controls should be a higher priority.

47 Representative Jesse Jackson Jr pointed this out, in offering a much more progressive alternative to the Africa Growth and Opportunity Bill, called HOPE for Africa, for which he mustered support from 70 colleagues in early 1999.

6

The Death of the Washington Consensus?

ROBIN BROAD AND JOHN CAVANAGH

Between the early 1980s and the late 1990s, an élite consensus swept the globe that unfettered free markets provided the formula to make rich countries out of poor. In policy circles, this formula came to be known as the 'Washington Consensus'.

At the onset of a new century, however, deep cracks have appeared within the Consensus. Its legitimacy has come into question in the face of an increasingly effective citizens' backlash in North and South, and growing dissension within the ranks of once-ardent backers of the Consensus as financial crisis strikes around the globe. While not yet dead, the Consensus has been wounded – potentially fatally.

This article analyzes the reign of the Washington Consensus and what the authors see as its loss of legitimacy in the global economic upheavals of recent years. It is written neither to help rebuild the Consensus nor to mourn its possible fall. Let us be clear from the start: the authors were never part of the Consensus. In numerous articles written over the last decade and a half, we chronicled the human and environmental wreckage of Consensus policies. Our goal here is to dissect the reign, to analyze the cracks, and to reflect upon the lessons learned in terms of a new development agenda. And, as we will argue, what is needed is not a new Washington-driven and Washington-dominated consensus but a vibrant new debate, involving the supposed beneficiaries of development – workers, farmers, urban poor, indigenous communities – over the vision, goals and policies of new paths to development.

The Reign of the Washington Consensus

In the first three decades following the Second World War, there was a lively debate over the relative roles of government and market in the development process. Prior to the 1980s, most developing countries favoured a strong government role in development planning and policies, fearing that unfettered markets in a world of unequal nations would put them at a disadvantage. As a result, most of these governments maintained trade restrictions of some sort, gave preference to national over foreign investment, and regulated capital flows in and out of the country. In the United Nations, these countries backed a 'new international economic order' agenda to close the North–South gap through collective government action to raise commodity prices and stimulate technology transfers and development assistance. Particularly during the 1970s, the US government rallied rich-country governments to oppose most of these proposals.

This debate was extinguished with the emergence of the governments of Ronald Reagan, Margaret Thatcher, and Helmut Kohl in the early 1980s. With strong corporate support, these governments championed free trade, free investment, deregulation, and privatization as the best route to growth. Exxon, Ford, and the rest of the Fortune 500 flourished as they spread their assembly lines, shopping malls, and US culture around the world. In 1990, economist John Williamson (then of the Institute for International Economics and now of the World Bank) summed up this growing policy consensus in ten areas of economic reform that reflected free-market strategies to achieve export-led growth, with specific policies ranging from trade liberalization to privatization of parastatals.[1] This 'Washington Consensus', he argued, was shared by 'both the political Washington of Congress and senior members of the administration and the technocratic Washington of the international financial institutions, the economic agencies of the US Government, the Federal Reserve Board, and the think tanks'.[2]

The power of the Washington Consensus over development theory and practice in the 1980s and 1990s is hard to overstate. That once-vibrant debate about development all but disappeared as the Consensus took on almost religious qualities. The high priests of the Consensus - the US Department of Treasury, the International Monetary Fund (IMF), and the World Bank - were in Washington. Converts to the religion spread far beyond the 'beltway' – like other religions, by a combination of the appeal of the Consensus's simplicity, proselytizing by its believers, and outright coercion. Indeed, beginning in 1982, the majority of developing countries lost substantial leverage over their economic destiny as external debts incurred in the previous two decades fell due at a moment of historically high interest rates. The US government, working with the governments of other rich nations, pressed developing countries into the free market paradigm as a condition for new loans. The IMF was assigned the role of enforcing the policies; the World Bank urged similar reforms through its new policy-oriented 'structural adjustment' loans.

As a result, by the 1990s, most developing country governments – with the exception of such East Asian 'tigers' as South Korea and Taiwan – had become converts to free market policies. Over the course of the 1980s and 1990s, developing country governments substantially reduced trade barriers and many removed long-standing restrictions on capital inflows and out-flows.

The high priests of the Washington Consensus were arrogant – acting as if there was no further need for debate and discussion about what develop-ment entailed or how to make it happen. They saw little need for country-specific experts, and detailed field studies were deemed a waste of time. One of us worked as an international economist in the Treasury Department from 1983 to 1985; it was taken as an article of faith that the IMF and World Bank formula, if properly followed, was the only route for countries to follow. In fact, during the reign of the Consensus, those of us daring to criticize the Consensus were treated like heretics.

By the early 1990s, the Consensus was like a steamroller in changing the face of development policy and practice across the globe. Its backers pressed successfully for an acceleration of corporate-friendly globalization rules, leading to the passage of the NAFTA in 1993 and the creation of the WTO in 1995. Each victory whetted the appetite of Consensus backers for more. The IMF and World Bank, in tandem with the US Treasury Department, pressed for investment liberalization in South Korea, Thailand, the Philippines and elsewhere. Governments launched a flurry of negotiations for a Multi-lateral Agreement on Investment (to outlaw governmental 'affirmative action' in favour of domestic industry over foreign) and for regional agreements on the NAFTA model.

Attack on the Consensus: the Discrediting of Free Trade

Yet, even as the steamroller ploughed on, the Consensus never gained wide-spread legitimacy in the developing world outside a technocratic élite. As the 1980s unfolded, citizen groups in the South, often campaigning in collabora-tion with Northern environmental, labour and anti-poverty groups, exposed the adverse development impacts of the World Bank and the IMF, the two institutions that have enforced Washington Consensus policies most zealously. Across the globe in Africa, Asia, Latin America and the Caribbean, anti-Consensus groups such as the Freedom from Debt Coalition in the Philippines and the Malaysia-based Third World Network became forceful actors on the global stage. They raised questions about both the goals and the impact of Consensus policies.

By its own admission, the Washington Consensus was focused solely on providing economic growth. As Williamson bluntly admitted in hindsight, 'I deliberately excluded from [my] list [of the 10 areas] anything which was primarily redistributive ... because I felt the Washington of the 1980s to be a city that was essentially contemptuous of equity concerns'.[3] Likewise, noted Williamson, the Consensus 'had little to say about social issues ... and almost nothing to say about the environment'.[4] But, on the ground in those countries that were recipients of Consensus policies, it turned out that these social impacts could not be separated from the economic. From the Philippines to Mexico to Ghana came evidence that these free-market policies left unacceptable consequences for workers, the environment and equity.

Inequality

As attested to by numerous United Nations and other studies, growing inequality has accompanied liberalization in the majority of countries. To dramatize the stark reality of this, critics charted the growing divide between the wealth of the world's billionaires and the world's poorest. As researchers at the Washington-based Institute for Policy Studies calculated, by 1999 the combined wealth of the world's 475 billionaires well exceeded the income of the poorest half of the world's people.[5]

Environment

Twenty years ago, many developing countries, from Chile and Brazil to the Philippines and Indonesia, were still endowed with abundant natural resources – lush tropical forests, rich fishing banks and mineral veins, and fertile lands. In these and other countries, the heightened emphasis on export-led growth brought long-term environmental costs that had not been factored into the Washington Consensus's measurements of economic success. Indeed, in country after country, export-led growth depended on the plunder of these resources. Forests were cleared, for example, as Costa Rica was encouraged by the World Bank to expand cattle production for meat exports and as Indonesia expanded palm oil production. And, with the widespread destruction of natural-resource systems, the very survival of the poorest populations of these countries, those who live off the natural resources, was threatened.

Workers

The Washington Consensus encouraged countries to adopt policies to woo foreign investment. As a result, factories exporting apparel, electronics, toys, and other products have sprung up in southern China, Vietnam, Guatemala, Malaysia and dozens of other countries. Indeed, an average of close to one factory each day has been opening along the 2,000-mile US–Mexico border since the advent of NAFTA in 1994. Yet, as countries have competed with each other for new investments in what critics dubbed a 'race to the bottom,' workers in most of the Third World's new global factories have been underpaid, overworked and denied fundamental worker rights, including the right to organize and strike and the right to a safe working environment.

Citizen outcry against Washington Consensus free-trade policies was never limited to Southern countries. Northern environmentalists began launching campaigns against the environmental impacts of the World Bank in the early 1980s. Labour unions joined the critics as companies used the threat of moving production to China or Mexico to bargain down Northern wages and benefits in a dangerous downward spiral.

As free-trade policies implemented in the South rebounded adversely to affect factory workers, small farmers and small businesses in the North, public opinion polls in the United States began to show a majority of Americans were sceptical of the merits of free trade. By the end of 1998, the US public was not simply opposed to expansion of the free trade agenda: according to a December 1998 *Wall Street Journal*/NBC News survey, 58 per cent of Americans polled indicated that 'foreign trade has been bad for the US economy'.[6] This widespread popular opposition was fed by unions, environmentalists, small farmers and citizen leaders such as Jesse Jackson and Ralph Nader, who echoed their Southern counterparts' critiques that free trade undermined workers, the environment, farmers, communities, sovereignty and equity.

This broad public opposition in the North gained backing in diverse élite circles during the 1990s battles over free trade. In the United States, many Democratic members of Congress called for 'fair trade' – a critique that in many ways mirrored the Southern NGO cry. On the other side of the aisle, roughly 60–70 Republican members of the US Congress consistently opposed free-trade agreements. While the Republican and the 'fair trade' backlash against free trade diverge dramatically on an alternative vision to the Washington Consensus, the two camps have, on key occasions, joined forces to slow the Washington Consensus steamroller.

Indeed, by the late 1990s, anti-free trade forces were strong enough to stall new free trade and investment initiatives from the US government (for example, the Congressional defeats of 'fast track' trade authority) and at the global level (for example, the 1998 derailing of negotiations for the Multilateral Agreement on Investment). But the combined strength of these outside critics only slowed the momentum of the Washington Consensus; it was the 1997 Asian financial crisis that shook its very foundations.

Cracks in the Consensus:
Hot Money and the Wall Street–Treasury Complex

In order to understand the actual cracks that have appeared within the Consensus, one has to understand the roots of the financial crisis. Over the past decade, the World Bank, the IMF and the US Treasury expanded their initial focus from the free trade and long-term investment planks of the Consensus to the financial, pressing governments around the globe to open their stock markets and financial markets to short-term investments from the West. The resulting quick injections of capital from mutual funds, pension funds and other sources propelled short-term growth in the 1990s, but also encouraged bad lending and bad investing. Between 1990 and 1996, private financial flows entering poorer nations skyrocketed from $44 billion to $244 billion. Roughly half of this was long-term direct investment, but most of the rest – as recipient countries were soon to discover – was footloose, moving from country to country at the tap of a computer keyboard.

In mid-1997, as the reality of this shortsighted lending and investing began to surface first in Thailand, then South Korea, and then several other countries, Western investors and speculators panicked. Their 'hot money' fled much faster than it had arrived – leaving local economies without the capital they had come to depend on. Big-time currency speculators such as George Soros exacerbated the crisis by betting against the local currencies of the crisis nations, sending local currency values to new lows. IMF policy advice seemed only to quicken the exodus of capital and the plunge of domestic currencies. Currencies and stock markets from South Korea to Brazil nosedived; and as these nations slashed purchases of everything from oil to wheat, prices of these products likewise plummeted. The financial crises stalled production and trade even in large economies such as Indonesia, Russia, South Korea and Brazil, leaving in their wake widespread pain and dislocation. Exact figures are hard to come by but the main international trade union federation estimates that, by the end of 1999, some 27 million workers will be unemployed in the five worst-hit Asian countries: Indonesia, South Korea, Thailand, Malaysia and the Philippines.[7]

As economies collapsed, élite support for the Washington Consensus began to crumble. In the pages of the *Wall Street Journal*, former Secretary of Defence Robert McNamara likened the crisis to the Vietnam War, implying that then-Treasury Secretary Robert Rubin, his deputy (and successor) Larry Summers, (now retired) IMF Managing Director Michel Camdessus and the other top managers had lost control.

Two sets of élite actors began launching critiques at Rubin, Summers and Camdessus – not quietly, but in a very public and vocal fashion, often using the opinion pages of the *New York Times*, the *Wall Street Journal* and the *Washington Post*. A first set of élite critics supports free markets for trade but not for short-term capital. This group is led by highly regarded free-trade economists such as Jagdish Bhagwati of Columbia University, Paul Krugman of the Massachusetts Institute of Technology (MIT) and (then) World Bank chief economist Joseph Stiglitz. It also includes well-known Washington figures such as Henry Kissinger. Bhagwati has argued that capital markets are by their nature unstable and require controls. Krugman has outlined the case for exchange controls as a response to the crisis. As dramatically interventionist as some of these proposals are, however, and as heated as the debate may sound, overall the group largely seeks to restore the Consensus by allowing national exchange and/or capital controls under certain circumstances.

Some within this first set of Washington Consensus reformers focus more on the folly of IMF policies during the crisis. Prominent Harvard University economist Jeffrey Sachs, himself once a proponent of 'shock therapy' in Russia, faulted the IMF for prescribing recessionary policies that transformed a liquidity crisis into a full-fledged financial panic and subsequently into a collapse of the real economy in an expanding list of countries. As Sachs put it, 'Instead of dousing the fire, the IMF in effect screamed fire in the theatre'.[8] While still subscribing to the goal of free trade, Sachs and others argue that the IMF needs to revise its standard formula for economic reform, as well as to be more transparent in its decisions and actions, and more publicly accountable for the impact of its policies.

A second set of Washington Consensus insider dissidents goes further in criticisms of the IMF, arguing for its abolition. Rooting their critique in an extreme defence of free markets, they fault the IMF for interference in markets. They charge that IMF monies disbursed to debtor governments end up being used to bail out investors, thus eliminating the discipline of risk in private markets (a phenomenon called 'moral hazard'). This group is led by long-time free trade institutions such as the Heritage Foundation and the Cato Institute (whose opposition to publicly funded aid institutions is nothing new). Its ranks have recently swelled, however, with well-known, vocal converts such as former Citicorp CEO Walter Wriston, former Secretary of State George Shultz, and former Treasury Secretary William E. Simon.

These two main camps of élite dissent within the Consensus in the United States have a growing set of counterparts in other rich nations and among some developing country governments. Western European economies, while not in the dire straits of Japan and much of the rest of the world, continue to be plagued by high unemployment and a shaky start for their new joint currency, the euro. The European Union has also been in widely publicized trade disputes with the United States, several involving the European public's growing scepticism over genetically engineered foods. As a result, a number of politicians from new centre-left governments in many European countries have raised their voices to question parts of the Consensus. Even Clinton's closest ally, Tony Blair, has a reform plan that includes a new intergovernmental global financial authority to help prevent future financial crises. Most Western European governments support at least limited versions of capital controls. And, along with counterparts in Europe, some in the Canadian parliament are exploring an international tax on foreign currency transactions to discourage speculative transactions.

So too is close US ally Japan looking for openings to rewrite parts of the Consensus. The Japanese government is both weakened and disillusioned after a decade of recession. It has waged high-profile wars with the United States not only over the creation of an Asian economic fund (Japan lost), but also over who should lead the WTO – a Thai candidate backed by Japan and much of Asia, or a New Zealander backed by most of the West.

In the developing world, there have also been a number of recent instances where élite actors have departed from specific aspects of the policies of the Consensus in practice. In Hong Kong, long-heralded by Washington Consensus adherents as a supreme example of free-market trade and finance policies, the government reacted to the financial crisis spreading through Asia by intervening in the stock market and acting to prevent currency speculation. Malaysia grabbed the world's attention in 1998 by imposing a series of capital and exchange controls that were successful in stemming short-term speculative flows. Several developing country governments have moved beyond their discontent over certain IMF prescriptions to question openly whether the WTO should heed US and European calls for new trade talks to further liberalize nations' investment rules and agricultural protection policies.

The combination of these criticisms and actions has begun to influence even the IMF and the World Bank. In Indonesia, where the crisis has been particularly brutal, the IMF implicitly acknowledged that there were occasions when the costs of Washington Consensus policies were likely to be unacceptably high. Initially the IMF hung tough – until riots greeted the removal of price subsidies on fuel[9] and precipitated a chain of events that led to the fall of long-reigning Indonesian dictator Suharto. In its dealings with the post-Suharto government, the Fund acquiesced to greater social spending and the maintenance of fuel, food and other subsidies. At the World Bank, President James Wolfensohn has taken small steps to distance himself and his institution from the more orthodox policies of the Fund. In 1997, he and several hundred NGOs convened by the Development Group for Alternative Policies (DGAP) agreed to carry out a multi-country review of the Bank's structural adjustment policies. More recently, Wolfensohn's speeches and Bank publications have included what amount to blistering attacks on the social and environmental costs of Washington Consensus policies.

Despite all of this dissent, it is important to point out that, by and large, these élite dissenters share a strategic goal: to salvage the overall message of the Washington Consensus while modifying the pillar of free capital flows. Indeed, the heat of the debate between these élite critics and Consensus adherents Michel Camdessus of the IMF and Treasury Secretary Larry Summers over capital mobility has made it easy for observers to overlook a key reality: the Consensus still largely holds over trade policies. Egos and quests for publicity notwithstanding, the arguments are essentially between orthodox and reform branches of the Consensus, and are primarily over just one aspect of the Consensus, that of the freedom of capital flows.

Further Openings in the Consensus

The goal of the new insider dissenters is not to kill the Consensus. But dissent from within the ranks had been unheard of in the last two decades of Consensus reign. And – a crucial *caveat* – in their quests to tinker with the Consensus's ten commandments and to capture the limelight, élite critics are not only undermining the legitimacy and credibility of the Consensus, they are also unwittingly opening the door to the broader mass-based, anti-free trade criticism. In at least three key areas, these élite critiques open deep wounds in the Consensus, wounds that could be fatal if pried further open by the anti-free trade, citizen group opponents.

First, in whose interests are Washington Consensus policies sculpted? The language some use in their élite critiques is raising questions about the narrow interests that the Consensus serves. Free trade champion Jagdish Bhagwati of Columbia University, writing in *Foreign Affairs*, has decried free capital mobility across borders as the work of the 'Wall Street–Treasury complex' (a term that builds on President Eisenhower's warnings of a 'military-industrial complex').[10] Bhagwati points fingers at individuals who have moved from Wall Street financial firms to the highest echelons of the US government and who, in Bhagwati's words, are 'unable to look much beyond the interest of Wall Street, which it equates with the good of the world'.[11] This should create ammunition for the broader critique of outsiders: if the US Treasury (and the international financial institutions) are not able to look beyond such narrow 'special interests' in terms of capital, why should they be trusted to do so with broader trade and other policies?

Second, what goals should economic policies serve and who should determine these goals? One of the élite critics, World Bank chief economist Joseph Stiglitz, has recently begun to call for a 'post-Washington Consensus' that moves beyond the narrow goal of economic growth to the more expansive goal of sustainable, equitable and democratic development.[12] In speeches that have surprised many observers, Stiglitz has argued that the debate over countries' economic policies and the debate over the new global economy must be democratized. Workers, he says, must sit at the table to decide the economic policies of individual countries in order to argue against policies that hurt them. So too, Stiglitz acknowledges, must the institutions of the global economy be democratized. This framework moves closer to the critique of the citizen groups outside the Consensus. Outside critics need to push for Stiglitz's words to be turned into action. Why debate this only among the élite? Why not invite in workers – and environmentalists, farmers and others who should be seen as representing broader national interests?

Third, the élite dissenters are reigniting the Keynesian belief that the state has a legitimate role in development. Indeed, whatever comes of the global financial crisis, the widespread fear of an unregulated global casino that can devastate individual economies overnight is negating the Washington Consensus rejection of an active state role. While most élite critics allow for a government role only in the realm of short-term financial flows, outside critics should use this crack to open up a larger debate about government intervention. With the acknowledgment that government is needed to check markets in one realm, there should be more intelligent debate over government roles in other arenas. The development debate, so lively in the 1960s and 1970s and so stifled in the 1980s and 1990s, can be revived.

In the face of the spreading dissent and criticism, the US Treasury Department is attempting to hold the line. Triumphant in its booming stock market, its low unemployment and inflation, and its 'victory' in Kosovo, the US government is trying to reassert a Wall Street-centred consensus that differs from the old one only in minor details. Mild US Treasury proposals to increase disclosure by financial institutions and improve surveillance by the IMF won the day at the June 1999 meeting of the G8 in Cologne, Germany. New Treasury Secretary Larry Summers and his minions attempted to consolidate their agenda and glue the cracks at the late September IMF and World Bank meetings in Washington.

Whether Summers wins the day with this *status quo* menu depends at least partially on a number of factors that are quite beyond his control – and the control of his critics, inside or outside. First, does the US economy continue to hum in aggregate terms and the US stock market continue to soar? Any significant downturn in either will strengthen the critics both inside and outside the Consensus. Second, can the beleaguered economies of Russia, Indonesia, Brazil and elsewhere get back on their feet under the current set of rules? Summers and the IMF point to rebounding stock markets and currencies in several of these crisis countries, yet in country after country the job and ecological crises remain acute. On the other hand, the future of a global economy in which inequality in growing, and only the United States and the world's wealthy are beneficiaries, is inherently unstable, both economically and politically.

Talk to most leading Washington Consensus pundits – outside of the ranks of the IMF and the US Treasury Department – and you find the begrudging acknowledgement that the Washington Consensus has lost much of its legitimacy with the public, and that there is a need to factor more social and environmental concerns into policy. In this climate of élite discord, there is greater space for the citizen groups on the outside to press more far-reaching and desperately needed reforms in global economic institutions. We know that, at key moments in the recent past, unions, environmentalists and other citizen groups have grown strong enough to stall the implementation of Consensus policies, as seen in the fights over the 'fast track' and the MAI. Their challenge is to exploit the internal discord, to link with dissident voices within governments, to spread debate around development goals and government roles. If they proceed wisely, they should be able to turn the cracks in the Consensus into gaping chasms.

A New Development Debate

Yet, what are these citizen groups for? Philippine social scientist Walden Bello sums up the citizens' clamour for change around the world with this sentence: 'It's the development model, stupid' (see Chapter 1 of this volume). New development proposals from citizen groups are based on both more expansive goals and a very different set of trade and finance policies that shift beneficiaries from a narrow group of corporations and wealthy individuals to a much broader swath of the public.

Collectively, these proposals suggest that local and national governments be given greater authority to set exchange rate policies, regulate capital flows and eliminate speculative activity. A priority at the international level is the creation of an international bankruptcy mechanism outside the IMF. When a country cannot repay debts, the mechanism would oversee a debt restructuring whereby there is a public and private sharing of costs. As the next Indonesia, Russia, or Brazil teeters on the brink of deep financial crisis, it would go to this facility, not to the IMF. With such a facility in place, the IMF could return to its smaller and more modest original mandate of overseeing capital controls as well as providing a venue for the open exchange of financial and economic information.

Anti-Washington Consensus groups, led by religious coalitions in many countries rallying under the banner of Jubilee 2000, have also argued that current debt reduction initiatives should be expanded substantially to cover a more significant amount of bilateral and multilateral debt, and that debt reduction should be delinked from IMF and World Bank conditions. Finally, many critics are picking up on an old proposal by Nobel Prize winner James Tobin of Yale University, who suggested a tiny global tax on foreign currency transactions. In today's flourishing global financial casino, Tobin's tax would both discourage harmful speculation and generate revenues that could help the crisis nations (see Chapters 14 and 15 of this volume).

The growing strength of citizen opposition, however, does not yet translate into the ability to create a new overall consensus around these proposals. Much as we would like to be town criers reporting the death of the Washington Consensus, such news is premature. Too much of the élite, particularly in the United States, still clings to the precepts of the old Consensus. And yet, in some key areas, the cracks have brought about debate and actions that have deeply wounded that Consensus. Another global economic downturn would spread the wounds. But the future of these opposition proposals depends most centrally on the political sophistication of their proponents. Can citizen movements translate growing discontent into effective political pressure both at a national level and jointly in the WTO, IMF and World Bank? Can they shift the debate beyond the confines of the Washington Consensus and its free market religion?

In the closing months of the Second World War, a small group – primarily men from the rich countries – sketched the architecture of the post-war global economy. The institutions created from these meetings are not serving the needs of the majority of people on earth. At the close of the twentieth century, there is the possibility of a larger, more representative group to create new global rules and institutions for the twenty-first century.

Notes

1 The ten areas in which Williamson noted consensus in terms of neoliberal, free-market policies are: fiscal discipline (policies to combat trade deficits); public expenditure priorities (to cut expenditure through the removal of subsidies); tax reform; financial liberalization (towards market-determined interest rates); competitive exchange rates; trade liberalization (to replace licences with tariffs and to reduce tariffs); foreign direct investment (removing barriers); privatization; deregulation (of impediments to competition); and property rights. Williamson, John (1990) 'The Progress of Policy Reform in Latin America' in *Policy Analyses in International Economics No. 28*, Institute for International Economics', Washington, DC, January. Williamson's 1990 monograph builds on a paper entitled 'What Washington Means by Reform,' which he presented at a conference in November 1989.

2 Williamson, John (1990) 'The Progress of Policy Reform in Latin America', in *Policy Analyses in International Economics No. 28*, Institute for International Economics, Washington, DC, January.

3 Williamson, John (1993: 1329) 'Democracy and the Washington Consensus', *World Development*, Vol. 21, No. 8.

4 Williamson, John (1990: 83) 'The Progress of Policy Reform in Latin America', in *Policy Analyses in International Economics No. 28,* Institute for International Economics, Washington, DC, January.

5 Calculated by the Institute for Policy Studies from data in *Forbes*, 5 July 1999 and United Nations Development Programme (1999) *Human Development Report*, UNDP, New York.

6 *Wall Street Journal*, 10 December 1998. Pre-free trade think tanks dismiss such poll results as coming from an ill-informed public plagued with 'globaphobia'. See Burgess, Gary, *et al.* (1998) *Globaphobia: Confronting Fears About Open Trade*, Brookings Institute, Progressive Policy Institute and Twentieth Century Fund, Washington, DC.

7 International Confederation of Free Trade Unions, ICFTU Online, 21 January, 1999.
8 Sachs, Jeffrey (1998: 17) 'The IMF and the Asian Flu', in *American Prospect*, No. 37, March–April.
9 See Shari, M. 'Up in Smoke', in *Business Week*, 1 June 1998, p. 66.
10 Bhagwati, J. (1998: 7) 'The Capital Myth: the Difference between Trade in Widgets and Dollars', in *Foreign Affairs*, Vol. 77, No. 3, May–June.
11 *Ibid.*, p.12.
12 Stiglitz, J.E. (1998) 'More Instruments and Broader Goals: Moving towards the Post-Washington Consensus', 1998 WIDER Annual Lecture. World Institute for Development Economics Research, United Nations University, Helsinki.

7

Can the IMF Be Reformed?

RICHARD LEAVER AND
LEONARD SEABROOKE

The sound of bursting bubbles that echoed throughout East and Southeast Asian currency and capital markets after July 1997 has changed totally the manner in which debates about Asian development must henceforth be framed. One central aspect of that new agenda must focus inevitably upon the intersection of national policy with the role and purpose of the multilateral infrastructure, most notably the IMF. During recent decades, when debates about Asian development largely consisted of a fascination with a succession of apparent national miracles, any real consideration of the role of the IMF was almost totally absent.[1] This absence must always have seemed decidedly odd to those concerned with the prospects for development in other places, for one of the first questions asked in Latin America and Africa concerns limitations upon the room for local manoeuvre that arises as a consequence of the Fund's role as financial overseer. Now that as a range of once-miracle Asian performers have been returned 'back to the Third World',[2] it will be necessary to fill that void with well-considered views about the proper role of the multilateral infrastructure in supporting national development.

Certainly critiques will not be hard to find. One has only to look at the performance of the Fund through the crisis to see how the critique will flow. The *prima facie* evidence for the prosecution is well known, and now almost universally accepted across the region. It runs as follows. Having failed to anticipate the onset of the crisis, the Fund then reacted in ways which tended to compound it. While its interventions were soon setting new records,[3] they were founded on two fundamental diagnostic errors. First, it responded to the crisis with the same package of policies traditionally dispensed for current account nosedives – high interest rates and reduced government expenditure. These measures (intended to deflate the ailing economy and its import bill, so producing the current account surplus needed to service external debt) are believed to have had the effect of converting a liquidity crisis into an insolvency crisis.[4] Meanwhile, on the diplomatic sidelines, the IMF defended

96

its turf over the shape of adjustment policies, helping the US Treasury put down early Japanese ideas about an Asian Monetary Fund (AMF) – ideas that, while sketchy, appeared likely to dispense funds more leniently,[5] so giving Japan a chance to distance itself from the perception of the IMF as an 'instrument of US financial diplomacy in the high-profile cases'.[6] Second, it insisted on wide-ranging liberalization, especially across the capital account, as a precondition for its support. When the full details of one set of these preconditions was publicly exposed – the January 1998 second Interim Agreement between the Fund and the Suharto regime[7] – a number of governments that previously had stood behind the Fund expressed the diplomatic equivalent of amazement and dismay. In that sense, this disclosure marked the first in a number of steps towards a widespread regional consensus that the *modus operandi* of the Fund needed to be looked at again.

A well-grounded critique is very useful, and especially so in this case, since it accurately describes both what the IMF actually did, and with what effect. Indeed, many of the above-listed charges have been at least implicitly acknowledged by the Fund. Consequently, it has for some time been willing to allow its Asian supplicants to lower domestic interest rates and rack up relatively large internal deficits, either to stimulate domestic growth or alleviate immediate poverty concerns. Along with many other agencies from the OECD world, its earlier insistence upon early capital account liberalization has been moved back into the more distant future, if not quite recanted.[8] Its senior officials, furthermore, have made signs of 'understanding', if not quite supporting, restrictions on capital movement such as those unilaterally implemented by the Malaysian government under Mohamad Mahathir.[9]

A widely accepted critique like this can do many things: it can aid in amending, sometimes quite fundamentally, pre-existing views, and thereby radically reshape the direction of policy. The one thing that a critique cannot do, however, is back-fill a void. Where there is nothing to amend, a critique operates in a vacuum – and, by implication, perpetuates the void. This, indeed, is precisely the political message intended by most of those who utter the critique – that the region would have been better off without the Fund's interventions.[10]

The quiescence of regional governments through mid-1998 when the House Republicans held the future of the Fund in their hands suggests that this implicit message was pretty close to official preference, and it is more certain that most non-governmental agencies felt this way.[11] But if there is no going back to the policy patterns of the past, then an abolitionist critique is an exercise in romanticism. It tells us nothing about what normative purpose should be served by the Fund's policies.

While we have no doubt about the extraordinarily poor performance of the Fund during the current crisis,[12] this chapter seeks to argue a contrary normative viewpoint about the Fund, one largely informed by an appreciation of the Fund's historical significance. The impetus to create the IMF was one of the noblest reactions to the Great Depression. It gave governments the option to do something other than immediately adjust the overall contours of domestic policy to the shape of their most recent current account outcome. Henceforth they were able to finance a temporary deficit by borrowing from the Fund the hard currency that would allow them to purchase their own national currency. In this way, the IMF created considerable room for domestic manoeuvre that was not evident previously under the fixed exchange rate system of the classical gold standard.[13]

Furthermore, at a time where the word 'globalization' stands in bad odour around the region, it should never be forgotten that there has hardly ever been a more positive moment in the 'economic emasculation' of the state than this. States, even by the niggardly criteria of Adam Smith's nightwatchman, had always assumed an inalienable right to issue money – and, by implication, to play a correspondingly large role in determining its relative value. But in 1944, the collective of non-communist states voluntarily surrendered up that right, a right that many had used (and abused) regularly during the previous two decades. They vested their powers in an untried international institution, which henceforth they would have to approach with cap in hand whenever 'the fundamentals' seemed to require a new value for their national currency. The moment of creation of the IMF therefore constitutes an important qualification to simplistic narratives about globalization. Globalization may have been 'down hill all the way' since then, but the postwar stanza of the fable kicked off with the creation of new global norms that effectively redefined the powers and prerogatives of states in relation to each other, their respective civil societies, and a newly invented multilateral infrastructure.

There is, finally, a strong practical reason for not yet abandoning the idea of the Fund, a reason which derives from the ontology of the crisis. While most debates about the nature of the crisis continue to revolve around the two policy-oriented poles of excessive globalization versus excessive cronyism, much of the larger historical context gets lost. Of particular note in this regard are the spectacular currency fluctuations in both directions between the dollar and the yen that go back at least to the 1985 Plaza Agreement. When the yen was initially on its way up, the topic on everyone's lips concerned the positive uses that might be made of the capital surpluses emanating from the modern Japanese prototype of a 'civilian power'.[14] Quantum increases in foreign aid, the greening of global politics, and the root-and-branch redevelopment of post-communist societies were some of the better causes persistently mentioned in dispatches from that time. But any realization of those better causes rested on a presumption that those surpluses could in fact be directed towards desired ends.

The presumption was not unreasonable historically, since 'administrative guidance' over the uses of capital had indeed been one of the most basic ingredients of 'the Japanese miracle'.[15] Those surpluses are, of course, still there; roughly one third of total global savings by individuals continues to be made in Japan alone,[16] sustained partly by the new fear of recession. What has lapsed totally is the ability of the Japanese bureaucracy (let alone the government) to control them. The low interest rates that started with the Plaza process and were compounded by Japan's post-bubble recession have now combined with successive waves of financial liberalization to push more and more Japanese money offshore, with less and less of it going in long-term forms. If one wants to understand the extraordinary hyper-growth of short-term capital movements in the mid-1990s,[17] then all roads lead to Tokyo.

This conjunction between the powerhouse of world savings and the frail, porous financial structure of an immature creditor country has only one historical parallel, and it is deeply disturbing; namely, with the United States after the Great War.[18] If, now as then, we must contemplate the dangers of a deflationary spiral,[19] then something like the IMF will have to be created to deal with collective action problems. So why divert attention to an open-ended debate about 'new financial architecture' when, at best, it might end up codifying powers to control capital that already exist?[20] And why seek to destroy something that eventually would have to be made again?

Avoiding the Void

One way of breaking out of the dead-end of a pre-emptive critique is to inquire into how that void was constituted in the first place. The fact that debates about Asian development contain virtually no reference to the role of the Fund should remind us of one of the historic achievements of most 'miracle' economies – their ability to generate and maintain substantial surpluses on both the trade and current accounts. These surpluses generally kept the wolf of structural current account deficits which activate the IMF outside the sturdy Asian house of bricks, so providing the regional micro-climate in which the illusion that the Fund did not matter could flourish.

But the void also highlights the salience of geopolitical determinants, for the history of recent Asian development was never totally deficit-free. There were important moments when the wolf did indeed get behind the door – in Indonesia during the mid-1960s, in South Korea during the early 1980s, and in the Philippines on a more regular basis. These problems were individually solved in a variety of ways that, despite their differences, complemented the simultaneous hardening of views about Asian miracle economies. In the last case, such was the regularity of IMF interventions that the Philippines required geographical exile; its generic pattern of development was therefore deemed to be more 'Latin' than 'Asian'.[21] But in the remaining cases, the financing of deficits was arranged under American auspices outside the multilateral framework. For post-Sukarno Indonesia, 'vast and steady infusions'[22] of (largely Japanese) capital routed through the Intergovernmental Group on Indonesia (IGGI) came to the rescue.[23] And for South Korea, the financial resources of the Nakasone government were committed to ends that Reagan deemed appropriate for a grateful, surplus-ridden Cold War ally.[24] Needless to say, both of these rescues of important client states in the Cold War context were done on notably superior terms than could have been obtained multilaterally.

This should cause us to acknowledge that the economic crisis now upon the region has two distinctively different dimensions. The first and most obvious one is about the shortcomings of the process of financial globalization, and the relative importance of those shortcomings in relation to the institutional peculiarities of 'crony capitalism'. The other dimension – very much neglected – concerns the total failure of the geopolitically animated back-up system that previously protected the region in second-best financial circumstances. While the first dimension is still capable of being construed as evidence of the continuing vitality of American strengths,[25] the second unambiguously represents their substantial reduction. Which of these two dimensions will ultimately prove to be the more important over the long term is still very difficult to say.

Looking at the void from the standpoint of this second dimension also underscores the pertinence of a series of questions whose answers lead towards a more normatively capable viewpoint. Why is it that the world's largest debtor economy, with massive structural deficits, gets to call the shots inside the Fund about its *modus operandi*? Don't creditors rather than debtors usually run banks? And why, in a global economy that is ultimately a closed circle, should East Asian current account surpluses ever have been regarded as good? Answers to these questions emerge by understanding just a little about what the Fund was designed to do, and how, over the years, it set about meeting its brief in changing contexts.

Questions of Power ...

The first reason commonly advanced to explain both the IMF's pattern of behaviour and its seeming resistance to reform is effective United States control over its operations. In theory, the adjective 'multilateral' suggests that organizational outcomes should be determined by principles that are superior to the raw distribution of political power. But, as with the UN system in general, political power inside the Fund has never been distributed on the basis of equal national representation. Instead, voting power is primarily allocated in proportion to the quotas of subscriptions that member economies make to the Fund, and these quotas in turn reflect the relative importance of countries within the world economy. Since the United States had been the world's largest economy for fifty years prior to the Second World War, and as it expanded by a further 70 per cent during that war at a time when all other national economies contracted, the Bretton Woods institutions were negotiated when the US enjoyed a position of economic preeminence never before seen (and unlikely to be equalled by any state in the future). It therefore was the dominant presence within the Fund, controlling more than 30 per cent of votes on its executive board.

The political significance of this sizeable minority of US votes was qualitatively enhanced, moreover, by the provisions agreed to regarding 'special decisions' of the Fund – the kinds of issues that concerned its operating procedures. Here, a steep super-majority of 80 per cent of quotas was required to effect any change. The US's original quota was therefore sufficient to veto any fundamental change within the Fund. Hence, although Washington could not unilaterally nominate changes, it did have the ability to block – the power to dispose, if not to propose.[26]

The long-term consequence of this investment of veto power in Washington is that the Fund has become subject to 'regulatory capture' by its most important member. For as any casual observer of the debates about US decline knows, the relative sizes of national economies soon began to shift around quite markedly, with the pronounced hierarchical character of the 1945 version of the world economy yielding a much flatter distribution of national capacities. The most spectacular changes were associated with 'the rise of East Asia'. So, for instance, while the US economy was ten times larger than Japan's in 1950, by 1970 it was merely five times as large[27] – and, by 1981, only 1.5 times as large.[28]

This movement towards a more equal distribution of economic capacities was also reflected in the shifting size of members' quotas within the IMF. By the early 1970s, the voting power of the US within the Fund had declined from over 30 per cent and was fast approaching the 20 per cent threshold protecting 'special decisions'. Japanese governments, in particular, were seeking to upgrade their diplomatic presence within the multilateral framework and thus achieve recognition as the world's third-largest national economy. At more or less the same time, the sharp rise in oil prices associated with the 1973 OPEC shock effectively shifted about 2 per cent of global GNP into the hands of oil exporters as a group – a movement that also demanded recognition in the distribution of quotas. The accommodation of both these changes would have stripped Washington of its power to dispose, potentially exposing the operation of the Fund to an indeterminate political bargaining process.

This was something that Washington would not tolerate. It stonewalled at a review of the Fund's quotas, drawing out the process. But in the end a deal was struck with the Japanese and Europeans. The voting power of the US was indeed reduced to 19 per cent, but the super-majority requirement for 'special decisions' was ratcheted up to 85 per cent.[29] This extraordinary double movement provided the precedent for a similar deal inside the World Bank a decade later,[30] so setting one of the major parameters of the distribution of political power governing the Fund through the period of the Latin and Asian debt crises.

This also explains some important dimensions of the Fund's current status and behaviour. The continuing US veto accounts for the inordinate amount of time that non-US diplomats spend lobbying Washington with the argument that their most recent regional or local problems do indeed have global (that is, US) ramifications. More importantly, the veto has contributed materially in two ways to the long-term run-down in the relative size of the Fund. First, while the executive arm of the US government constitutionally enjoys freedom of action in determining international monetary policy,[31] Congress is inevitably involved in appropriating any monies needed to fund quota increases. In addition, the periodic fashion for unilateralist impulses in monetary policy within the executive sometimes works to the same end. Since it is pointless for other Fund members to act on their desires for quota increases until the US muddle has been clarified, the veto imposes a tortuous burden which, by its very nature, usually becomes manifest in the midst of some systemic crisis. The long-run result is a strong tendency to run down in the Fund's subscribed base of working capital.[32] Hence the sum total of IMF quotas expressed as a proportion of the value of world exports exhibits a decline from 13 per cent in the early 1960s to under 4 per cent at the beginning of the Latin debt crisis.[33] Similar low levels, verging on insolvency, were reached early on in the Asian crisis.[34]

All dimensions of this time-honoured political game have been manifest in a particularly sharp form during the current crisis. Low assessments of the direct exposure of US banks to the Asian financial collapse (best expressed in Clinton's November 1997 remark that the crisis was nothing more than 'a few little glitches in the road'[35]) plus administration reticence to test the patience of the Republican-dominated Congress after its somewhat devious engineering of the 1995 Mexican bail-out,[36] kept Washington out of the envelope of government financiers that stood behind the IMF's rescue package for Thailand.

This apparent signal of US aloofness[37] brought forward the ill-fated Japanese proposal for an Asian Monetary Fund and the subsequent exercise to preserve the prerogatives of the IMF at Hong Kong. But after the Fund's subsequent record disbursements rapidly diminished its working capital and brought about the need for a hefty quota increase, those Republican Congressmen nonetheless found themselves in temporary possession of Washington's power to dispose. As they toyed with that power, the run-down of its financial capacity forced the Fund to turn to the almost forgotten General Agreement to Borrow[38] in order to address the needs of the Russian government – needs which the Fund had previously rejected, but which Washington regarded as too important politically to ignore.[39] Its bare cup-board then became a contributory cause of further currency instability as the crisis moved on to Latin America. And since the exposure of US banks in Latin markets was high rather than low, the administration and the Congress ultimately did find grounds for agreeing that something ought to be done to return the Fund to a state of at least semi-solvency.

A focus upon raw political power within the Fund therefore offers considerable insight into why and how the Fund acted as it did during the crisis. But it also exposes a fundamental anomaly – namely, that the largest economy with a structural current account deficit is none other than the United States. How is it that the normal operating procedures, implemented so mechanically for other deficit economies, can be waived entirely for the US? And how is it that a bank can be bullied by the one country that most flagrantly violates its prescriptions? Arguing at this point that 'power is the explanation of the distribution of power' introduces a self-referential circularity that is excessively political. A more satisfying solution to the anomaly emerges by looking at the Fund's purposes.

... and Questions of Purpose

The maintenance of currency stability requires comprehensive consideration of both the sources of potential instability and the creation of robust mechanisms capable of fairly apportioning the costs of adjustment between national economies. One deficiency in the treatment of these issues during the Anglo-US negotiations that conceived the Fund is well known, if only because the crisis has reminded us so dramatically of its continuing pertinence – namely, the relative neglect of principles that might enforce systemic controls on the movement of capital across borders.[40] Given that inter-national capital movements had very nearly dried up during the Great Depression and subsequent world war, this defect reflected an inability to see very far beyond the conditions in which the negotiations were couched.

So although the Bretton Woods design did enable currency controls to be enacted, all such restrictions were unilateral acts not buttressed by congruent and complementary policies from other member states. Each state that resorted to such restrictions therefore found itself in a position of 'not-so-splendid isolation' in its dealings with foreign capital – a structural weakness in bargaining strength over the long (if not the short) run. Not surprisingly, the willingness to implement such restrictions therefore tended to diminish over time.

There was also a second flaw in the design that tends to be neglected these days, although its continuing pertinence is once again underscored by the crisis. As James Tobin and Gustav Ranis have rightly observed, 'the architects of the IMF ... did not presume that currency difficulties were the victim's fault'.[41] Its designers all thought that the pursuit of current account stability required that discipline be exerted over both deficit and surplus economies. In its most highly developed form, this amounted to an implicit notion of moral equivalence, and a rejection of the commonsense proposition that a current account surplus was a good thing. Keynes in particular regarded countries that accumulated long-run surpluses as being equally culpable in creating pressures to realign the relative value of currencies. Since the global economy was ultimately a closed circle, every surplus implied a corresponding deficit. Keynes therefore sought, and thought he had obtained, disciplinary powers that the Fund could exercise against surplus economies. Although not his first preference, the 1944 articles of agreement on the IMF nonetheless included a 'scarce currency clause' that, amongst other things, enabled economic sanctions to be applied against a structural surplus economy.[42] This would force governments with structural surpluses into reflation, so increasing their volume of imports and reducing the tendency to surplus – and also the corresponding pressures towards deficit that would necessarily be building up elsewhere inside the global economy.

The scarce currency clause, however, hardly figures at all in the history of the Fund's operations. Because it was then running massive current account surpluses, at the first substantive meeting of the Fund the US used its power to neuter the interpretation (let alone the implementation) of the scarce currency clause.[43] Twenty years later, however, the relatively much smaller US economy had firmly embraced structural deficits on the current account, while the locus of current account surpluses and increased economic throw-weight was shifting towards East Asia, with Japan first cab off the rank. These are the countries that currently enjoy relief from the disciplines of multilateral adjustment, bequeathed to them by Washington's self-interested action in 1946.

In their heart of hearts, US administrations now understand the para-doxical nature of their bequest, since they never tire of lecturing Japanese governments about the need for domestic reflation that will leaven their seemingly intractable trade surpluses.[44] Indeed, their willingness to bring economic sanctions up to the front line of possible trade wars with East Asian surplus economies seems to recapture something of the original intentions of the IMF's architects. The fact that they have never followed through on that intention, however, points to an implicit bargain between Washington and Tokyo based around the avoidance of direct eye contact. By not pressing the point about Japanese current account surpluses, Washington ensures that Tokyo will continue to turn a blind eye to US deviance on structural deficits. To further lubricate this mutual neglect, the US also enjoys the lion's share of the benefit arising from Japan's surpluses in the form of a healthy inflow of long-term capital[45] that appears consistently immune to unfavourable movements in 'the fundamentals' in either economy.

Hence, the world's two biggest national economies are both able to continue flouting different aspects of multilateral principles of adjustment by tacitly 'privatizing' their grievances and rewards into bilateral channels. Bilateralized benign neglect does have costs, however, and Raymond Vernon alluded to the general pattern of their distribution in his analysis of the dynamics of the US–Japanese bilateral relationship: they are displaced onto outsiders.[46] How long the bilateral trans-Pacific bargain will continue to deliver the goods to Tokyo and Washington, and how long third party interests can continue to be ignored, are matters to which we now turn.

The End of the Game?

Visions of 'people-centred economics' of the kind that animate this volume appear, at first, to be considerably removed from the 'top-down' analytics of this paper. There are, however, real prospects for narrowing the gap, once one appreciates where the crisis has come from and where it is likely to go. A temporary respite from the turmoils of mid-1998 (induced by the lowering of the dollar in the face of a possible credit crunch) provides a good opportunity to look at this issue.

As previously suggested, the crisis is best understood as a long-term resolution of tensions established in the funding of the second Cold War. The US policies associated with that early 1980s recrudescence of superpower rivalry – most notably the combination of high military spending and a highly valued dollar – quickly became essential ingredients in the making of three yawning deficits: an internal US budget deficit, an external US current account deficit, and the (largely) Latin American debt crisis.[47] By the mid-1980s, any one of these had the potential to bring the global economy to its knees.

During 1985, in the face of record trade deficits both bilaterally with Japan and multilaterally with the world, the Reagan administration suddenly abandoned its previous preference for a high-dollar policy in favour of an orderly devaluation, aiming to avert a disorderly collapse. To this end, it sought the monetary cooperation of both Germany and Japan through the agency of the Group of Seven (G7). The ensuing dollar devaluation still stands as the major achievement in the whole history of the G7, for during the next eighteen months the yen rose from 260:1 to 120:1 against the dollar. The consequence was that the threat of systemic financial collapse associated with the debt crisis was contained, while the rate of expansion of America's trade deficit was capped and pushed down at the margins.

The important thing to remember about this operation is that its economic costs were borne almost entirely by the Nakasone government, which spent somewhere in excess of US$130 billion in this controlled manipulation of currency markets.[48] Given that US sentiment was becoming steadily more attached to the proposition that Japan was a 'free rider' on containment, this has to be seen as perhaps the most important supportive move by any US ally in the whole history of the Cold War.[49] Needless to say, US criticisms of Japan's 'chequebook diplomacy' did not abate in the least (indeed, they went on to reach new heights around the Gulf War).

The Nakasone government, of course, did not find this supportive role easy to enforce upon the one political constituency that really mattered to it – big business. Domestically located and export-oriented, Japanese industry now faced a highly unfavourable exchange rate environment for international trade. For some industries, especially those facing relatively high labour costs, the only option was to move offshore. Consequently, in the second half of the 1980s, Japan's outward-bound foreign direct investment grew at an average annual rate of more than 50 per cent per annum, rising from a yearly total of only US$6.5 billion in 1985 to US$48 billion in 1989, thereby making Japan the world's largest source of FDI. Although the US was the major destination for this sharp jump in outward-bound capital, Asia's share of the total increased over time, and tended to exhibit a higher concentration in manufacturing.[50] By 1997, one-third of all international loans to Southeast Asia were made with Japanese capital.[51] For those Japanese industries that stayed at home, however, other forms of compensation were required for their acquiescence to dollar devaluation. This was largely achieved by a policy of cheap money implemented through the Ministry of Finance.

These two consequences of Japan's role in managing the dollar – the outward movement of capital, and the domestic cheapening of money – now stand intimately associated with the genesis of the Asian crisis. The former helped pump up growth rates and industrial capacity in the newest phalanx of industrializers within the ASEAN area,[52] thereby contributing (with the fullness of time) to the production of over-capacity in those sectors where the incentives for going offshore were strongest. The latter, although ostensibly targeted narrowly at industrial upgrading and the embrace of robotics, soon lost its tight focus on that laudable objective and became the major force behind the evolution of the bubble economy. When, in due course, the bubble broke to yield a domestic Japanese recession, already cheap money became progressively cheaper, with capital outflows increasingly assuming the more volatile and shorter-term forms that turned up in mid-1997 as some of the most worrying characteristics of the debt profiles of ASEAN economies.

Japanese banks effected much of this pronounced movement towards more volatile forms of external financing (as their high exposure, revealed in the ASEAN downturn, all too clearly demonstrated). But cheap Japanese capital was a gold mine for financial institutions of all kinds. At the centre of the action was the so-called 'yen carry trade', where cheap yen loans were converted into other currencies and thereby made available for a range of off-shore investments.[53] The volume of this particular trade is unknown, but it was clearly of sufficient magnitude to help keep the yen moving down after 1995 against a strong and rising tide of export surpluses that should have pushed it up. Its political significance is partly confirmed by the revelation during the second half of 1998 that a number of hedge funds were big players in this trade.

In this respect, the crisis has closed a previously open circle within the world economy: it has brought the problem of external deficits back home to the region where the vast majority of the world's external surpluses are also aggregated. The closing of the circle partly explains why ideas about an Asian Monetary Fund continue to float near the surface of Japanese economic diplomacy and to entertain the enthusiasts for regionalism of one or another kind.[54]

Whether the deeply entrenched problem of asymmetry in the burden of adjustment to monetary imbalances can be closed off geographically in East Asia must be doubted for two reasons. First, it requires a sustained reversal of the present trend whereby the yen has been of decreasing relevance as a unit of account in international payments[55] (a trend likely to be further reinforced in the near future by the rise of the euro). Second, it demands some stability in the value of the yen. Certainly, the yen's value cannot afford to be continually sacrificed at the altar of Japan–US relations.

Ever since the two 'Nixon shocks' of the early 1970s,[56] questions about the circumstances under which Japanese governments would find it necessary to make the dramatic policy moves that would establish it as 'a more normal country' have been a recurrent theme in the international politics of the region. While these questions continue to pervade the political and strategic aspects of East Asian regional order,[57] the economic crisis under-scores their continuing pertinence in the bluntest possible way, because it is now clear that what is on the line is nothing less than the survival of the Japanese economy. A volatile yen will continue to bounce Japan's famed economic institutions between the two unacceptable poles of a low value (which drags down the balance sheets of its financial houses) and a high value (which threatens the export prospects of its major corporations). It thereby helps diminish the room for policy manoeuvre available to its governments.

This domestic dimension of policy exhaustion in the face of a third year of recession is particularly apparent at the moment. Stimulus packages totalling nearly US$1 trillion have been implemented during the last decade without notable positive effect (other than, perhaps, to increase the rate of personal savings, an outcome which comes close to counter-productive). Meanwhile, on the monetary front, options are almost totally exhausted, with interest rates reduced recently to 0.03 per cent. Yet in spite of these orthodox exertions, Japan's economy still shrank throughout 1998 by nearly 3 per cent, while the recorded rate of unemployment rose to a record high – a result that raised serious doubts about the credibility of the government's modest growth target of 0.5 per cent for the following year.[58] While progressing down that road, the government has accumulated a public sector debt problem that now exceeds one full year of GDP. More will undoubtedly be added to this total, in part because political authorities remain committed to fiscal stimulus. But new debt will also be created through the recapitalization of the financial sector, where non-performing loans totalling nearly US$1 trillion were revealed at the beginning of 1998.

The critical issues that loom ahead have profound international and domestic dimensions. There is serious doubt about the ability of a profit-recessed Japanese private sector to absorb all the bonds necessary to finance this debt. There is certainty that this financing process will set the yen tumbling once again, and that the low water mark of 150:1 which was identified in June 1998 as critical to Beijing's policy on devaluation will be sorely tested. And there is the possibility that asset sales (especially US Treasury bonds) will be used to moderate the volume of new debt.[59] If this does eventuate, it is likely to deliver a short-arm jolt to Clinton's 'new economy' and put US interest rates on an upward trajectory that will expose the accumulated private debt which underpins it.

As the current Indian summer of the crisis begins to recede, revealing a global economy where the pace of growth is slowing and most of yesterday's 'strong men' are now looking weak at the knees, the international implications of the means used by the Obuchi government to address its domestic recession and solvency problems will move into the foreground. As this shift occurs, the questions of financial stability posed by Japan's ongoing backing for the idea of the AMF are likely to infuse the agenda of the IMF. Then, perhaps, we can begin to contemplate the possibility that the Fund will deliver in a more balanced way on all the elements of its articles of agreement.

Notes

1 Apart from casual historical observations about the importance for East Asian exports of the favourable exchange rates endorsed by the IMF during the post-war fixed exchange rate system, and more recent musings about the propensity of many regional governments for mercantilist behaviour under the floating rate system, very little was heard about either the IMF in particular or the issue of monetary stability in general. At best, it is depicted as part of the IFIs that provide loans to governments – or, in the case of Vietnam, withholding funds in compliance with US embargoes. For a selection of books which demonstrate a limited understanding of the importance of the IMF, see Kim, Y.C., ed. (1995) *The Southeast Asian Economic Miracle*, Transaction Publishers, New Brunswick; World Bank (1993) *The East Asian Miracle: Economic Growth and Public Policy*, Oxford University Press, New York; and Arogyaswamy, B. (1998) *The Asian Miracle, Myth, and Mirage: the Economic Slowdown is Here to Stay*, Quorum Books, Westport.

2 This apposite phrase comes from Walden Bello: see his 'Back to the Third World? The Asian Financial Crisis Enters Its Second Year', *Focus on Trade*, No. 27, July 1998. See <http://focusweb.org/focus/pd/apec/fot/fot27.htm>

3 At least two records were set in South Korea alone: for the largest IMF funding package measured in US dollar terms (supplanting the previous Mexican record), and for the largest agreement in relation to the recipient's quota with the Fund. See Butler, S., Omestad, T. and K.T. Walsh (1998: 42) 'The Year of the IMF: As Seoul Struggles with Reforms, Capitol Hill Takes Aim', *US News & World Report*, Vol. 124, No. 1, 12 January.

4 Support for the notion of insolvency crisis can be found in McKibbin, W. (1998: 10) 'The Crisis in Asia: an Empirical Assessment', Research School of Pacific and Asian Studies, Australian National University and Brookings Institution, Washington, DC, 16 February (revised 25 March).

5 As Treasury Secretary Robert Rubin later expressed his (and the Fund's) objection, the creation of the AMF might lead to 'reform shopping': see his 'Remarks to Students and Faculty of Georgetown University', *Federal News Service,* 21 January 1998. For more general analysis of the September 1997 version of the AMF, see Altbach, Eric (1997)'The Asian Monetary Fund Proposal: a Case Study of Japanese Regional Leadership', *JEI Report*, No. 47, 19 December. On Rubin's support for the IMF's involvement in the Asian financial crisis and its critical importance to 'the economic well-being of the American people', see Rubin, Robert (1998: 421–6) 'Strengthening the Architecture of the International Financial System: the Financial Crisis in Asia and the IMF', *Vital Speeches*, Vol. 64, No. 14.

6 Testimony of Walden Bello before Banking Oversight Subcommittee, Banking and Financial Services Committee, US House of Representatives, 21 April 1998. Available from <http://www.house.gov>. For its part, the IMF argued that Japan, rather than supporting the establishment of an AMF, would be better served by adopting 'energetic measures for the rehabilitation of its banking sector, tax relief, public investment, and the opening up and deregulation of its economy', for the sake of the region and to lessen pressure upon the United States to restore growth; see Camdessus, M. (1998) 'From the Asian Crisis Toward a New Global Architecture', address to the Parliamentary Assembly of the Council of Europe, Strasbourg, France, 23 June.

7 'Indonesia – Memorandum of Economic and Financial Policies', Jakarta, 15 January 1998, available from the Homepage of *Asienhaus Essen* at <http://www.asienhaus. org/asiancrisis/ imf_indonesia.htm>.

8 According to Wyplosz, the liberalization of capital movements in developing states is a source of blame for the crisis since it breaks the 'iron law of macroeconomics' – that a country have only two of the following: full capital mobility, monetary policy independence, and a fixed exchange rate. See Wyplosz, C. (1998: 4) 'Global Financial Markets and Financial Crises', paper presented at the Forum on Debt and Development, 'Coping with Financial Crises in Developing and Transition Countries: Regulatory and Supervisory Challenges in a New Era of Global Finance', Amsterdam, 16–17 March.

9 For Camdessus's concessions, see 'IMF Chief Admits Errors in Preventing S-EA Crisis', *Business Times*, 24 September 1998. The most recent, and perhaps the most amazing, display of the Fund's new 'human face' has come through its qualified vote of confidence in the August 1998 stock market intervention by the Hong Kong Monetary Authority. Furthermore, it has advised the SAR authorities to consider the merits of a deficit budget to counteract their slump, despite financial secretary Donald Tsang's obvious aversion to any red ink in his budgets: see Brooker, M. 'IMF in Guarded Vote of Confidence', *South China Morning Post*, 12 February 1998.

10 As with all large-scale counterfactuals, this is a difficult issue that may or may not prove to be true (and thankfully, the ultimate verdict is beside the point of this paper). However, those bent on pursuing the issue might be tempted to compare the medium-term trajectories of Russia and Indonesia (where the Fund's labours proved too little and too late) with Thailand and South Korea (where IMF remedies were more or less swallowed early and whole).

11 Zitner, A. 'Critics Taking Aim at Bailout Work of IMF', *The Boston Globe*, 7 October 1998 and Lambro, D. 'Swinging with the Bailout Rhythm', *The Washington Times*, 23 July 1998.

12 Or, for that matter, in many previous crises. However, it does seem that the Fund played a marginally more positive role in the Latin debt crisis than it has in the Asian one – in that it at least prevailed upon the banks to maintain some inflows of new money to help debtors meet their most pressing obligations. Although there has been repeated talk about this during the last twelve months, nothing of significance has yet happened. This shift in emphasis from the IMF can be attributed partially to the new reliance upon international 'best practices' in banking, including the signing of the Bank for International Settlement's Basle Accord on capital adequacy standards. In theory, the existence of such regimes decreases the need for a more active role in swaying the interests of the banking community. See Camdessus, M. (1998: 19) 'IMF Asian Programs', *Presidents & Prime Ministers*, Vol. 7, No. 1, January–February.

13 For more detailed analysis, see Ruggie, J.G. (1983: 205–6) 'International Regimes, Transactions, and Change: Embedded Liberalism in the Postwar Economic Order', *International Regimes*, ed. S. Krasner, Cornell University Press, Ithaca.

14 On the theme of 'civilian powers' and Japan's place within the genre, see Maull, H.W. (1990) 'Germany and Japan: The New Civilian Powers', *Foreign Affairs*, Vol. 69, No. 5; Funabashi, Y. (1991) 'Japan and the New World Order', *Foreign Affairs*, Vol. 70, No. 5; and Nye, J.S. Jr, 'What Sort of Japan Holds Best Promise for Long Run?', *Los Angeles Times,* 20 December 1992.

15 For one of the best arguments on this score, see Eccleston, B. (1986) 'The State, Finance and Industry in Japan', *State, Finance and Industry*, ed. A. Cox, Wheatsheaf, Sussex.

16 As Ken Courtis has recently observed, the aggregate savings of Japanese households are roughly twice as large as the GNP of the US; see his 'Big Bang or Wee Whimper? Restructuring Japan's Financial Sector', *Harvard Asia Pacific Review*, Winter 1997–8, <http://www.hcs.harvard.edu/~hapr/w9798/courtis.html>.

17 One of the more accessible ways of grasping the sheer magnitude of this hyper-growth is suggested by Jeffrey Winters: namely, that private capital flows to developing countries in just 1996 and 1997 were numerically greater than the total flows from the World Bank Group to the global periphery in its first 50 years: see his 'The Financial Crisis in Southeast Asia', paper presented to the conference 'From Miracle to Meltdown: The End of Asian Capitalism?' Asia Research Centre, Murdoch University, Perth, August 1998.

18 This metaphor is explored at greater length in Leaver, R. (1998) 'Moral (and Other) Hazards: The IMF and the Systemic Asian Crisis', paper presented to the conference 'From Miracle to Meltdown: the End of Asian Capitalism?' Asia Research Centre, Murdoch University, Perth, August. Historical comparisons of the inefficacious actions of an immature creditor country also extend to the US's refusal of Keynes's proposal to make substantial loans to Germany in the 1920s. Keynes's suggestion at the Paris Peace Conference was that greater access to funds would support democratic reform. While today's political and economic climate is substantively different, the IMF and others must consider the political

ramifications of a capital-starved economy. See Mardick, J. (1998: 39) 'The IMF Approach: the Half-Learned Lessons of History', *World Policy Journal*, Vol. 15, No. 3, and also Dieter, H. (1998: 14) 'Crises in Asia or Crisis of Globalization?', 1998, *CSGR Working Paper* No. 15/98, November.

19 On this and other things, see Krugman, P. (1999) 'The Return of Depression Economics (Similarities between the Economic Conditions of the 1930s and 1990s)', *Foreign Affairs*, Vol. 78, No. 1, where the 'liquidity trap' in mature economies is emphasized.

20 As Krugman has noted, 'when you don't have money you talk about architecture'; see Lachia, E. 'Get Used to Recessions, Economist Says', *Asian Wall Street Journal*, 5 October 1998.

21 On problems in the Philippines, see Manzo, A. and Harris, S. (1999: 30–2) 'The Philippines: Another IMF Casualty', *Dollars & Sense*, No. 221, January–February. For a misguided view from the East Asia Analytical Unit (a division of the Australian Department of Foreign Affairs and Trade) on how the Philippines has recently 'found the path of East Asian growth', see Macrae, M. (1998: 1) 'Philippines Passes Test', *International Business Asia*, Vol. 6, No. 9, 18 May.

22 This apposite phrase comes from Benedict Anderson: see his 'From Miracle to Crash', *London Review of Books*, 20 (8), 16 April 1998 <http://www.lrb.co.uk/v20n08/ande2008.htm>.

23 The infusions are still happening, although they are now overwhelmed by their task. IGGI's successor, the Coordinating Group on Indonesia (CGI), continued to provide cheap aid to the Suharto regime, with a last-gasp commitment of US$6.5 billion in February 1998. And with pre-commitments for US$2.4 billion in yen-denominated loans obtained a year later, Habibie's Indonesia is now positioned to emerge as the major recipient of aid under Japan's Miyazawa Plan; see Earl, G., 'Japan to the Rescue: $2.4bn', *Australian Financial Review*, 8 February 1998.

24 As Meredith Woo-Cumings has correctly observed, the 1983 Japanese loan of US$4 billion was, in relative terms, fully half the size of the IMF credits extended to Seoul 16 years later: see her 'Bailing Out or Sinking In? The IMF and the Korean Financial Crisis', paper presented at the Economic Strategy Institute, 2 December 1997, <http://www.asienhaus.org/asiancrisis/woo-cumings.htm>.

25 The word 'still' is used advisedly, for on this central issue the tides of opinion have been shifting. Especially after the September 1998 debacle of the bail-out of Long Term Capital Management, virtually everyone was willing to admit that the free movement of capital was not always a good thing. One of the more thoughtful (if less noted) of these critiques from high places has been made by the Reserve Bank of Australia, previously not out of place as a repository for Luttwak's scourge of 'central bankism' (see Luttwak, E. (1996) 'Central Bankism', *London Review of Books*, 14 November). For samples of its recent move to more enlightened modes of thinking, see the arguments of its Deputy Governor, Stephen Grenville, in particular his 'Capital Flows and Crises', talk to the Credit Suisse First Boston Australia conference on 'The Global Financial System – the Risks of Closure', 13 November 1998 <http://www.rba.gov.au/speech/sp_ind4.html>.

26 For a classic analysis that gives emphasis to similar themes, see Strange, S. (1974) 'IMF: Monetary Managers', *The Anatomy of Influence*, eds R. W. Cox and H. K. Jacobson, Yale University Press, New Haven.

27 See Saxonhouse, G.R. (1988: 226) 'Comparative Advantage, Structural Adaptation, and Japanese Performance', *The Political Economy of Japan, Volume 2, The Changing International Context*, eds T. Inoguchi and D.I. Okimoto, Stanford University Press, Stanford.

28 Krasner, S.D. (1985: 70) *Structural Conflict: the Third World Against Global Liberalism*, University of California Press, Berkeley. Put in a slightly different and broader context, Japan's share of world GNP was 3 per cent in 1960, but by 1980 it weighed in at 10 per cent; see Spero, J.E. (1990: 78–9) *The Politics of International Economic Relations*, Fourth Edition, St Martin's Press, New York.

29 Yoshiko Kojo (1992: 296–8) 'Burden-sharing Under US Leadership: the Case of Quota Increases of the IMF Since the 1970s', *Power, Economics and Security*, ed. H. Bienen, Westview Press, Boulder.

30 See Rapkin, D. P., Elston, J. U., and J. R. Strand (1997: 177) 'Institutional Adjustment to Changed Power Distributions: Japan and the United States in the IMF', *Global Governance*, Vol. 3, No. 2.

31 The historical and theoretical implications of this executive freedom of action over monetary policy, and of the sharp contrast with the rights of the Congress to make trade policy, are fleshed out by Stephen Krasner in his 'US Commercial and Monetary Policy: Unraveling the Paradox of External Strength and Internal Weakness', *Between Power and Plenty: Foreign Economic Policies of Advanced Industrial States*, ed. P.J. Katzenstein (1977), University of Wisconsin Press, Madison.

32 Without greater funding (with different strings attached) the IMF is unable to reform its current 'repo' man function without the support of the 'Wall Street–Treasury Complex'; see Veneroso, F. and Wade, R. (1998: 3–22) 'The Asian Crisis: the High Debt Model versus the Wall Street–Treasury–IMF Complex', *New Left Review*, 228, and also Preston, P.W. (1998: 241–3) 'Reading The Asian Crisis: History, Culture and Institutional Truths', *Contemporary Southeast Asia*, 20.

33 Madison, C., 'IMF Boost No Bailout, Administration Insists', *The National Journal*, Vol. 15, No. 12, 19 March 1983.

34 Recent figures reveal slightly lower levels (3.6 per cent) than during the Latin debt crisis; see International Monetary Fund, *International Financial Statistics*, Vol. 50, No. 12, December 1997, pp. 10 and 62, and International Monetary Fund, *International Financial Statistics*, Vol. 51, No. 12, December 1998, pp. 10 and 62.

35 This remark was further amplified by virtue of being uttered at the Vancouver APEC Summit; see Press Conference by the President and Prime Minister Chretien of Canada, Pan Pacific Hotel, Vancouver, British Columbia, United States Information Agency, 23 November 1997. As presidential adviser Sandy Berger later sought to explain, the word 'glitch' was 'an undefined term' that expressed the president's desire not to overstate the severity of the situation or to suggest it was insurmountable: see transcript, Berger, Tarullo, Steinberg, Summers briefing, 'Clinton, APEC Leaders Committed to Manila Framework', United States Information Agency, file ID: 97112501.EEA, 25 November 1997.

36 For details of executive–legislative gamesmanship during the tequila crisis, see Schwartz, A.J. (1997) 'From Obscurity to Notoriety: a Biography of the Exchange Stabilization Fund', *Journal of Money, Credit and Banking*, Vol. 29, No. 2.

37 This was generally interpreted to mean that 'in financial matters, Asia is Japan's responsibility': see Masahiko Ishizuka, 'Japan's Economy Must be Model for Region', *The Nikkei Weekly*, 29 September 1997.

38 This rarely used mechanism had been created in 1961 to coordinate the defence of the fixed exchange rate system amongst the industrialized countries, and was last invoked in 1978 to assist the Carter administration stabilize the dollar.

39 Previously the IMF had rejected support for the Russian economy. Yeltsin, however, dispatched Anatoly Chubais to Washington to lobby the Clinton administration so that Russia could have its way with the Fund. The eventual agreement delivered Russia three times more IMF credits than the Fund previously had been willing to contemplate. For a compelling account of the politics of this lobbying process, see Gordon, M.R. and D. E. Sanger (1998), 'Rescuing Russia', *New York Times*, 17 July.

40 For extensive analysis, see Helleiner, E. (1994) *States and the Reemergence of Global Finance: From Bretton Woods to the 1990s*, Cornell University Press, Ithaca, especially Chapter 8.

41 Tobin, J. and G. Ranis (1998), 'Flawed Fund', *The New Republic*, 9 March.

42 For recent reflections, see Gavin, F.J. (1996: 186) 'The Legends of Bretton Woods', *Orbis*, Vol. 40, No. 2.

43 Keynes was thoroughly depressed at this, so much so that some regard his subsequent death as a direct consequence of what was done at the Savannah River conference. See Moggridge, D. E. (1992: 835–6) *Maynard Keynes: an Economist's Biography*, Routledge, London.

44 For further analysis of this and related issues, see Reich, S. (1998) 'Miraculous or Mired? Contrasting Japanese and American Perspectives on Japan's Current Economic Problems',

CSGR Working Paper, No. 21/98, Centre for the Study of Globalization and Regionalization, University of Warwick, December. Available as a pdf file from <http://www.warwick.ac.uk/fac/soc/CSGR/>.

45 Some 40 per cent of the quantum leap of outward-bound foreign direct investment that emanated from Japan after 1985 ended up in the United States. See also Mochizuki, M.M. (1992: 342–6) 'To Change or to Contain: Dilemmas of American Policy Toward Japan', *Eagle in a New World: American Grand Strategy in the Post-Cold War World*, eds K.A. Oye, R.J. Lieber and D. Rothchild, Harper Collins Publishers, New York.

46 Vernon, R. (1990) 'The Japan–US Bilateral Relationship: Its Role in the Global Economy', *The Washington Quarterly*, Vol. 13, No. 3.

47 Epstein, G. (1985) 'The Triple Debt Crisis', *World Policy Journal*, Vol. 2, No. 4.

48 For the most detailed account of the operation and its costs, see Funabashi, Y. (1989) *Managing the Dollar: From the Plaza to the Louvre*, 2nd edition, Institute for International Economics, Washington DC.

49 For highly pertinent reflections on this and other things, see Kataoka, T. (1995) 'The Truth About the Japanese "Threat": Misperceptions of the Samuel Huntington Thesis', *Hoover Essays*, No. 9, Hoover Institution on War, Revolution and Peace, Stanford University.

50 On this, see Bernard, M. and J. Ravenhill (1995) 'Beyond Product Cycles and Flying Geese: Regionalization, Hierarchy and the Industrialization of East Asia', *World Politics*, Vol. 47, No. 2.

51 Peek, J. and E.S. Rosengren (1998: 2) 'Japanese Banking Problems: Implications for Southeast Asia', paper presented at the Second Annual Conference of the Central Bank of Chile, 'Banking, Financial Integration, and Macroeconomic Stability', Santiago, Chile, 3–4 September.

52 Japan was not, however, a significant player in the inflows of FDI into China.

53 See Klee, K., 'The Buck is Bruised', *Newsweek*, 19 October 1998 p. 58, and also Roach, S. (1997: 102–3) 'Angst in the Global Village', *Challenge*, Vol. 40, No. 5. Furthermore, Japanese banks have carried a 'Japan Premium' since 1995 on eurodollar and euroyen interbank loans, a premium which reflects concern about the solvency of Japanese banks and securities companies. The emergence of this premium compounded solvency (and competitiveness) problems within Japanese banks, who were buying up US Treasury bonds to meet the capital adequacy provisions of the Basle Accord rather than putting capital to work through foreign lending. The 'Japan Premium' also reflects a lack of faith in the ability of the Japanese government to provide security for its banking system. Peek, J. and E. S. Rosengren, 'Determinants of the Japan Premium: Actions Speak Louder than Words', Federal Reserve Bank of Boston Papers. Available from Eric.Rosengren@bos.frb.org or Peek@bc.edu.

54 See, for instance, the proposal for an Asia Pacific Monetary Fund (APMF) recently advanced by C. Fred Bergsten, former Chair of APEC's Eminent Persons' Group; 'Reviving the "Asian Monetary Fund"', *International Economics Policy Briefs*, No. 98-8, Institute of International Economics, December 1998, <http://www.iie.com/NEWSLETR/news98-8.htm>.

55 According to the Ministry of International Trade and Industry (MITI), the yen is 'nowhere achieving the status of a truly international currency': cited in Bergsten, C.F. (1997: 91) 'The Dollar and the Euro', *Foreign Affairs*, Vol. 76, No. 4.

56 Schaller, M. (1996) 'The Nixon "Shocks" and US–Japan Strategic Relations, 1969–74', *Working Paper*, No. 2, US–Japan Project Working Paper Series, The National Security Archive US–Japan Special Documentation Project, <http://www.seas.gwu.edu/nsarchive/japan/schaller.htm>.

57 Clinton's June 1998 visit to Beijing, for instance, was directly reminiscent of the Nixon shock in that an American President went to East Asia without visiting Japan.

58 Hartcher, P. and A. Cornell, 'Japan's Rescue Remedy no Match for the Malaise', *Australian Financial Review*, 16 March 1999.

59 Some important players have been calling for Japanese sales of US treasury bonds for a considerable time: see, for instance, Ohmae, K., 'Not Another Hashimoto, Please!', *Newsweek*, 27 July 1998.

8

Can Global Finance Be Regulated?

MANFRED BIENEFELD

In the 1920s, as the world was tilting towards disaster, the League of Nations was single-mindedly promoting liberalization of the global economy as the recipe for prosperity and stability. But the more it succeeded, the more unstable the global economy became. Growing instability led to increasing uncertainty and that, in turn, led to greater risk and increased opportunities for 'irrational enthusiasms' in the world's financial markets.

As this process gathered pace, speculators made enormous fortunes, even as their 'irrational' wagers enmeshed the real world economy in a disastrous web of impossible financial obligations. Eventually the world's financial markets became increasingly unmanageable: real growth faltered, income inequality exploded, social cohesion was eroded and political stability was undermined. In response, those who were getting rich beyond their wildest dreams were adamant in claiming that the problems were due to the fact that we had not liberalized enough. It was only by liberalizing far more radically that we could hope to regain the stable, rapid growth paths that could provide the foundation for steadily improving living standards for the people as a whole. And for those that were not persuaded by this logic, they were quick to add that 'there was no alternative' since finance was now so global national authorities could no longer regulate it. Meanwhile, a leading British historian (A.J. Toynbee) declared the nation state a 'parochial prejudice' and a leading economist (von Mises) deemed sovereignty a 'ridiculous illusion'.[1]

But this was to ask governments to do a job that they could not do, and would not do. It was to forget that financial regulation and management is, first and foremost, a political matter, not an economic or technical one. Indeed, it is only once the political questions have been answered, that the technical questions and the economic management issues can be addressed effectively. After all, efficiency in the pursuit of politically illegitimate or questionable ends is no virtue.

In the 1920s the push for a 'self-regulating market' was led by bankers seeking to re-establish the gold standard. Their efforts focused on four demands: balanced budgets, independent central banks, free capital flow and the gold standard. It is no accident that, apart from the demand for the gold standard, these same slogans dominate today's policy debates, which should come as no surprise, especially to those who profess to believe that human behaviour is largely self-interested. But, now as in the 1920s, these demands are a recipe for disaster and they are at the heart of Asia's current crisis.

Can and Should Global Finance be Regulated?

Before discussing the nature of this crisis further, let me comment briefly on the question of whether global finance can be regulated. This question is extremely popular in some circles because it invites the answer that regulation by national authorities is no longer possible in a global world. But the question is a highly misleading one; and that particular answer is quite indefensible. Indeed, to ask whether global finance can be regulated is like asking whether murder can be prevented, or whether value added taxes can be collected. In each case the answer is obviously: yes it can, but never completely or perfectly. In other words, this is not an either–or question. The questions that we really need to address are: how important is it for national political authorities to regulate their financial systems? What factors tend to make such regulation more, or less, difficult? And what forms should such regulation take?

I will focus attention on the first of these questions, namely: why the national regulation of money and of financial systems is of absolutely over-riding importance for political, social and economic reasons. I'll also look at the related question of why 'self-regulation' by the financial institutions, or regulation by international agencies, is not a substitute for national regula-tion. On this basis I will then comment briefly on the other two questions, which cannot be addressed seriously until the importance of such regulation has been established.

The Standard Argument for Financial Deregulation

Before making my argument, let me briefly comment on the main counter-argument: that political 'interference' in financial markets is highly undesirable (hence the need for 'independent central banks') and that the minimum of regulation that is absolutely required should either be turned over to 'independent' global authorities like the Bank of International Settlements and the IMF, or should be achieved by improving the risk management capabilities of the financial institutions themselves (as reflected in the BIS's recent decision to set aside its capital adequacy ratios for larger banks with sufficiently sophisticated 'in house' risk management models to be allowed to make their own judgments regarding the consolidated risks embedded in their total operations).

My critique of this position does not deny that political regulation entails serious risks that can often lead to unwise decisions. But it argues that these risks have to be managed by improving a country's political and administrative processes or institutions. They cannot be avoided by shifting the responsibility for regulation to 'the market' or to certain supranational agencies, because this is not simply a technical task. In fact, it is slightly absurd to suggest that such a shift of responsibility 'depoliticizes' financial regulation; it merely locks it into a particular 'politics' and then takes that decision out of the reach of the democratic debate. Indeed, the fact that the task of financial regulation has been misrepresented so widely as a largely technical one reflects the degree to which the financial institutions themselves dominate this particular policy debate, partly because they have privileged access to the more technical aspects of this task.

The argument that governments, even democratically elected ones, should not have power over monetary policy, or over financial regulation, is basically specious. The same argument could be applied to any other sphere of public policy, since the same alleged weaknesses of the political process would impair their ability to make 'rational', 'efficient' decisions in these areas. So should these responsibilities also be given to more 'rational' supranational authorities? The absurdity of this argument, with its nasty imperialist undertones, should lead one to ask why money and finance are treated so differently. The answer is that they are implicitly treated as largely technical matters and that they are deemed 'too important' to be left to 'the people'.

The imperialist undertone of the argument for 'international stewardship' in the financial sphere raises an issue that requires comment. Certainly the historical record provides a basis for thinking that such arguments tend to have a racist element. After all, there is no doubt that 'other' races and 'other' cultures have been more readily declared incompetent to govern themselves 'responsibly'. Nor can one doubt that there is a racist undertone to the glib claim that the current Asian crisis is largely due to the corrupt and cronyist nature of its financial systems. Although racism inevitably does play a role, it would be a grave mistake to conclude that this is primarily a racist issue, however, for that would be analytically wrong and would only allow the opposition to these processes to be divided along racial lines.

The truth is that the forces that drive these processes have truly global ambitions. And as they seek to create an increasingly integrated global economy, they are actively extending the argument that national governments cannot be trusted to behave rationally or efficiently to ever more countries and to ever wider ranges of the policy debate. In response, they support the creation of ever more powerful, activist and intrusive international rules and institutions, with the power to override national decisions or to impose sanctions on those who fail to comply with their definition of rationality. And this process ultimately knows no boundaries of race or culture. The argument for independent central banks is also applied to the industrial countries. The rules of the WTO, and of the proposed Multilateral Agreement on Investment, were also intended to constrain those governments. And although it is true that the enforcement of those rules will always discriminate to a degree in favour of the powerful, power is being shifted to corporate institutions and entities and away from public authorities around the world.

Soon after being elected in 1984, the new Tory government of Canada actively began to explore the possibility of a free trade deal with the United States, even though the idea never appeared on the Conservatives' election platform, and Prime Minister Brian Mulroney actually ridiculed it when seeking the party leadership. 'Free trade with the United States is like sleeping with an elephant,' he said. 'It's terrific until the elephant twitches and, if it rolls over, you're a dead man.... It affects Canadian sovereignty and we will have none of it, not during the leadership campaign or at any other time.'[2]

When the Minister for International Trade was asked by a journalist why the government now thought that Canada might need such an agreement, she replied that 'the main reason' was to ensure that no future Canadian government could ever return to the discredited 'nationalist' policies of the past![3] In other words, a minister was announcing that her government was seeking to enter into an international agreement specifically in order to ensure that the Canadian electorate would not have certain choices open to it in the future, because this government deemed these undesirable. The most amazing thing is that neither the minister nor the government had to resign, and that the free trade agreement is actively in force today, in the even more restrictive form of the North American Free Trade Agreement. This particular process is widely known as 'locking in' – as in, locking a country into a particular policy regime. And no country, except the US, is immune.

Moreover, the corporate and financial interests that are driving this process are quite clear as to its importance and its implications. Thus in the early 1990s *Business Week* posed a rhetorical question to President Clinton: what should be the main objective of American foreign policy now that the Cold War was over? And in the answer it gave to its own question, it summarized that global project very effectively. According to *Business Week*, that main objective should be a relentless attempt to establish an increasingly unified market around the world. Moreover, the editors warned the President that this would be no easy task. He would have to be prepared to take occasional tough actions to achieve this objective, since there would be 'opposition from those dispossessed in this process'.[4] Moreover, they would probably articulate their objections in nationalist terms, precisely because the struggle was over the ability of national societies to establish different priorities from those of the unified global market. Thus nationalism was to take the place of communism as the main enemy. And nowhere was this more evident than in the world's financial markets.

It is therefore no surprise that the demand for the further deregulation of global financial markets has been prominent in global policy debates. But there is a fatal flaw in the argument of those who extol the virtues of deregulated financial markets and advise countries to open their domestic financial systems to competition from foreign financial institutions in order to increase domestic efficiency while improving access to foreign capital. The advice is usually given with a *caveat* in the form of an exhortation that, as governments follow this advice, they must be sure to 'make adequate provision for prudential regulation'. But this glib advice raises two problems: one fundamental, the other practical.

The fundamental problem is that one cannot argue that 'financial markets know best' and also accept the need for 'prudential regulation' by some authority that must oversee and second guess the risk assessments made by the actors in the market. The fact is that if such authorities do, or can, exist, then the market does not know best. Thus, there is no obvious reason why the role of such authorities should be restricted to risk supervision.

The practical problem is that it is a tall order for any country, much less a developing one, to exercise 'adequate prudential regulation' over a financial sector that has been opened up substantially to foreign financial institutions, since that will make such regulation virtually impossible. At first glance, this may appear to contradict my earlier statement that the regulation of global finance is always possible, but that is not the case. What may become virtually impossible is 'adequate prudential regulation' within a situation in which a national financial system has been extensively liberalized. Liberalization is itself a policy choice, however, unless it is imposed on countries by external institutions. In other words, the contradiction does not reside in my argument, but in the argument of those who insist on the overriding importance of 'adequate prudential regulation' while advocating the extensive liberalization of a country's financial system.

So let me now turn to my main argument. National regulation of finance is possible. It is also so important that the obstacles that stand in its way, and that are being erected by the day, have to be overcome, where necessary, by adopting policies that will entail significant short-term costs.

The Problem of Regulating Finance in an Increasingly Global World

To understand this issue, we need first to establish why it might be desirable to regulate money and finance from a national perspective. The following reasons lead me to conclude that such regulation is essential:

1 Credit-based economies have to answer three critical questions: who has the right to create credit? What risks are they allowed to take? Who pays when things go wrong? There are no 'correct' answers to these questions. The answers are essentially political and can be given only on the basis of a legitimate political process, such as generally exists only at the level of the nation state (though conceivably at a regional level).

2 The value of money and the rate of interest and profit are critically important determinants of income distribution – and hence of desired patterns of resource allocation. This is an inherently political question that requires political legitimization. That is why history is replete with examples of economies that integrate themselves into a larger economic and monetary space only to find that they have tied themselves to a system within which their resources are systematically alienated to meet 'demand abroad' because that is where the 'effective demand' – backed by gold or hard currencies – is found.

3 As Keynes pointed out so consistently, free capital flows are inherently political precisely because they respond to policies in accordance with the priority that these give to the interests of capital.

4 The most important aspect of any development policy is its internal coherence at the national level. This means, the coherence between industrial, trade, finance, social and sectoral policies. Sustaining that coherence requires 'policy flexibility' – the use of a wide range of policy instruments in order to deal with unforeseen shocks and disturbances.

5 Investment needs to be guided by relatively long-term considerations and depends heavily on stability and predictability. Moreover, there are many advantages to a situation in which the rate of interest in an economy broadly reflects the level of profitability in that same economy. Such congruence makes it easier to manage economic disturbances, and that makes it easier to maintain a clear link between effort, risk and reward – which is ultimately important for securing the system's perceived political legitimacy in the longer run.

6 Capital is not a homogeneous concept. Foreign capital cannot be freely substituted for domestic capital, except if 'national' capital has become so delinked from its national social or economic base that it behaves exactly

like any other form of international capital. In reality, capital inflows are frequently not positive, productive additions to the capital stock. They may be aggressive and potentially destructive interventions by competitors, largely speculative forays, or attempts to acquire valuable resources at knockdown prices from distressed or corrupt governments. Moreover, they inevitably influence and ultimately distort the domestic political process and erode its capacity to make policy from a national perspective. A comment by Oliveira Campos, the architect of the Brazilian miracle of the 1970s, is a good example of this. Just as the second oil crisis was coming over the horizon in 1980, Campos said that Brazil needed to make some difficult decisions, but he was afraid that it would be unable to do so because its leading industries were dominated by multinationals who would have no interest in supporting those decisions.[5]

7   The value of a national currency should ultimately reflect the strength and the structure of that economy. If collective investment decisions are to be made in a responsible manner, then the system must ensure that those who pay the taxes to finance those investments have reason to believe that they will reap the eventual benefits. Equally, those who refuse to pay such taxes should have reason to believe that they will have to live with the negative consequences of those decisions. Citizenship must be an integrated concept that includes rights and responsibilities. Taxes are not an extraction by governments of something that rightfully belongs to the individual. To a large extent, they represent the income that accrues to the social investments that the individual uses to generate that income. Hence, incomes are always a 'joint product', based on the individual's efforts and the social investments on which the individual draws. In such a world there can be no such thing as an 'inalienable right of the individual to make the best use of their personal assets anywhere in the world', as a Deputy Director of the Bank of Canada once claimed in a debate with me.[6]

Factors Making National Financial Regulation More or Less Difficult

Once we have established that national financial regulation is of great importance, we need to address the obstacles that stand in its way. There are three types of factors to be considered here: internal structural and political conditions; external rules and regulations; and technical parameters. Each will be considered briefly.

Internal conditions

- Ideological perceptions of the rights and obligations of citizenship, and hence of the legitimacy of imposing national control on the financial system in the national interest (no law is enforceable unless most citizens see it as legitimate).

- Economic structure: the role of multinational corporations (MNCs), foreign financial institutions, etc.

- Political representation: capacity of popular voices to influence priorities, to ensure reasonably equitable income distribution, to ensure benefits of growth are shared widely.

- Capacity to mobilize resources and savings and to allocate these effectively to productive activities from a longer-term perspective (that is, dynamic comparative advantage).

- Capacity to ensure significant levels of competition within the domestic economy to maintain momentum and technological dynamism.

- Administrative capacity to formulate and to implement policies from a national perspective and to maintain popular support in the process.

International conditions

- Access to international finance on reasonable terms and under conditions in which creditors substantially share the risks of failure.

- Rules regarding the ability to maintain capital controls and other forms of intervention in domestic financial markets.

- The scale and nature of the 'buffers' that are established to help countries overcome large unforeseen disturbances in the global, or the domestic, economy.

- Freedom to use a wide range of policy instruments pragmatically in the pursuit of a strategic national development objective without being subjected to retaliation or sanctions.

- Reasonable access to external markets in a growing international economy.

- The ability to acquire technological expertise through joint ventures on reasonable terms.

Technical factors

Although the technical changes that have reshaped the way in which international finance functions are often cited as a critical obstacle to regulation, this is probably the least important factor, since electronic transfers actually make it easier to trace transactions where there is a political will to do so. The impact of the new technologies on communications, however – and hence on the way in which 'national' perceptions of these problems are shaped in actual practice – may constitute a serious obstacle to rebuilding the capacity for national regulation of finance.

Conclusions

The main conclusion is that national regulation of finance continues to be of the greatest importance. Because of this, the significant obstacles that now stand in the way of such regulation have to be addressed and ultimately overcome. There is no doubt that such regulation is still possible, though the degree to which this is so will vary from country to country. In Asia it should still be relatively high.

Asia must understand that its previous success was based on its ability to pursue coherent national policies in a context where finance was relatively controlled. Moreover, today's crisis is directly linked to the fact that it lost control over those processes, and that this effectively destroyed the capacity of various countries to manage their domestic economies – socially, economically and politically.

If Asia's people allow themselves to be persuaded that their politicians were the central problem and that they should cede control of their financial systems to international rules and institutions, they will be making a dramatic mistake, ensuring the 'Latin Americanization' of Asia. Where politicians *were* a large part of the problem – and that is true in many cases – the response must be to deal with that problem politically: to bring back to power governments that are capable and willing to pursue relatively integrated, equitable and culturally defensible national development strategies that can improve the quality of the lives of their citizens. There is no other solution.

Notes

1 Polanyi, Karl (1944: 189) *The Great Transformation*, Boston: Beacon Press, 1957 edition.
2 Bakan, J., 'The Crisis in Canadian Democracy', *The Toronto Globe and Mail*, 19 August 1988 p. A7.
3 *The Globe and Mail*, 30 October 1987.
4 *Business Week*, 17 January 1994, p. 102.
5 Campos, O., 'New and Old Industrial Countries', a paper given at an international conference at the University of Sussex, 1980.
6 'The Advisability of Capital Controls', Working Dinner at the North South Institute, Ottawa, Canada.

9

Putting People before Profits
Proposals for the Regulation of Foreign Investment

JESSICA WOODROFFE

Like lambs to the slaughter, governments are signing away their right to regulate inward investment, leaving multinational corporations with more and more power. While the Southeast Asian crisis shone the spotlight firmly on the dangers of unregulated financial flows, the chronic problems of longer-term foreign investment remain largely ignored.

This is the issue of the next century. Foreign investment is the largest source of financial flows to the Third World, and increasing rapidly.[1] Decisions taken now will determine the future. If nothing is done, inequality will continue to increase at an obscene rate. Or we can choose finally to harness the pursuit of profit, making it subservient to the pursuit of poverty eradication. It is still possible that foreign investment, including that of multinational corporations, could deliver real benefits, but only if governments are willing to face up to their responsibilities.

The World Development Movement (WDM) is proposing a framework for the regulation of foreign investment which complements national rules with an international investment agreement. We argue that liberalization agreements are benefiting multinationals. Only through regulation can the worst abuses of multinationals be stopped, and foreign investment moulded to provide a positive contribution towards society.[2]

The Problem

That foreign direct investment is desirable is a pervasive assumption which has turned into an obsession among many international decision makers. It seems clear that the role of foreign investors needs to be de-emphasized. It is much less clear just what the acceptable role of FDI should be. Perhaps it should be the fuel – but not the engine – for sustainable, equitable growth.

Most foreign investment comes from multinationals. There is mounting evidence that some of these multinationals are wreaking havoc in the Third

World. People around the world can attest to these abuses. Burmese, Nigerians and Colombians suffer human rights abuses while oil companies turn a blind eye and reap huge profits; banana workers are intimidated for joining trade unions in Costa Rica; workers die in a toy factory fire in Thailand; African babies become sick due to artificial breast milk; and across Asia children get hooked on cigarettes.[3] Workers' rights have been abused, lands destroyed, consumers lied to and national laws broken.

In the worst cases, multinationals are persuading governments to lower standards in return for the promise of investment. A downward spiral is occurring where Third World governments compete with one another to provide the cheapest labour, or fewest environmental regulations, as the most effective way of attracting foreign investment.

Multinationals are also guilty of applying double standards. While conditions may be better in their factories than in local ones, they still fail to meet the minimum standard considered acceptable in their home country.

The tragedy is that potentially foreign investment could play a valuable role, providing jobs, capital and technical know-how. But in reality the positive impact is often limited. Our task, then, is to rule out the worst abuses of foreign investment and find ways of ensuring that any potential benefits are realized. To this end, WDM is proposing a framework of national and international mechanisms for the regulation of foreign investment.

Getting It Right

Recent discussion of the regulation of foreign investment has been framed within the global liberalization agenda. Little time has been spent on considering the purpose of such agreements beyond the context set by the liberalization assumption.

The first question is: what should be the objective of foreign investment regulation? On this there appears some consensus; few would pronounce themselves openly against poverty reduction or environmental sustainability. In the UK, the government is clear that 'social and environmental' objectives should now be part of any investment agreement, and has made very clear its support for the OECD target of halving world poverty by 2015.

The second question is: how should this be achieved? The *status quo* is failing the poorest. The gap between rich and poor is increasing. Three billionaires now have more than the combined income of the 48 poorest countries.[4] Investment is not always contributing to pro-poor growth, and is in some cases responsible for gross human rights abuses and increasing poverty.

True believers in the free market agenda argue that the problem is market distortions. If government interference in the market is removed, everything will run smoothly. Foreign investment can then make its full contribution to equitable development. There is, however, scant evidence for this hypothesis. At best, the market allocates resources 'efficiently' in order to maximize output. Left to its own devices the market does not and cannot meet social goals like poverty reduction and equity.

The crisis in Southeast Asia provided more evidence, if any were needed, that markets are not always that smart, even when it comes to economics. No one has ever claimed that markets have a conscience. Clearly help is needed. Replacing blind ideological adherence to blanket liberalization with across-the-board regulation is not the answer. A far more pragmatic approach is needed which starts with the goal of poverty reduction and then develops a new relationship between markets and the state. In this, governments will need to be able to select what types of investment they attract, and to regulate that investment selectively to maximize its contribution to equitable, sustainable development.

WDM is proposing, rather than a single solution, a framework of regulation using:

International agreements
- An International Investment Agreement (IIA);
- UN conventions.

National government action
- Domestic laws holding companies accountable for operations overseas;
- Pro-poor national development strategies.

Increasingly economic activity is global while legal and political worlds are still organized at a national level. Even the UN is made up of national representatives. International law applies almost exclusively to governments, not individuals or companies. Meanwhile, multinationals flow around the world beyond the reach of national legislatures. Clearly, enforceable international regulation is needed.

But much still can, and should, be done at a national level. One of the dangers of globalization is that the nation state is being weakened, without being replaced by democratic structures. Corporations are all still registered nationally and are thus responsible to the governments in those states. Perhaps most importantly, if foreign investment is actually to play a positive role it will have to fit into the national development strategies of host governments, which must be allowed to regulate.

The concept of regulating corporate activity is nothing new. It is taken for granted that there should be rules governing the operation of corporations domestically. In the UK the factories act on child labour was passed as early as 1833. Similar international rules are a practical response to the internationalization of economic activity. Nor is the concept of international regulation a new one. Rules which promote liberalization and protect companies are strictly enforced. Enforcing the rights of individuals should not be beyond our abilities.

Some advocate 'civil society regulation' through which consumer groups and trade unions put pressure on companies to improve their performance, for example through codes of conduct. Such action clearly has a role to play. Trade unions in particular have won valuable victories. Many companies have now recognized the need at least to appear ethical. Some of the more responsible companies can set 'best practice' targets for the industry. But this will never be enough. Enforcement is dependent on the continued vigilance of a small group of campaigners, and the worst companies can easily choose not to comply. Increasingly, 'ethical' companies are also concerned that less scrupulous competitors are able to undercut them. Complementary mandatory regulation by governments will always be needed.

An International Investment Agreement

Discussions on FDI in the OECD and WTO start from the assumption that investment regimes should be liberalized. The goal for the agreement becomes the execution of a particular political ideology, rather than sustainable development or poverty reduction. It is not surprising that the outcomes have been deeply flawed.

Much has been written elsewhere on the Multilateral Agreement on Investment, the OECD's ill-fated attempt at liberalization that was finally abandoned in 1998. The collapse was due in part to the steadfast commitment of the French to their film industry, but it was also due to activists who exposed the absurdity of the agreement, which had been negotiated secretly by the unelected bureaucrats of the rich world.

Following the demise of the MAI, British Trade Minister Brian Wilson called for future debates to take place 'on the basis of a fresh agenda with clearly defined objectives which take full account of social and environmental concerns'.[5] While this is a promising start, a really useful agreement will need to go further. There has been a sterile debate over whether there needs to be a rules-based system for foreign investment. Clearly the answer is yes. The real debate is about what those rules should be.

WDM proposes two objectives for an International Investment Agreement to meet the needs of developing countries:

1 *Enable governments to attract high-quality investment as part of a sustainable development strategy.* A rules-based system is needed to provide sufficient stability to attract FDI to developing countries, while at the same time maintaining sufficient flexibility to allow developing country governments to find high-quality investment that contributes to pro-poor growth.

2 *Protect basic rights through global standards for the operations of foreign investors.*
Corporations, rather than governments, would be responsible for complying with standards, based on existing UN agreements, to protect the
rights of individuals and communities.

Enabling Governments to Attract Quality Investment

WDM proposes that a new international investment agreement should start
with the responsibility of governments to ensure that foreign investment
promotes the welfare of their citizens. Most developing countries want
foreign investment. The primary concern of many is how to increase FDI,
since most of it is concentrated in a handful of countries. Rightly or wrongly,
FDI is perceived as a way of providing much needed capital and technical
expertise. While the benefits have been exaggerated, there does seem to be a
role for 'quality' investment and it is important that any investment agreement does not preclude developing countries from being able to attract such
investment if they so choose.

Investors need rules to reassure them that their investment will be safe,
particularly in developing countries. Certain guarantees – for example, fair
compensation after expropriation – will be necessary. However, the need to
protect corporate rights has been exaggerated. Investors choose their location for all sorts of reasons, including potential access to new markets, infrastructure and a skilled workforce. In the process of designing a new agreement, work is needed to identify just what rules are required.[6]

A new IIA, therefore, will need to include basic protection of investors in
order to ensure the continued expansion of investment flows globally,
without unnecessarily tying the hands of governments. But quality matters
more than quantity. There is no point in attracting large-scale foreign investment if it is not beneficial. The quality of inward investment is crucial in
determining the extent to which it contributes to a country's development.
Investment can be valuable, but not always. It is government action that can
make the difference. Protection for investors needs to be balanced with
enabling governments to ensure that investment is actually beneficial.

UNCTAD has argued that an international investment agreement must
leave developing countries with sufficient space to pursue their own development strategies. 'One of the challenges facing countries is therefore ensuring
that IIAs are sufficiently flexible to serve, in addition to the specific objectives of each instrument, the development needs of developing countries.'[7]

Foreign investment needs to contribute to a government's own national
development strategies. Pro-poor growth is growth that provides jobs to
those who need them, pays poor producers a decent price for their produce,
and ensures that women as well as men receive income. It is also growth that

provides sufficient income, through taxation, for the government to provide those social services which it can provide better than the market. None of this happens automatically. It requires governments to lay down certain rules or 'performance requirements' for corporations, ensuring that governments have effective economic strategies and that foreign investment fits within these frameworks.

For example, mergers may provide more technology transfer but fewer new jobs than a greenfield site. Investment in the manufacturing sector may well fit better with a country's long-term development strategy than extractive industries. Performance requirements may be necessary to maximize technology transfer or prevent FDI creating a net outflow of foreign exchange.

Proposals were made to include labour and environmental clauses within the MAI, but these missed the central concern that governments' ability to promote sustainable development would be constrained. What is often referred to as the 'social and environmental' dimension within investment agreements has focused on ruling out the worst impacts of investment. WDM wants to go beyond this to look at the 'developmental' aspects of investment – considering how investment can actually be harnessed to make a positive contribution to developmental goals like equity and poverty reduction.

In practice this is a defensive proposal, arguing that any IIA should not include rules prohibiting governments from discriminating among investors and enforcing entry requirements or performance measures. Governments would retain the right to discriminate between that investment which is damaging and that which would contribute to sustainable development. They would also retain the right to require certain measures of corporations – in relation to technology transfer, for example, or employment of locals, or location of research and development functions – even if such measures appear to discriminate against foreign investors.

IIAs cannot guarantee that governments will pursue sensible economic policies which ensure that the potential benefits of foreign investment are maximized, but it is vital that they leave the space for those governments that wish to do so.

Maintaining Standards

Another function of an IIA is to stop the downward spiral of standards, establishing a floor below which it is not acceptable for multinationals or their subcontractors to operate. It is, of course, the job of governments to protect the basic rights of their citizens by establishing such standards, but, as is only too evident, this is not always possible. Pressure from potential investors is difficult to resist when they are now more powerful than many governments.

While all developing countries want to attract foreign investment many, their desire is not unconditional, as the Ghanaian Ambassador explains:

In return for providing an 'attractive investment climate', multinational enterprises can be expected by the host government to behave in accordance with international directives and host domestic laws. They would also be expected to show an understanding of, if not empathy with, the developmental objectives of the host country and due regard for its culture.[8]

WDM is proposing a set of core standards for multinationals, based on existing international agreements, with which companies would have to comply. A key departure from existing international arrangements is that companies as well as states would accept responsibility for complying with the standards, and would be monitored by an international body. It is companies who commit the crimes, yet in the past it is governments who have been responsible for maintaining the standards.

Crucially, governments would still own the agreement, thus rooting the mechanism in existing national legal and political systems. Governments would give to the international body permission to monitor the operations of its domestically registered companies, and the companies operating under its jurisdiction.

To avoid lengthy debate, the proposal is to base the core standards on existing agreements. They cover the areas of basic human rights; working conditions; equality in employment; consumer protection; the environment; local communities; business practices and sovereignty (see Appendix: The Core Standards at the end of this chapter).

The standards would be the minimum expected of companies and it should be normal business practice to meet them. They would set lower standards than most of the voluntary codes of conduct. It would also be possible to start with an even more modest proposal, that companies should be held responsible at an international level for negligence causing bodily harm. This would be most straightforward where the standards were based on criminal law.

Beyond the Core Standards

The discussion gets more complicated when we look beyond minimum standards to the corporate practices that legitimately can be expected of multinationals. As the biggest companies merge and remerge they have the power to set prices and call the shots, and consumers lose out. They can also by-pass national taxes by transferring income internally, and demand higher and higher incentives before they deign to set up shop.

Many governments have a competition policy to remove 'market distortions' such as monopolies. Multinationals are able to bypass these laws by operating across national boundaries. If focused on the increasing market domination by a few multinationals, however, competition policy could still prove a valuable part of an investment agreement.

The leading Indian consumer organization, Consumer Unity and Trust Society (CUTS), is proposing that alternative investment agreements should include competition policy as a way of achieving developmental goals. As companies get larger they have an increasing ability to dominate the market. Competition policies can help consumers by preventing monopolies fixing high prices, or help local firms by preventing cartels from pushing them out of business. They can also stop restrictive business practices such as transfer pricing which deprive governments of the taxes they are owed. Transparency and rules on disclosure are also important components in regulating multinationals. Proposals include changes to reporting requirements and an audited corporate report.

The present bias appears to be toward protecting corporations through competition policy, however, rather than promoting developmental objectives. Moreover, some 'market distortions' will be necessary to allow governments to govern. Therefore, the focus should be on removing the distortions created by corporations rather than those created by governments.

The Enforcer

One of the criticisms of past agreements has been the lack of democratic process. There is however a growth of literature suggesting alternatives involving civil society.[9]

Meanwhile, the debate continues in global institutions. With the failure of the OECD to secure agreement for the MAI, attention has now turned towards the WTO. The European Union is pushing for investment to be firmly on the WTO's agenda, to the dismay of opponents of the MAI who see the agreement re-emerging with a new name but otherwise largely intact.

So far, the WTO has seemed unlikely to produce an investment agreement that leaves governments with flexibility and protects citizens against the worst abuses of the multinationals. Instead, recent WTO decisions have put multinationals' profits before the livelihoods of Caribbean farmers and the health of European consumers. The WTO has an explicit mandate for liberalization that disqualifies it from the necessary pragmatic approach. It also has a democratic deficit, with many developing countries excluded from key negotiations.

Another alternative is UNCTAD, long seen as the only development-friendly forum on trade or investment. While this may well be the forum for some useful debate and analysis, it has no teeth. But the absence of an obvious institution to house an agreement should not deter us. It is lack of political will, rather than technical details, which stands in the way.

WDM has proposed a possible mechanism for the enforcement of core standards simply to show that it is feasible. We are not wedded to this enforcement model, however, believing that it would be futile to become bogged down in enforcement mechanisms before establishing the principles for an IIA. The ideal would be to use existing mechanisms, but these all require compliance by governments, not companies. In addition to the commission proposed below, two other avenues are worth pursuing.

Guarantees for investors have so far come without corresponding responsibilities. One proposal is that investors should only have the right to protection under an international agreement if they comply with basic standards. Under a 'Denial of Benefits' clause, an investor would not receive the benefits of an international agreement if it was in breach of the relevant codes attached to the agreement. For example, a baby food company would not be able to complain that it had not been given national treatment (equivalent to that of local firms) in relation to health services or hospital contracts, if it had been in breach of the World Health Organization (WHO) code on breast-milk substitutes. This could even be taken further, so that the investor would lose all investment rights under the agreement, not just those related to that particular code violation.[10]

The International Criminal Court may also provide an interesting precedent: under its procedures, third parties are subject to international law and can be tried either in domestic courts or by the international court.

A Core Standards Commission

The proposal for a Core Standards Commission (CSC) attempts to provide a model for international enforcement, without undermining the role of nation states. Ideally, all states would ratify the conventions from which the core standards are taken and therefore include them in their own domestic law. At present many states have agreed to the conventions, demonstrating their commitment to comply, but have not yet ratified them. Because waiting for ratification could severely delay the process, WDM is proposing an enforcement mechanism that does not depend on ratification.

The proposal is for an international body which monitors compliance with the core standards and, where offenders are also in breach of domestic law, assists individuals and communities in taking these companies to court.

Under the international agreement on Core Standards for Corporate Responsibility, a Core Standards Commission would be established. This could comprise representatives from business, trade unions, governments and the law. Its remit would cover all the core standards. Governments would have to ensure it had access to the necessary information in the countries involved.

The CSC would hear complaints against companies accused of breaching the internationally agreed core standards. Complaints would be made in writing by anyone who considered that their rights had been violated under the core standards. The commission would have the right to investigate the breach. If upheld, the first stage is for the complaint to be registered.

The CSC will then take the advice of local legal experts. If, *prima facie*, there is a breach of local law then the Commission is entitled to issue proceedings against the company in the local courts. The Commission will be acting on behalf of the victim and will only proceed if their permission is received. Governments could also enforce the decision themselves through their own courts.

For this model to work, participating states would have to agree to allow the CSC to investigate complaints in their jurisdiction, and to allow the CSC to issue proceedings in their courts. The international agreement would need to include a definition of multinational enterprises (as in the OECD guidelines). Under this model, the CSC would only investigate complaints against multinationals.

This model has a number of advantages. Action can be taken even if not all states have actually ratified the various international agreements. National legislation should be strengthened rather than undermined. Although the register of breaches against the core standards will have no sanction, they should prove a deterrent and a source of warning to prospective host governments. At the same time the Commission should build up a valuable knowledge base which can be used in improving the system in the future.

The model does not yet solve the problem of the 'corporate veil' – but could in the future add the proposal that host courts could recover assets from the rest of the 'group' or parent company.

WDM's proposal is that the standards should apply to multinational corporations. We believe that it is possible to require performance standards of major corporations in a way that would be unrealistic for small local industries. OECD guidelines already attempt a definition of multinational enterprises. On signing the core standards, governments would be agreeing that their domestically registered multinationals should abide by the standards, as should multinationals operating in their territory.

Balancing National Sovereignty and Individual Rights

There has been an understandable concern among Third World countries that any kind of standards within an international agreement are merely a device to legitimize new forms of protectionism by industrialized countries, banning imports from any country which does not comply. This fear is particularly acute where the process is to be adjudicated by the WTO.

Strengthening rather than weakening governments is crucial in the face of the liberalization onslaught. But the current situation is that some governments are bargaining away their sovereignty in an anxious attempt to attract foreign suitors; nor do governments always protect individual rights. The proposal for an IIA attempts to protect the rights of individuals and communities in relation to corporations, while at the same time maintaining a government's ability to govern. It is companies, not countries, that are sanctioned for transgressions against the standards; moreover, a key element in the standards is the protection of governments' right to pursue their own development strategies.

Complementary International Action

Existing international agreements, mostly covering traded products, play a valuable complementary role. Such agreements have to be enforced by individual governments, and tend to be highly specific, but can be useful in establishing best practice in particular areas. International organizations can also facilitate and encourage governments to enforce the codes. The WHO has codes on the marketing of both pharmaceuticals and breast-milk substitutes, and is promoting an International Framework Convention on Tobacco Control.[11] The Food and Agriculture Organization (FAO) agreed to the Rotterdam Convention on the export of hazardous chemicals. Strengthening the International Labour Organization (ILO) is of central importance in protecting workers' rights.

The OECD guidelines for multinational enterprises are currently under review. Although to date the guidelines have had little impact, with few corporations having any idea of their content, they could still be of some value. Modernized and extended, they would provide a valuable indicator to companies of what is expected of them by their OECD governments. In its submission to the review process WDM has recommended that the responsibilities of multinationals be laid out clearly, with progress toward effective enforcement. To be effective, the guidelines must apply to companies' operations outside as well as within the OECD.[12]

National Action

While a global agreement may be necessary to regulate companies operating globally, it is only one part of the framework. We have made it clear that an IIA can only leave space for national development strategies; it is then up to host governments to implement them. But industrialized countries or 'home' governments have a role too. Companies are still registered at a national level, and subject to the laws of that country.

Almost all multinationals are based in industrialized countries, where it is accepted that domestic laws will govern what they do and what form they take as corporate entities.   But as soon as they move their operations overseas, governments turn a blind eye, or make toothless requests for ethical behaviour. In doing so they lag behind Northern consumers, investors and trade unions who are already expressing a demand for tougher action. There is enormous scope for home country governments to take responsibility for the operations of their domestically registered companies overseas. In return for incorporation or legal recognition, basic requirements should be made of companies.

Groundbreaking cases in the UK have highlighted a central issue. Under British law companies are expected to provide a 'duty of care' to their employees and those affected by their operations. The law firm Leigh, Day and Co. has brought three cases on behalf of South African and Namibian workers who claim that British companies failed to exercise this duty of care. If accepted, the principle is simple and potentially devastating: a company owes a duty of care to all its workers, wherever they live. If key decisions which lead to a dangerous act are taken in the UK, then the victim can sue the company in the UK. Hiding beyond subsidiaries would be much more difficult.

Moreover, the concept of duty of care is based not just on the laws of the country in which it operates, but also on all the information to which the British directors have access . That legal standards are lower abroad (in this case on safe levels of asbestos exposure) is no excuse if information is available in the UK showing that higher standards are required for basic health and safety. The days of double standards could finally be numbered.[13] In the rest of the European Union it is already accepted that a claimant can sue a company in the country in which it is registered if he or she so chooses.

In the US, legal action has been taken against oil company Unocal for alleged violations of human rights in Burma. The case is potentially significant as the company is accused of human rights crimes that are usually attributed only to governments.[14]

A second opportunity also exists in the UK. The Department of Trade and Industry is conducting a review of company law, which provides an opportunity to modernise the British government's understanding of corporate activity. At present, only shareholders are recognized as legitimate stakeholders in the operations of a company. It is actually against the law for directors to sacrifice commercial advantage for ethical motives. Non-governmental groups are arguing that workers, consumers and local communities, both at home and abroad, are also legitimate stakeholders. Moreover, WDM is proposing that under a new Act the government should ensure that the rights of these stakeholders are protected by law.

Because multinationals use the complex web of relationships between parent company, subsidiaries and subcontractors to hide from their responsibilities, transparency is key.

Sanctions are a last resort. A small number of regimes are so heinous that any kind of investment in them will inevitably compromise human rights. Where there is a democratic opposition to the regime, calling for sanctions, as in Burma, we argue that the British government, and others, should enforce such sanctions legally.[15]

Finally, there is the overwhelming need for host country governments to be able to regulate the activities of multinationals in order to ensure that the potential benefit of foreign investment is maximized, and its cost minimized. It is through these national government decisions that the impact of investment on development can really be shaped. This is true in the industrialized countries as well as in the Third World. In both Wales and Scotland increasingly nuanced and selective approaches to inward investment have been adopted. But here incentives can be used. It is in developing countries that the ability to regulate is most needed.

Governments need to attract foreign investment which supports rather than undermines domestic production and which provides training, technology transfer and research and development functions located in the host country.

In all, foreign investment tends to be more beneficial if it meets the following criteria:

- Provides new capital rather than buying out an existing company;

- Contributes to economic development by introducing industries which are higher up the value-added chain;

- Transfers technology and management skills to the local population;

- Provides high quality jobs appropriate to the skills of the local workforce and is prepared to train local people;

- Supports local business by sourcing locally, requiring the kind of inputs which can be provided by local business, and is prepared to support its development;

- Does not undermine local business. In this respect industries which intend to export their product may be better than ones which want to produce for the domestic market;

- Improves the balance of payments and provide foreign exchange.

In some cases governments will be able to target those multinationals which provide the most benefit. In others, they will need to make certain requirements of the foreign investor before they set up shop. These might include rules that: a specified amount of local goods (local content) is used in the production process; that technology transfer occurs; that a proportion of key personnel are local employees; or that a proportion of the product is exported.

The UNCTAD Expert Meeting on Existing Agreements on Investment and their Developmental Dimensions (May 1997, Geneva) produced a list of criteria for 'development-friendly' investment ·similar to the one above. It included the following advice:

> Frameworks should take into account host countries' developmental objectives, reserving for those countries the ability to pursue economic development.... Frameworks should not make it difficult for developing countries to protect their culture, environment, economic mechanisms and social goals.[16]

An enabling IIA, which gives governments the freedom to pursue such strategies, is not enough. Third World governments are already being constrained by other international institutions. IMF-designed structural adjustment programmes are the prerequisite for most aid and debt relief. Despite mounting evidence against such a strategy, the IMF continues to 'persuade' governments to deregulate and liberalize, exposing economies to even deeper penetration by multinationals.[17]

Reducing governments' reliance on foreign exchange would also help. Increasing international debts and diminishing aid flows have increased the dependence of developing countries on foreign investors, further reducing their bargaining power.

Of course not all governments would pursue pro-poor development strategies if left to their own devices. Local democratic movements therefore have an important role to play. But the tragedy is that even where governments are willing and able to pursue pro-poor paths of development they will find themselves increasingly constrained by more and more international agreements standing in their way in the name of liberalization.

Liberalization is an ideology which favours corporations over governments and their citizens. Foreign investment by multinationals potentially has a valuable role to play, but not in a world without rules.

Appendix

The Core Standards

The World Development Movement believes multinational companies should abide by basic standards in all their operations and ensure that their subsidiaries and subcontractors also comply. Such standards give the business community a stable, agreed international framework for its operations, and they enable countries and their peoples to maximize the benefit and minimize the cost of multinational companies' operations.

Below is a proposed list of such standards. Under each of the proposed standards we have listed the existing international agreements from which the standard was derived. We have not attempted to be exhaustive but, rather, to present a basis for further debate. (A full list of annotated sources is available from World Development Movement, 25 Beehive Place, London, SW9 7QR, England.)

Basic human rights

Multinational companies should respect the right of everyone to life and liberty; no one should be subjected to torture, cruel treatment or arbitrary arrest. Companies should promote basic human rights, ensuring they are universally and effectively observed. Companies must ensure any security forces working for them abide by basic standards.

Universal Declaration of Human Rights: Preamble, Articles 3 and 5.
UN Code of Conduct for Law Enforcement Officials.

Working conditions

Multinational companies should uphold the rights of workers to form and join trades unions and bargain collectively, and to a safe working environment. Multinational companies must not use child or forced labour.

ILO Conventions 29, 87, 98, 155, 105 and 138.

Multinational companies should offer the best possible wages, benefits and conditions; these should be no less favourable than those offered by comparable firms, when such are present.

ILO Tripartite Declaration 34, 33.

Multinational companies should maintain the highest health and safety standards, bearing in mind their experience within the whole company, including knowledge of special hazards. They should inform representatives of the workers and the government about health and safety standards they observe in other countries.

ILO Tripartite Declaration 37.

Equality

Multinational companies should uphold the right of women and men to have equal pay. Companies should not discriminate in employment on the grounds of sex, race, beliefs or origin.

ILO Conventions 100 and 111.

Consumer protection

Multinational companies should uphold the right of the consumer to accurate marketing and information on products, safe goods, instructions on their proper use and information on all risks.

UN Guidelines for Consumer Protection.
WHO codes on breast-milk substitutes and on promoting pharmaceuticals.
FAO convention on pesticides.
Food standards of Codex Alimentarius.

The environment

Multinational companies have responsibilities to undertake environmental impact assessments; to prevent and clean up pollution; and to meet their responsibilities on climate change, biodiversity, the sea, and ozone-depleting substances. Prior informed consent is needed for the export of toxic waste or banned pesticides.

Rio Declaration.
Agenda 21.
Conventions on climate change, biodiversity and the law of the sea.
Basle agreement; Montreal protocol; Rotterdam convention.

Local communities

Multinational companies should uphold the right of indigenous people to control their own development. They should respect their rights over land, the environment, and natural and mineral resources. Companies should act to compensate people relocated with their consent and to ensure effective protection at work.

ILO Convention 169 on Indigenous and Tribal Peoples 7,14, 15, 16, 20.

Business practices

Multinational companies should not abuse market power or limit competition, through practices such as price fixing, predatory take-overs or collusive deals, and should provide the authorities with all necessary information.

UNCTAD Rules for the Control of Restrictive Business Practices (D 1–4).

Sovereignty and development strategies

Multinational companies should respect every state's right to choose its own economic system and to regulate foreign investment and the activities of transnational corporations within its jurisdiction.

UN Charter of Economic Rights and Duties of States, Articles 1 and 2.

Multinational companies should take account of countries' policy objectives, including development and social priorities. They should pay due regard to using technologies that generate employment, and consider giving contracts to national companies, using local materials and promoting local processing.

ILO Tripartite Declaration of Principles Concerning Enterprises and Social Policy 10, 19, 20.

Notes

1 Foreign direct investment grew by 27 per cent in 1997, according to the UNCTAD World Investment Report, United Nations, New York, 1998.

2 This chapter refers only to foreign direct investment – that investment taking a lasting stake in a project. Speculative investment has no role to play in sustainable development and should not be protected by investment agreements. Portfolio investment should also be treated separately as its value is less clear.

3 Information on all these campaigns is available from the World Development Movement at wdm@wdm.org.uk.

4 United Nations Development Programme (1999) *Human Development Report*, Oxford University Press, New York and Oxford.

5 Chatham House, London, 29 October 1998.

6 Some commentators have referred to the 'rights' of corporations in an investment agreement. WDM is deliberately not using such language. We are concerned only with those rules needed to maintain the flow of investment.

7 'International Investment Agreements: Concepts Allowing for a Certain Flexibility in the Interest of Promoting Growth and Development', note by the UNCTAD secretariat (circulated in TD/B/COM.2/EM.5/2) Geneva, 24–26 March 1999.

8 Her Excellency A.Y. Aggrey-Orleans, Ambassador and Permanent Representative of Ghana in Geneva, 8 March 1999, London.

9 Polaris Institute (1998) 'Towards a Citizens' MAI', Polaris Institute, Canada, April.

10 Proposed by Sol Picciotto, University of Lancaster.

11 For more information see *Burning Issue*, WDM Briefing, September 1998.

12 WDM Submission to the Review of the OECD Guidelines, WDM, August 1998.

13 See *A Law Unto Themselves*, WDM Briefing, September 1998.

14 *Earthrights News*, April 1997.

15 The Burma Campaign (UK) has produced legal evidence that such sanctions are possible.

16 The UNCTAD Expert Meeting on Existing Agreements on Investment and their Developmental Dimensions, May 1997, Geneva.

17 See *Stop Sapping the Poor*, WDM Briefing, May 1999.

10

Why Capital Controls and International Debt Restructuring Mechanisms are Necessary to Prevent and Manage Financial Crises

MARTIN KHOR

On 1 September 1998 Malaysia became the first Asian country affected by the economic crisis to announce the new track of imposing foreign exchange controls in a bold attempt to lay the ground for a recovery programme. Until recently capital controls were a taboo subject. With its action, Malaysia broke the policy taboo; only a week earlier, the US economist Paul Krugman had broken the intellectual taboo by advocating that Asian countries should adopt exchange controls.

The Malaysian move involved measures to regulate the international trade in its local currency and to regulate movements of foreign exchange with the aim of reducing the country's exposure to financial speculators and the growing global financial turmoil.

The new Malaysian policy package included:

- Officially fixing the ringgit at 3.80 to the US dollar, thus removing or greatly reducing the role of market forces in determining the day-to-day level of the local currency. (The ringgit's value in relation to currencies other than the dollar will still fluctuate according to their own rates against the dollar.) This measure largely removes uncertainties regarding the future level of the ringgit.

- Measures relating to the local stock market, including the closure of secondary markets so that trade can be done only via the Kuala Lumpur Stock Exchange (this is to prevent speculation or manipulation from outside the country); and the measure that non-residents purchasing local shares have to retain the shares or the proceeds from sale for a year from the purchase date (this is to reduce foreign speculative short-term trade in local shares).

- Measures to reduce and eliminate the international trade in ringgit, by bringing back to the country ringgit-denominated financial assets such as cash and savings deposits via the non-recognition or non-acceptance of

140

such assets in the country after a one-month dateline. (Permission will be given, however, under certain conditions.)

- Resident travellers are allowed to import ringgit notes up to RM1,000 only and any amount of foreign currencies, and to export only up to RM1,000 and foreign currencies only up to the equivalent of RM10,000.

- Except for payments for imports of goods and services, residents are freely allowed to make payments to non-residents only up to RM10,000 or its equivalent in foreign currency (previously the limit was set at RM100,000).

- Investments abroad by residents, in any form, and payments under a guarantee for non-trade purposes require approval.

- Prescribed manner of payment for exports will be in foreign currency only (previously it was allowed to be in foreign currency or ringgit from an external account).

- Domestic credit facilities to non-resident correspondent banks and non-resident stockbroking companies are no longer allowed (previously domestic credit up to RM5 million was allowed).

- Residents require prior approval to make payments to non-residents for purposes of investing abroad for amounts exceeding the equivalent of RM10,000 in foreign exchange.

- Residents are not allowed to obtain ringgit credit facilities from non-residents.

- Measures imposing conditions on the operations and transfers of funds in external accounts. Transfers between external accounts require prior approval for any amount (previously freely allowed); transfers from external accounts to resident accounts required approval after 30 September 1998; sources of funding external accounts are limited to proceeds from the sale of ringgit instruments and other assets in Malaysia, salaries, interest and dividends, and the sale of foreign currency.

In general, the ringgit is still to be freely (or at least easily) convertible to foreign currencies for trade (export receipts and import payments), inward foreign direct investment, and repatriation of profit by non-residents. Convertibility up to a certain limit is also allowed for some other purposes, such as financing children's education abroad. But convertibility for autonomous capital movements for purposes not directly related to trade is limited.

The Malaysian Prime Minister Datuk Seri Dr Mahathir Mohamad explained the rationale for the move. When asked by a journalist whether the exchange control measures were regressive, he said they were not; instead it was the present situation, marked by currency instability and manipulation, that was regressive. He said that when the world moved away from the Bretton Woods fixed-exchange system, it thought the floating rate system was a better way to evaluate currencies.

> But the market is now abused by currency traders who regard currencies as commodities which they trade in. They buy and sell currencies according to their own system and make profits from it but they cause poverty and damage to whole nations. That is very regressive and the world is not moving ahead but backwards.[1]

The Malaysian measures, he added, were a last resort.

> We had asked the international agencies to regulate currency trading but they did not care, so we ourselves have to regulate our own currency. If the international community agrees to regulate currency trading and limit the range of currency fluctuations and enables countries to grow again, then we can return to the floating exchange rate system. But now we can see the damage this system has done throughout the world. It has destroyed the hard work of countries to cater to the interests of speculators as if their interests are so important that millions of people must suffer. This is regressive.[2]

Explaining the move to make the use of offshore ringgit invalid, Mahathir said that typically offshore ringgit were used by speculators to manipulate the currency. They hold the ringgit in foreign banks abroad and have corresponding amounts in banks in Malaysia.

Mahathir also said that with the introduction of exchange controls, it would be possible to cut the link between interest rates and the exchange rate. 'We can reduce interest rates without speculators devaluing our currency. Our companies can revive. If our currency is revalued upwards, the companies can buy imports as they don't have to pay so much.'[3] He added that the country would not be affected so much by external developments such as the crisis in Russia.

Asked if the IMF would be unhappy with the measures, Dr Mahathir said the agency's actions had benefited the foreign companies but were not in Malaysia's interests.

> They see our troubles as a means to get us to accept certain regimes, to open our market to foreign companies to do business without any conditions. It says it will give you money if you open up your economy, but doing so will cause all our banks, companies and industries to belong to foreigners.[4]

He said the Malaysian measures were aimed at putting a spanner in the works of speculators, to force them out of currency trading. He added that the period of highest economic growth was during the Bretton Woods fixed exchange system. But the free market system that followed the Bretton

Woods system had failed because of abuses. There are signs that people are now losing faith in this free market system, but some countries benefit from the abuses; their people make more money, so they don't see why the abuses should be curbed.

A Brief Analysis of the Malaysian Measures

The Malaysian measures should be seen as a bold attempt to give that country's economy a reasonable chance to recover. By restricting the availability of the ringgit in offshore markets and the international trade in that currency, the measures are aimed at greatly reducing the conditions and opportunities for speculators to make profits out of fluctuations in its value.

The move to have the ringgit's rate fixed by the financial authorities, rather than by the market, will also restore greater financial stability by reducing the uncertain conditions under which businesses and consumers now have to operate. Instead of fixing the exchange rate through a currency board system (where money supply and domestic interest rates are determined by the foreign reserves and inflows and outflows of funds), Malaysia has chosen the route of controlling the flows of ringgit and foreign exchange.

The great advantage of this approach is that it allows the government greater freedom to determine domestic policy, and in particular to influence domestic interest rates. It can now reduce interest rates without being overly constrained by the reaction of the market and fears of the ringgit falling. Since the introduction of the measures, interest rates have fallen by 4–5 per cent. This has eased the debt-servicing burden of businesses and consumers (especially house buyers), and the financial position of banks.

The decision to make ringgit held abroad invalid after one month will encourage an inflow of ringgit returning to the country. It will also dry up the sources of ringgit held abroad that speculators can borrow to manipulate the ringgit, for example by 'selling short'. No doubt some Malaysians who hold ringgit accounts abroad, or who travel frequently and who need to transfer funds abroad may suffer some inconveniences. But these personal sacrifices can be taken as a contribution to generating the necessary conditions to get a serious recovery going.

The Malaysian exchange control measures are a response to the basic causes of the crisis afflicting both the country and the region. The crisis began with funds being allowed to move freely in and out of the affected countries. Those countries had recently liberalized their financial systems, allowing locals and foreigners alike freely to convert foreign currency into local currency, and vice versa. In the past this currency convertibility had been allowed to finance current transactions of trade and direct investment; now, however, this freedom was extended to the capital account – for example, for short-term flows such as investment in the stock markets; loans from and to abroad; remittances abroad by individuals and companies for savings or property purchases overseas. By introducing this 'capital account convertibility', countries exposed themselves to autonomous inflows and outflows of funds by foreigners and locals, subjecting their local currency to speculation as well as exchange rate volatility.

The crisis was sparked by speculation and a stampede of foreign funds moving out – followed shortly by locals also sending their money abroad, whilst the local currencies fell sharply. Now that the countries are in deep recession, capital account convertibility is causing another equally vexing problem. It has prevented them from implementing the policies they need for recovery. A major policy priority is to lower interest rates (to relieve consumers and companies from their heavy debt-service burden) and to increase spending (creating greater demand for businesses and incomes for workers). The government is constrained from this line of action, however, because speculators may again attack the local currency. Also, some residents may be tempted to send more of their savings abroad in search of higher interest rates.

The possibility of funds exiting in an environment of free capital account convertibility of the local currency thus puts a damper on the measures needed for a recovery. This is why it is logical for the affected countries to reimpose a degree of control over the convertibility of the local currency, controlling the conditions in which currency speculators can operate profitably, checking the exit of funds and discouraging the inflows of undesirable forms of short-term capital. Many observers point to China and India as countries that have not been subjected to volatile capital flows and currency instability because they do not allow full convertibility of their currencies. The lesson is that developing countries seeking to shield themselves from externally generated financial crises should retain (or regain) some controls over the convertibility of their currency.

Until recently, however, the option of reintroducing capital controls has not been discussed openly because it is considered a 'taboo' subject. The prevailing ideology held and spread by the IMF and the G7 is that countries should liberalize their capital accounts, and that those that have done so will suffer damage if they reimpose controls. Policy makers in the affected countries are worried that if they even discuss the advantages of capital control, their countries will be blacklisted by the IMF, the rich countries and financial speculators. Yet if they keep silent, their countries will continue to be subjected to the views and interests of 'market players', to suffer the consequences of a relatively high interest rate policy, and to be denied a speedy recovery.

Some Responses to the Malaysian Move

Since Malaysia's announcement, its policy measures have been received controversially abroad. The IMF has been particularly hostile, and so have monetary authorities in many Western countries. The Japanese authorities, however, have given at least some support. Policy makers in many developing countries are watching closely to see if the measures work. If they do, it can be expected that pressures will build for other countries to reassert capital controls.

The IMF expressed dismay, pronouncing that any restrictions on the movement of capital would damage investor confidence. Generally reflecting the views of the financial establishment in the rich countries, the IMF is the main upholder of the prevailing strong orthodoxy that countries must allow the unrestricted inflow and outflow of capital. It has been advising (and in cases where it provides loans, it has been insisting as a condition for the loans) that countries should liberalize and open up their economies to the free flows of funds. Some analysts, especially those connected with investment funds that depend on free capital movements to make speculative or investment gains, have been vitriolic in their criticism. But there were many bouquets as well. Business groups, consumer groups and trade unions in the country supported the measures and the local stock market went up. Foreign investors in the country, through the Malaysian International Chamber of Commerce, also expressed support.

Controls on short-term capital would give crisis-hit countries greater monetary flexibility, making banking reform easier, whilst lower interest rates would give a boost to growth. Without controls, the Asian countries have had great difficulty restructuring their banks whilst maintaining tight monetary policies in order to keep their currencies stable. The *Financial Times* cautioned, however, that while judicious use could be made of capital controls, they should be temporary; they should be used to assist in economic reforms and not to avoid them: in this view, capital controls are a double-edged sword, creating better conditions for reforms but lessening the incentive for undertaking them.

Krugman: Breaking the Academic Taboo on Capital Controls

On the academic level, the taboo was broken in August 1998 when the Massachusetts Institute of Technology (MIT) economist Paul Krugman advocated that Asian governments should reimpose capital controls as the only way out of their crisis. Krugman is a renowned trade economist, a believer in free trade, and no wild-eyed radical, so that made his advocacy more newsworthy.

In his *Fortune* article, entitled 'Saving Asia: it's time to get RADICAL', Krugman agrees with the IMF critics that high interest rates imposed by the IMF would cause even healthy banks and companies to collapse. Thus, there is a strong case for countries to keep interest rates low and try to keep their real economies growing. As Krugman points out, however, the problem is that the original objection to interest rate reductions still stands, and that the region's currencies could again go into free fall if the interest rate is not high enough. 'In short, Asia is stuck: its economies are dead in the water, but trying to do anything major to get them moving risks provoking another wave of capital flight and a worse crisis. In effect, the region's economic policy has become hostage to skittish investors.'[5] Krugman says there is a way out – what he calls Plan B – 'but it is a solution so unfashionable, so stigmatized, that hardly anyone has dared to suggest it. The unsayable words are exchange controls.'[6] Exchange controls, he adds, used to be the standard response of countries with balance of payments crises.

> Exporters were required to sell their foreign-currency earnings to the government at a fixed exchange rate; that currency would in turn be sold at the same rate for approved payments to foreigners, basically for imports and debt service. Whilst some countries tried to make other foreign-exchange transactions illegal, other countries allowed a parallel market. Either way, once the system was in place, a country didn't have to worry that cutting interest rates would cause the currency to plunge. Maybe the parallel exchange rate would sink, but that wouldn't affect the prices of imports or the balance sheets of companies and banks.[7]

Krugman points out some problems posed by exchange controls in practice, such as abuse by traders and distortions, which incline economists to think these controls work badly. 'But when you face the kind of disaster now occurring in Asia, the question has to be: badly compared to what?'[8]

Asking why China hasn't been as badly hit as its neighbours, Krugman answers that China 'has been able to cut, not raise, interest rates in this crisis, despite maintaining a fixed exchange rate; and the reason it is able to do that is that it has an inconvertible currency, a.k.a. exchange controls.'[9] Those controls are often evaded, and they are the source of a great deal of corruption, but they still give China a degree of policy leeway that the rest of Asia desperately wishes it had (see Chapter 12 in this volume).

> In short, Plan B involves giving up for a time the business of trying to regain the confidence of international investors and forcibly breaking the link between domestic interest rates and the exchange rate. The policy freedom Asia needs to rebuild its economies would clearly come at a price, but as the slump gets ever deeper, that price is starting to look more and more worth paying.[10]

A press release by *Fortune* also carried Krugman's warning that if Asia did not act quickly, the crisis could worsen into a depression similar to that experienced in the 1930s, and that IMF programmes requiring higher interest rates to stop a currency freefall had made the matter worse. The statement pointed out that, as a long-time colleague of IMF deputy managing director Stanley Fischer and US deputy treasury secretary Lawrence Summers, Krugman had moved with due caution towards proposing such an extreme measure as exchange control. Krugman also discusses the implicit 'gag rule' that prevents not only officials but anyone associated with the current strategy (bankers, major institutional investors) from being too vocal about an alternative strategy.

Krugman is certainly not the first person to advocate capital controls as a part of the solution to the Asian financial crisis. Indeed he is, as he admits, a new convert. But he is such a prominent part of the economics establishment that his proposal has sufficient weight to break the taboo against considering foreign exchange controls as a serious policy option. As more economists like Krugman speak up, capital controls are being recognized as a respectable option for governments wanting an effective policy instrument to prevent further financial turbulence.

After the announcement of the Malaysian measures, Krugman published an open letter to the Malaysian Prime Minister stating that he fervently hoped the dramatic policy move would pay off. He warned however, that these controls are risky, with no guarantee of success. He gave four guidelines: that the controls should aim at minimal disruption of business; that they be temporary; that the currency should not be pegged at too high a level; and that they serve to aid reforms and not be an alternative.

The Tide Turns against Free-Market Orthodoxy

Interestingly, although the majority of market analysts and international commentators have condemned the market interventions, some serious and influential components of the economics profession and the Western media have looked more favourably upon attempts to regulate the financial markets. This represents the beginning of a shift of opinion, indeed a shift of paradigm, about the net benefits and costs of allowing financial markets to operate in a *laissez-faire* manner.

Although the Malaysian policies were the most radical and prominent, indicating a systemic change, recently other countries have introduced measures aimed at limiting the exposure of their markets to speculation and sudden shifts in capital flows. They include the free-market champions Hong Kong and Taiwan (which both tightened regulations against manipulation) and Russia (which was forced to default on some of its debts and at one stage suspended all trade in the rouble).

In September 1998 the Hong Kong authorities reportedly spent over

US$14 billion to buy shares in the local stock market to prop up the Hang Seng index in an attempt to defeat speculators that had placed heavy bets on a fall in the index. It also introduced measures to curb the short-selling of Hong Kong shares. The new rules are aimed against speculators who have been short-selling shares whilst at the same time speculating that the currency will drop. First, the stock exchange reinstated a rule that shares in a company can be sold short only when they are rising. Second, the exchange also announced it had temporarily banned short sales on the shares of three of Hong Kong's biggest companies, HSBC Holdings, HK Telecommunications and China Telecom (Hong Kong). Third, the Hong Kong Securities Clearing Co. increased regulations on settlement of stock trades, giving brokers two days after a deal is executed to deliver the shares. Previously more time was allowed.

According to the *Asian Wall Street Journal*, this change of rules will hurt speculators who had entered contracts to sell shares short without even having those shares on hand. Dealers, investors, analysts and commentators have warned that the series of interventions by the Hong Kong authorities will cause tremendous damage to Hong Kong's free market reputation. The authorities have replied that manipulation of the financial markets distorted the market in the first place, and has to be curbed.

It was also in September that the Taiwan authorities took measures to prevent the illegal trading of funds managed by George Soros, which have been blamed for causing the local stock market to fall. Although local sales by the Soros funds are banned, at least six local securities firms were selling those funds on proxy accounts, according to officials. The Securities and Futures Commission announced that securities firms would have their licences revoked and that dealers could face two years' jail for selling the unauthorized funds.

In Russia, meanwhile the country's experiment with the free market lies in tatters, with the government having to announce a default on government bonds and a temporary moratorium on external debt.

> Russia's economic upheaval has profoundly shaken the confidence of Russians in the goals of a free-market economy and democracy that the West championed. Perhaps more than at any time in Russia's quest over the last six and a half years to remake itself after the collapse of Soviet rule, the concepts of liberal market reform and democracy are in retreat.[11]

And in a front-page article entitled 'Acceptance of Capital Curbs is Spreading', the *Asian Wall Street Journal* of 2 September said:

> The failure of IMF orthodoxy to arrest the contagion sweeping through Asia has made ideas like capital controls intellectually respectable again. Policy makers can't help but notice that China and Taiwan both have capital controls and neither has succumbed to the region's contagion.[12]

The tide of deregulation and absolute freedom of financial dealing is now beginning to turn. Regulation of financial markets and capital/exchange controls have made a come-back. The battle between paradigms will now be watched closely by the public, the market and policy makers.

Using Capital Controls to Prevent and Manage Financial Crises

The need for developing counties to make use of capital controls to prevent and manage financial crises has also been stressed by UNCTAD. In fact, UNCTAD has warned consistently about the dangers of financial liberalization and the risks posed by a policy of allowing funds to flow freely in and out.

UNCTAD's 1998 Trade and Development Report makes the central point that, to protect themselves against international financial instability, developing countries need to have capital controls – a proven technique for dealing with volatile capital flows. This is a key part of the report's proposals on financial crises. It reaches this conclusion after surveying several other measures (such as more disclosure of information and greater banking regulation) that have been proposed by the industrial countries and the IMF. UNCTAD finds that these proposals have merit, but are inadequate to deal with the present and future crises (see Chapter 3 in this volume). It therefore stresses that developing countries should be allowed to introduce capital controls, as these are 'an indispensable part of their armoury of measures for the purpose of protection against international financial instability'.[13]

Although it was released on 16 September, the Trade and Development Report was finalized in July 1998. The writing of the report thus predates the sweeping capital control measures taken by the Malaysian Government on 1 September. The new Malaysian policy seems to be consistent with the rationale and advice provided by UNCTAD. This was the first time since the Asian crisis began that an influential international agency had called for the use of capital controls.

The Trade and Development Report notes that good economic fundamentals, effective financial regulation and good corporate governance are necessary to avoid financial crises, but that by themselves they are not sufficient. Experience shows that in avoiding these crises a key role is played by capital controls and other measures that influence external borrowing, lending and asset holding. Controls on capital flows are imposed for two reasons: first, as part of macroeconomic management (to reinforce or substitute for monetary and fiscal measures); and, second, to attain long-term national development goals (such as ensuring residents' capital is invested locally, or that certain types of activities are reserved for residents).

Contrary to the belief that capital controls are rare, taboo or practised only by a few countries that are somehow 'anti-market', the reality is that these measures have been used very widely. UNCTAD notes that they have been a 'pervasive feature' of the last few decades. In the early post-war years, capital controls were generally imposed on outflows of funds as part of macroeconomic policies dealing with balance of payments difficulties, and to avoid or reduce devaluations. Rich and poor countries alike also used controls on capital inflows for longer-term development reasons.

When freer capital movements were allowed from the 1960s onwards, large capital inflows posed problems for rich countries such as Germany, the Netherlands and Switzerland. They imposed controls such as limits on non-residents' purchase of local debt securities and on the bank deposits of non-residents. More recently, some developing countries facing problems due to large capital inflows also resorted to capital controls.

For example, when faced with a surge of short-term capital inflows in January 1994, Malaysia imposed these capital controls:

- banks were subjected to a ceiling on their external liabilities not related to trade or investment;

- residents were barred from selling short-term monetary instruments to non-residents;

- banks had to deposit, at no interest in the central bank, monies in ringgit accounts owned by foreign banks;

- banks were restricted in outright forward and swap transactions they could engage in with foreigners.

These measures were gradually removed from 1995 onwards.

When Chile was faced with large capital inflows in the early 1990s, it took measures to slow short-term inflows and to encourage certain types of outflows. The main step was that foreign loans entering Chile were subjected to a reserve requirement of 20 per cent (later raised to 30 per cent). In other words, a certain percentage of each loan had to be deposited at the central bank for a year, without deriving any interest.

To prevent excessive inflows Brazil and the Czech Republic both resorted to tax strategies. Brazil in mid-1994 imposed controls such as an increase in the tax paid by Brazilian firms on bonds issued abroad, a tax on foreigners' investment in the stock market, and an increase in tax on foreign purchases of domestic fixed-income investments. Faced with large inflows in 1994–5, the Czech Republic imposed a tax of 0.25 per cent on foreign exchange transactions with banks, and also imposed limits (and the need for official approval) on short-term borrowing abroad by banks and other firms.

Besides these specific cases, the 1998 Trade and Development Report lists examples of capital controls on both inflows and outflows. Controls on inflows of foreign direct investment and portfolio equity investment may take the form of licensing, ceilings on foreign equity participation in local firms, official permission for international equity issues, differential regulations applying to local and foreign firms regarding establishment and permissible operations, and various kinds of two-tier markets. Some of these controls can also be imposed on capital inflows associated with debt securities, including bonds. Such inflows can be subject to special taxes or be limited to transactions carried out through a two-tier market.

Ceilings (as low as zero) may apply to non-residents' holdings of debt issues of firms and government; or foreigners may need approval to buy such issues. Foreigners can also be excluded from auctions for government bonds and paper. UNCTAD also lists other controls commonly used to restrict external borrowings from banks. They include:

- a special reserve requirement concerning liabilities to nonresidents;

- forbidding banks to pay interest on deposits of non-residents, or even requiring a commission on such deposits;

- taxing foreign borrowing (to eliminate the margin between local and foreign interest rates); and

- requiring firms to deposit cash, amounting to a proportion of their external borrowing, at the central bank.

As for controls on capital outflows, they can include controls over outward transactions for direct and portfolio equity investment by residents as well as foreigners. Restrictions on repatriation of capital by foreigners can include specifying a period before such repatriation is allowed, and regulations that phase the repatriation according to the availability of foreign exchange or to the need to maintain an orderly market for the country's currency. Residents may be restricted as to their holdings of foreign stocks, either directly or through limits on the permissible portfolios of the country's investment funds. Two-tier exchange rates may also be used to restrict residents' foreign investment by requiring capital transactions be undertaken through a market in which a less favourable rate prevails, compared to the rate for current transactions.

Some of these techniques are also used for purchases of debt securities issued abroad and for other forms of lending abroad. Bank deposits abroad by residents can also be restricted through legal means. UNCTAD also notes a current trend to make accounts and transactions denominated in foreign currencies available to residents. It says that capital controls can include restrictions on residents' bank deposits denominated in foreign currencies and on banks' lending to residents in foreign currencies. Such loans and deposits can increase currency mismatching, which is a potential source of financial instability, as it enables large shifts between currencies during crises, putting pressure on the exchange rate and resulting in insolvencies among debtors.

Besides capital controls, UNCTAD also makes two other proposals for better managing of external assets and liabilities. First, it warns of the dangers of a country allowing its residents to undertake easy borrowing in foreign currencies, and allowing them to make bank deposits denominated in foreign currencies. To guard against this, UNCTAD says, there should be strict enforcement of prudential rules that match the currency denominations of financial firms' assets and liabilities with measures that increase the costs of foreign borrowing (through imposing taxes, special reserve requirements or cash deposits at the central bank). Also, limits can be placed on bank lending and deposits in foreign currencies. Non-interest-bearing reserve requirements can be imposed on bank deposits in foreign currencies, thus reducing or eliminating the interest paid on them and diminishing their attractiveness.

Second, UNCTAD says the Asian crisis starkly showed the risks of failure to enforce separation between the onshore and offshore activities of a country's banks. Some countries set up offshore centres whose activities are subject to lighter regulation and some tax privileges. One such centre, the Bangkok International Banking Facility (BIBF), set up in 1992, was a conduit for funds received from abroad which were recycled to the domestic market, much of it used to finance speculation in stocks and property. As much as 95 per cent of the funds raised by the BIBF were lent domestically. In contrast, Asian Currency Units (ACU), which conducts offshore banking in Singapore, has tighter rules which restrict the use of the Singapore dollar as an international currency and control the ACU's involvement in domestic banking business. In 1996, 63 per cent of the ACU's liabilities were from overseas sources and 42 per cent of its assets were loans to banks abroad. Pointing to this contrast between the Thai and Singapore offshore centres, UNCTAD says it is feasible to have measures that insulate offshore banking from the domestic market, and thus contribute to financial stability.

UNCTAD concludes that recent financial crises and frequent use of capital controls by countries to contain the effects of swings in capital flows point to the case for continuing to give governments the autonomy to control capital transactions, and it questions recent moves in the IMF to restrict that autonomy. It points out that ways have not yet been found at a global level to eliminate the cross-border transmission of financial shocks and crises that result from global financial integration and capital movements. For the foreseeable future, therefore, countries must be allowed the flexibility to introduce capital control measures, instead of new obligations being imposed on these countries to further liberalize capital movements through them.

The UNCTAD report has made out the case for capital controls quite clearly. It is important to note, however, that these controls should not be treated as a panacea: they cannot cure recession's ills by themselves. Capital controls can also have some disadvantages, as well as their own built-in limitations – but they can be an important part of a set of policies devised to protect a country facing a turbulent and hostile external threat and to reduce its exposure to financial and economic chaos, at least for some time.

Orderly Debt Work-out for Debt-Crisis Countries

Capital controls are especially useful for preventing a crisis. Should a country already find itself in a serious debt-repayment crisis, however, such controls need to be accompanied by other measures. The most important of these is an international mechanism for a fair and effective debt work-out.

Again, the 1998 Trade and Development Report makes the key point: countries that come under speculative attack, and want to avoid an uncertain economic recession or collapse, may have little choice but to resort to two presently unconventional measures – capital controls, and a 'debt standstill' (or temporary stop in servicing external loans).

In its chapter on the management and prevention of financial crises, UNCTAD says that theoretically there are four lines of defence an indebted country can employ if faced with a massive attack on its currency:

1   domestic policies (especially monetary and interest rate policy) to restore market confidence and halt the run;

2   maintaining sufficient foreign reserves and credit lines;

3   use of an international lender-of-last-resort facility to obtain the liquidity needed;

4   a unilateral debt standstill accompanied by foreign exchange restrictions, and initiation of negotiations for an orderly debt work-out.

Examining each of these options, UNCTAD finds that although the first three are theoretically feasible, in reality they either don't work or don't exist. Therefore, in the present crisis, the fourth option should be considered seriously.

The first option (tight monetary policy and high interest rates), favoured by the IMF, has not worked for ailing Asian countries. On the contrary, says UNCTAD, higher domestic interest rates increase the financial difficulties of the debtors and reduce their incomes and net worth, increasing the likelihood of default. 'Thus, they provide no incentive for foreign lenders to roll over their existing loans or extend new credits.'[14]

The second option (maintaining high reserves) might work if the reserves are large enough and have been built up through trade surpluses, as is the case in a few countries. But there are many problems if reserves are increased through borrowing: the cost for carrying such reserves would be very high, the reserves may not be enough to stem a big attack or large fund withdrawals and, moreover, the borrowed funds in the reserves are also vulnerable to withdrawals.

On the third option, there has not been an international lender of last resort to provide liquidity to stabilize currencies in developing countries facing currency crises. Instead, after the currency has collapsed, there have been IMF-coordinated bail-outs. These bail-outs, however, are designed to meet the demands of creditors and to prevent default, says UNCTAD, and they pose three problems. First, they protect creditors from bearing the costs of poor lending decisions, putting the burden entirely on debtors; second, they create 'moral hazard' for international lenders, encouraging imprudent lending practices; and third, the funds needed are increasingly large and difficult to raise.

UNCTAD thus proposes the fourth option: setting up an international insolvency procedure whereby a country unable to service its foreign debts can declare a standstill on payment and be allowed time to work out a restructuring of its loans. Meanwhile, creditors would agree to this 'breathing space' instead of trying to enforce payment. What UNCTAD is proposing is actually an extension of national bankruptcy procedures (similar to Chapter 11 of the US Bankruptcy Code)[15] to the international level for countries facing debt difficulties. Bankruptcy procedures are especially relevant to international debt crises resulting from liquidity problems, as they are designed to address financial restructuring rather than liquidation.

In the US code, no receiver or trustee is appointed to manage the debtors' business and debtors are left in possession of their property. The procedure is to facilitate a three-stage orderly work-out. In stage one, the debtor files a petition and there is an automatic standstill on debt servicing, giving debtors-in-possession a breathing space from their creditors, who are not allowed to pursue lawsuits or enforce debt payment. This prevents a 'grab race' by creditors, and the debtor can formulate a reorganization plan. In stage two, the code provides the debtor with access to working capital to carry out its operations, by granting seniority status to debt contracted after the petition is filed. This debtor-in-possession financing can be granted if approved by the court and does not depend on the existing creditors' agreement. Stage three sees the reorganization of the debtor's assets and liabilities and its operations. The plan does not need unanimous support by creditors (acceptance by 50 per cent of the creditors in number and two thirds in amount of claims is sufficient) and the debtor can get court approval of the plan.

These procedures are not used only for private debt. Chapter 9 of the US code deals with public debtors (municipal authorities), applying the same principles as those invoked in Chapter 11. The recent successful work-out of the Orange County debt was under Chapter 9 and there are similar arrangements in most other industrial countries. UNCTAD proposes an international mechanism using the same principles. One suggestion, by Kunibert Raffer (1990), is an international bankruptcy court that applies an international Chapter 11 drawn up in a United Nations treaty. The court would have powers to impose automatic stay, allow debtor-in-possession financial status and also restructure debt and grant debt relief.

UNCTAD says a less ambitious and perhaps more feasible option is to set up a framework to apply key insolvency principles (debt standstill and debtor-in-possession financing) combined with established debt-restructuring practices, with the IMF playing a major role. There are many objections to giving so much power to the IMF, however, on the grounds of conflict of interest (the IMF is also a creditor, and imposes conditionality on its loans; its shareholders, moreover, are countries affected by its decisions).

Another alternative which UNCTAD seems to favour is to set up an independent panel to determine if a country is justified in imposing exchange restrictions that have the effect of debt standstill, in line with the IMF's article VIII, section 2(b). The decision to impose a standstill could be taken unilaterally by the debtor country, then submitted to the panel for approval within a certain period. This would avoid 'inciting a panic' and would resemble safeguard provisions in the WTO allowing countries to take emergency actions.

These debt standstills should be combined with debtor-in-possession financing so the debtor country can replenish its reserves and get working capital. This would mean the IMF 'lending into arrears'. UNCTAD argues that the IMF funds required for such emergency lending would be much less substantial than the scale of bail-out operations. The IMF can also help arrange for private-sector loans with seniority status. As regards government debt to private creditors, reorganization can be carried out through negotiations with creditors, with the IMF continuing to play the important role of bringing all creditors to meet with the debtor government. For private sector debt, negotiations could be launched with private creditors immediately after the imposition of debt standstill.

The above proposal by UNCTAD is long overdue. In the absence of such an international system, developing countries have been at the mercy of foreign creditors and investors who have been liable to pull out their funds suddenly in a herd-like manner. Without protection, these countries face a liquidity crisis first; this in turn produces a solvency crisis, and then an economic crisis. If a Chapter 11 international bankruptcy procedure existed, a country facing the prospect of default could declare a debt standstill, get court clearance for protection from creditors, obtain fresh working capital, restructure its debts, plan for economic recovery, and eventually service the

debts adequately. With such procedures, countries facing a 'cashflow problem' could take action before it worsens and thus prevent a major crisis. Both
the debtor country and its creditors would gain.

Contrast this with the present messy situation. In the absence of a fair
system, all creditors rush to exit the country, each hoping to recoup its loan
before other creditors take out theirs. Then, when the debtor country has its
back to the wall, the creditors as a group usually demand, in a restructuring
plan, that the government not only pay higher interest on its loans, but also
take over or guarantee the payment of the loans contracted by private banks
and firms. It might be argued that a country already near default could
declare a unilateral debt moratorium and then dictate its own terms for debt
restructuring. Few countries have the courage to do so, however, as the
foreign banks may gang up and deny any new credit, thus threatening the
debtor country's capacity to pay for essential imports.

In 1998, however, a rapidly ailing Russia did declare a moratorium, not
only on its foreign debt but also on its domestic government bonds (most of
which are held by foreign investors). At the same time it floated the rouble,
which has since devalued sharply. It also stated the terms of debt restructuring. The foreign banks have expressed outrage at these terms and are
clamouring to negotiate with the government, and even threatening to seize
the assets of Russian banks located abroad. By taking unilateral action, Russia
was trying to preempt an even greater crisis; it was also forcing the foreign
investors and creditors to take their share of the loss. This ongoing drama
also shows the necessity of having an internationally agreed debt work-out
procedure. In its absence, the situation is bound to be messy, whether in the
case of a country unilaterally declaring a default and moratorium (as Russia
did), or in the case of countries that helplessly watch as the foreign creditors
pull their money out.

If the rich creditor countries are serious about reforming the global
financial system, then the international bankruptcy procedures put forward
by UNCTAD (and also by others in the past) should be considered urgently.
For there are many more countries presently facing the threat of capital flight
that could be on the brink of debt default. Action should be taken before the
financial bleeding spreads to these other countries.

Time for Regulation

Given an international environment of big financial players with huge con-
centrations of money for speculation and investment, financially small
countries are now subjected to great volatility and financial and economic
danger. For instance, the Long Term Capital Management[16] affair revealed
that a hedge fund with $4–5 billion in equity could manage to raise so much

credit that the banks were exposed to the tune of $200 billion. Few governments can withstand a determined bid by a few big hedge funds to speculate on their currencies and financial markets. And besides, the hedge funds are other gigantic investment funds (such as mutual and pension funds) as well as investment banks, commercial banks and insurance companies.

The almost total freedom given to international investors and speculators has wreaked financial and now economic and social chaos. The time has come to regulate these big players. But there are serious doubts whether there is the political will to act as the financial institutions and those that own and manage them are very powerful and it is in the vested interest of politicians and their parties to cater to these powerful institutions.

Meanwhile, developing countries need to protect themselves from the free flow of funds. Capital controls are thus a necessary element in the repertoire of economic instruments that must be an option. In these days of financial turbulence this economic instrument may even be a necessary option in itself. This does not mean, of course, that capital controls by themselves are a panacea or 'magic bullet'. They should be accompanied, for instance, by an international mechanism for debt standstill to help seriously indebted countries. Moreover, there are weaknesses and loopholes in capital controls – such as leakages through transfer pricing mechanisms, false invoicing, possible black markets, and so on. Nor should capital controls merely be a shield for a country to protect itself from having to carry out changes and reforms made necessary by the financial crisis, or structural reforms that are needed in the long run.

Thus, the success of efforts to revive an economy will also depend greatly on the effectiveness, efficiency and fairness (in burden sharing) of recapitalization, restructuring and reforms in the financial institutions and corporations. It will also depend on the right mix of monetary and fiscal policies to spur recovery without imposing greater financial or economic burdens on ordinary citizens, especially the poor. In other words, capital controls are a necessary but not sufficient condition to protect a country from an unresolvable crisis and to enable its recovery. They have to be accompanied by other measures. On the other hand, the fact that there are weaknesses in capital controls, and that other measures are also needed, does not make capital controls a wrong policy option, as some opponents of capital controls like to suggest.

Total freedom for capital flows is a principle championed by the big financial players and institutions that stand to gain from extreme financial liberalization. Capital controls to limit such freedom, on the other hand, can be supported from a scientific point of view and from the viewpoint of ordinary citizens who need to be protected from predatory speculation and economic chaos.

Notes

1 *New Straits Times*, 2 September 1998.
2 *Ibid.*
3 *Ibid.*
4 *Ibid.*
5 Krugman, Paul, 'Saving Asia: It's Time to Get RADICAL,' *Fortune*, August 1998.
6 *Ibid.*
7 *Ibid.*
8 *Ibid.*
9 *Ibid.*
10 *Ibid.*
11 *International Herald Tribune*, 31 August 1998.
12 'Acceptance of Capital Curbs is Spreading,' *Asian Wall Street Journal*, 2 September 1998.
13 UNCTAD (1998) *Trade and Development Report 1998*, United Nations, New York and Geneva.
14 *Ibid.*
15 See Zhiyuan Cui in Chapter 13 of this volume for further discussion.
16 Long Term Capital Management, a US-based hedge fund, ran into extreme difficulties in 1998, and was effectively bailed out by a consortium of New York banks – led by the Reserve Bank of New York. LTCM's board included several Nobel Prize economists and several of its largest investors were also directors of the banks which led the bail-out. Even the *Financial Times* and *Wall Street Journal* denounced this as 'crony capitalism'.

11

Capital Account Convertibility
Theoretical Issues and Policy Options
SUMANGALA DAMODARAN

The currency and banking crises experienced by several countries of East Asia in 1997, as well as those seen in Russia in 1998 and Brazil most recently, have again brought to the fore several issues that have a bearing on development strategies, liberalization patterns and experiences, and the consequences for individual countries, particularly developing ones, of linking up to international financial markets. One of the most important issues thrown up is that of the capital account convertibility (CAC) of the balance of payments of developing countries. Recently, the IMF has been considering a proposal to amend its articles of agreement to incorporate CAC as one of the obligations of Fund membership. It proposes to bring in the requirement that all member countries make their currencies freely convertible for all current as well as capital account transactions.[1]

This chapter presents a brief sketch of the basic theoretical issues that have arisen in international discussions on CAC. It does not purport to present a comparative evaluation of the various strands of thinking around the issue, but only seeks to outline the theoretical underpinnings of and the context in which various positions on the issue have been adopted. Discussions on CAC have revolved around the following aspects:

1 The question of whether or not international capital flows should be restricted and what exchange rate regime is compatible with free capital mobility or with effective restrictions on capital mobility.

2 The link between liberalization of other sectors of the economy and capital accounts.

After the Second World War, the Bretton Woods accords were devised around the basic thesis that free international mobility of capital is incompatible with the preservation of reasonably free trade and full employment. Accordingly, exchange rates were pegged and capital controls were considered necessary against currency speculation, which threatened exchange-rate stability. With the displacement of pegged exchange rates by a regime of floating rates in the 1970s, the new orthodoxy was born, which holds that free capital mobility is essential for maximizing global benefits from international trade and investment. The floating of exchange rates and the lifting of capital controls were considered essential steps in the establishment of an efficient international financial system.

Currently, however, even among those adhering to orthodox positions on capital mobility, there is no consensus on the exchange rate issue. The IMF defines CAC as the 'freedom from exchange controls on capital transactions in the balance of payments'[2] within either a fixed or a flexible exchange rate regime. In India, the Tarapore Committee, appointed by India's central bank (the Reserve Bank of India), looked into the issues and prospects of undertaking CAC in India. The Committee defines CAC in its widest possible sense as 'the freedom to convert local financial assets to foreign financial assets and vice versa at market determined exchange rates'.[3] In this paper we shall deal essentially with the arguments for and against international capital mobility, and not deal specifically with the question of choice of exchange rate regime.

As mentioned above, a vast part of the literature on CAC is concerned with *when and how* – in addition to the issue of *whether or not* – to liberalize capital account transactions. Literature that looks at this forms part of the general literature on economic liberalization and is mainly concerned with the speed and sequencing of the liberalization of different sectors of the economy and the evolution of optimum sequencing paths. Much of this literature has emerged in response to actual experiences with liberalization in developing countries.

Keeping the above in mind, this paper is structured as follows: the second section presents a brief sketch of the simple macroeconomics of balance of payments transactions, because an understanding of the link between the current and capital accounts is crucial to understanding the issues involved in discussions on CAC. The third section will review the theoretical arguments for and against controls on foreign transactions in general and on capital flows in particular. The fourth section deals with arguments on the pros and cons of CAC that have been put forward in the last five or six years.

Some Essential Concepts

The balance of payments of any country is a statement of all transactions that are undertaken between the residents of a country and the rest of the world. Briefly, these transactions take the form of exchange of goods (exports and imports of merchandise, or visible trade), exchange of services (export and import of services, or invisible trade), unrequited transfers, or exchanges such as gifts that do not involve a corresponding reciprocal transaction, and the exchange of capital. The current account consists of visible and invisible trade and unrequited transfer payments. The capital account records all international transactions that involve a resident of a country changing either his or her assets with, or liabilities to, a resident of another country and consists of short-term and long-term private and official loans, portfolio and direct investments, and changes in official reserves.

An essential difference between the two is that transactions on the latter necessarily involve domestic residents either acquiring or surrendering claims on foreigners, whereas those on the former do not. For example a country acquires foreign exchange when a multinational corporation (MNC) invests within its national boundaries, but this investment is in terms of the MNC buying land, houses, productive plants, etc. Similarly, when international investors acquire shares in a country, it involves the transfer of financial assets. Capital account transactions can therefore involve changes in the composition of the national capital of a country. The decision to allow the free flow of direct and financial foreign capital across national boundaries can thus have serious implications for the national sovereignty of a country as control over its national capital is put in doubt.

The aspects of capital flow that have provoked most debate are its causes, magnitude, direction and form; the mechanism by which a financial flow induces a corresponding real transfer of resources; and the consequences of capital flow. We will briefly touch upon some of these aspects here.

Relationship between the capital account and the current account

The following relationship holds between the current and the capital accounts:

Current account deficit = Capital account surplus + Drawing down of reserves

This means that if a country has a deficit on its current account, the country has spent more abroad than it has earned during the specified period. This can be settled by international borrowing, or by seeking capital flows in the form of direct or portfolio investment, or by depleting reserves of foreign currency that have built up over the years. This, however, is merely to address the condition that defines balance in the balance of payments. To be able to capture the implications of capital inflows or outflows, and their relationship to the current account, we could say that any changes in the capital account of the balance of payments, brought about particularly by autonomous capital flows, get reflected through changes either in the current account position or the reserve position. The implications of this are dealt with below.

The inflow of foreign capital to finance current account deficits can be beneficial to a country, and not undermine the viability of its balance of payments in the long run, if borrowing from abroad is used to finance capital formation in productive assets rather than consumption. Foreign capital can also be used to enhance export earnings in excess of debt-servicing requirements, or even for productive investment that does not generate foreign exchange, if there are accompanying policies that enhance export earnings in excess of debt-servicing requirements.

Even if the above conditions are satisfied, extensive literature shows that the medium- and long-term fundamentals of an economy may be distorted by a substantial inflow of foreign funds, a point that will be discussed below. Furthermore, even if economic fundamentals remain strong, the general perception associating an adverse impact with large current account deficits makes a country highly vulnerable to speculative attacks. Another very important aspect of the financing of current account deficits using foreign funds is the composition and relative volume of different kinds of capital inflows, and whether these flows are responsive to short-term swings in expectations or not.

Capital flows and the domestic economy

Large capital inflows or outflows affect the domestic economy in a variety of ways. It is difficult to trace precisely the developments that follow the liberalization of capital flows, inward or outward, because responses in the real economy would depend to a large extent on export and import elasticities (or the responsiveness of imports and exports to changes in their prices), dependence of export production on imports, etc. Some implications of inflows and outflows of capital that can occur in standard exchange rate regimes have been highlighted in the literature, however, and have been touched upon here.

First, in a flexible exchange rate regime, capital inflows result in an appreciation of the domestic currency. This, by making imports cheaper and exports more expensive, results in the possibility of an increasing current account deficit that can become unsustainable. This is because when capital flows in, the excess supply of foreign exchange makes domestic currency more expensive and results in its appreciation. In a fixed exchange rate regime, on the other hand, increased capital flows are not allowed to impact on the exchange rate; this results in the central bank adding the inflows to foreign exchange reserves and releasing an equivalent amount of domestic currency into the economy.

This excessive supply of money in the economy can spark off inflation, in turn leading to exchange rate overvaluation in real terms and subsequent erosion of competitiveness. In both cases, therefore, capital inflows result in currency appreciation, leading to the possibility of widening current account deficits. In a flexible exchange rate regime, capital outflows tend to depreciate the domestic currency, and could result in two possible outcomes. If export production and imports are responsive to the depreciation and exports are not very import-dependent, the result could be a narrowing of the current account deficit. If, however, export and import elasticities are not high, and exports are highly import-dependent (as is the case in many developing countries), then the impact of depreciation is felt more in terms of an increase in the cost of imports. This in turn can cause inflationary pressures and, through a real appreciation resulting in the possibility of a widening current account deficit, can induce capital flight. Capital outflows in a fixed exchange regime need to be financed through running down official reserves or through increases in foreign borrowing. Choices involving the exchange rate regime and whether and how to control capital flows thus become crucial determinants of how these processes work themselves out in different countries.

Second, in order for an economy to attract inflows of foreign portfolio capital, the domestic rate of interest needs to exceed the world rate of interest by at least the expected rate of depreciation of the domestic currency. The maintenance of high interest rates can adversely affect productive investment directly, and also have indirect effects through making the servicing of public debt more expensive. This, by squeezing the public exchequer, can lead to lower public as well as private investment and also reduce welfare expenditures. Thus, opening up to global portfolio flows can result in stagnation in the host economy. What is important to note is that capital flows in themselves can trigger off the various mechanisms mentioned above, without the need for the impulses to come from the real economy.

Some of the points raised above bring out the implications of linking up to international financial markets for individual countries. Discussions on all these counts have formed part of the debate on whether countries should liberalize capital account transactions and, if they do so, how this should be done.

The Pros and Cons of Capital Account Convertibility

Discussions on liberalization of the capital account of the balance of payments essentially revolve around whether or not to restrict the free movement of capital across national boundaries and, if a free flow is deemed a desirable objective, how and why it should be introduced, in the context of an overall liberalization programme. This section looks at:

1 the evolution of, and rationale for, exchange control measures and for capital controls in particular;

2 the mainstream critique of exchange control regimes and the arguments for economic liberalization and for capital account liberalization in particular;

3 differing perspectives within mainstream literature on the nature of financial markets and consequently the implications for policies relating to capital flows;

4   alternative perspectives on the desirability of freeing capital flows, based
    on alternative analyses of financial market behaviour and concerns about
    the autonomy of domestic economic policies.

Since a large part of the literature emerged in response to the actual
experiences of developing countries which embarked upon economic liberalization programmes, the discussion of the above topics will be largely
chronological.

Exchange control refers to the imposition by monetary authorities of
strictly defined limitations on international transactions or the conversion of
national currency into foreign currency. It occupies the middle ground between
the unrestricted convertibility of a country's currency and the total ban on convertibility, or autarky. Exchange control measures can aim to restrict transactions in the current account or the capital account, or both. Exchange control
measures that affect the current account typically involve restrictions on
imports such as quotas and tariffs, requirements to deposit export proceeds
with central banks, export quotas, etc. Capital controls involve restrictions on
various kinds of capital flows. We examine here the arguments for and against
exchange control in general and capital controls in particular.

At all times the theoretical arguments for exchange controls have emphasized their necessity for ensuring the preservation of the national autonomy
of a country from outside interference. The history of exchange controls
since the Second World War shows that they emerged in reaction to the
inability of standard exchange rate regimes to ensure stability in the balance
of payments of countries that were faced with imbalances such as excessive
deficits, debts, inflation triggered by the depreciation of the national
currency, or capital flight.

Exchange control measures emerged in response to the fact that neither
fixed nor flexible exchange rate regimes were successful in regulating international financial markets: the controls sought to correct these imbalances.
Different exchange rate regimes produced different imbalances, as demonstrated by the experience of the principal market economies from 1945: at
the beginning of the 1970s, these economies passed from a fixed exchange
rate system to a floating one.

As outlined previously, in a system of fixed exchange, the defence of
parities leads to vast movements of currency reserves by central banks,
inciting speculative movements of private capital which stake on the realign-
ment of parities. In a system of flexible exchange, an appreciation of the
national currency can worsen the current account deficit and incite speculative capital movements. These arbitrary movements reinforce constraints on
national policy autonomy, because domestic policies need to be tailored to
maintaining the most favourable conditions for the inflow of capital to be
ensured, or to prevent destabilizing currency fluctuations.

In exchange systems that permit the development of important imbalances, restrictions on convertibility seem the only means at the disposal of a country that seeks to preserve autonomy in domestic policy making, particularly if its currency does not play a significant role in the international monetary system. This, however, was not the sole reason for restricting international exchange. Exchange controls also emerged as part of policies geared towards the domestic market. In the current account sphere, controls sought to select particular productive activities in line with certain social goals and to shield domestic industries from international competition. This approach derived essentially from the understanding that the state would have to take responsibility for basic economic decisions concerning the level of investment and savings, the allocation of investment among competing uses, and the general distribution of income; and that a reliance on the market mechanism could not assure high rates of growth and other social objectives. As part of this understanding, it was felt that the financial system should be subordinated to the needs of production in order to promote growth, and controls on capital flows were advocated on the premise that free capital flows can endanger the autonomy of countries that seek to follow independent economic policies.

Different kinds of exchange control measures emerged to restrict transactions on the current and capital accounts. These included restrictions on the use of foreign exchange, including the use of multiple exchange rates. Restrictions on the current account included licensing requirements for exports and imports, the surrender of export proceeds, and tariffs on imports. Among the restrictions on the capital account were those on non-resident accounts and the licensing of inward and outward capital flows. Thus the arguments for exchange controls in general and capital controls in particular grew out of the need to preserve the policy autonomy of national governments, which it was assumed would not be assured by a reliance on market mechanisms alone.

In the late 1970s, studies by Bhagwati (1978) and Krueger (1978) on different forms of control on foreign exchange transactions in eleven developing countries provided the basis for arguments in favour of economic liberalization in developing countries. This is what has been referred to as the neo-liberal framework. Proponents of this perspective hold that attempts to 'thwart the market' are inefficient, if not ineffective, instruments to achieve virtually any objective and that state-led development episodes that tried to correct for market failures through state intervention have all ended in failure.[4]

The argument runs as follows: developing countries have been characterized as illiberal economies where controls that restrict buyers or sellers or both have existed in key markets such as those for finance, labour, foreign exchange and agricultural commodities. These controls distort market magnitudes and result in allocative inefficiencies, waste, and bias against the agricultural and trade sectors. According to this mainstream view, a large body of empirical evidence suggests that liberalized economies have outperformed repressed, illiberal and closed economies.[5]

In an ideal world with no imperfections or externalities, this view holds, the best liberalization policy would be to lift controls on all markets simultaneously in order to maximize welfare. In a non-ideal or second-best world, where distortions and externalities of various kinds exist, liberalization could mean policies that reduce the restrictiveness of controls, either through complete removal or the replacement of a more restrictive set of policies with less restrictive ones. There are well-founded conjectures, validated by empirical experience, that the liberalization of some markets only will also improve welfare. With the existence of various kinds of distortions, simultaneous liberalization might prove difficult and counter-productive, and therefore the speed with which liberalization is undertaken and the sequence in which different markets are liberalized become important. The second generation of models on liberalization therefore concentrated on devising optimum liberalization paths for countries.[6]

In the specific case of the foreign exchange market, controls in the prototype illiberal economy consist of a variety of price- and quantity-based controls on external transactions of the kind described earlier. In the particular case of capital controls, it is argued that over long periods of time they result in distortions and allocative inefficiency; prove ineffective, with the possibility of arbitrage and black markets; and are costly for the economy to maintain.

Free capital flows, on the other hand, are seen to have many advantages: first, they make available a larger capital stock to supplement domestic resources in terms of presenting the possibility of borrowing from the global market, for governments as well as private entities, and also accessing global savings in a variety of non-debt-creating forms. Second, they provide gains from trade in international financial assets as residents hold an internationally diversified portfolio, which reduces the vulnerability of income streams and wealth to domestic shocks. And third, they provide dynamic gains from financial integration: whereas competition intensifies between financial intermediaries and margins are reduced, the quality of financial assets improves due to greater liquidity and deeper markets.

The theoretical basis for the liberalization of international capital markets arises from a strong macro version of the Efficient Market Hypothesis (EMH). The EMH was developed to analyze financial market behaviour under conditions of repression in the domestic economy, in order to articulate the theoretical advantages of liberalization for domestic capital markets; it was then extended to the elucidation of how the international financial market works. It holds that, left to themselves, capital markets generate asset prices that, given available information, are best estimates of the present value of future income streams from capital assets. Errors in asset pricing, generated as a result of incomplete information, are removed by signals from excess demand and the correction squeezes out 'noisy traders' who can push prices away from equilibrium by speculating on price movements instead of evaluating assets on the basis of fundamentals.

Fundamentals and asset prices are altered by exogenous supply shocks due to technological, demographic and structural changes, and by demand shocks due to 'policy surprises' sprung by governments. While supply shocks are largely unavoidable, this approach decrees that demand shocks should be avoided by governments eschewing interventionist measures that disrupt market efficiency and cause asset price volatility.

While liberalization of international capital movements is essential and desirable, however, strong links exist between the current and capital accounts on the balance of payments which influence the way in which adjustments to the lifting of controls take place, and which therefore provide conditions under which liberalization can be effective. Issues of timing and sequencing in the case of the capital account need to address several issues:

1 Allocative efficiency issues, due to the fact that the process of liberalization of the capital account is a shorter process than that of the current account, because the asset market adjusts much faster than the goods market. Simultaneity is impossible in this scenario and sequencing becomes obvious, because in order to reduce distortions simultaneously in both markets, capital account liberalization needs to be lagged behind current account liberalization. The differential nature of the two markets itself necessitates sequencing in time.

2 It needs to be recognized that the opening of the capital account creates a sudden capital inflow leading to currency appreciation in real terms in a floating exchange rate system, in turn leading to a bias against tradeables through an increase in export prices and a fall in import prices, or to a capital outflow soon after. In the former case, trade liberalization, if already underway, can be undermined through a widening of the current account deficit, or even reversed. Capital account liberalization undertaken before trade liberalization is well advanced is therefore most likely to render trade liberalization itself unsustainable. This theoretical point, and the models that articulated it, were developed to explain what actually occurred in many Latin American countries in the early 1980s.

3 The relationship between the liberalization of the capital account and stabilization policy, where it is repeatedly emphasized that opening the

capital account should be undertaken only after stabilization policies have reduced inflation and reduced balance of payments imbalances.

Throughout the 1980s, therefore, mainstream literature maintained that as long as the capital account was liberalized in a regime of stable domestic policies and after trade liberalization was well under way, countries would benefit unequivocally through liberalizing capital account transactions of all kinds. The sequence was known, given initial conditions, and it was only the timing that mattered. The models suggested that it was possible for countries to devise ideal sequencing paths given certain combinations of initial conditions. The case of East Asia was cited as providing credence to the models that were put forward.

The question of the volume and volatility of capital flows, particularly short-term speculative flows, began to occupy mainstream theorizing from the time of the Mexican currency crisis of 1994, bringing into focus some of the aspects of financial markets that had been raised by Keynesian and radical economists time and again. This crisis, and the ones that followed in Argentina in 1995, East Asia in 1997 and in Russia and Brazil most recently, brought to the fore the questions of herd behaviour, of panic and contagion in international financial markets following speculative attacks on the national currencies of these countries. Since many of these countries have been following optimum sequencing paths as suggested by mainstream literature, the earlier prescriptions on timing and sequencing of the current and capital accounts have been shown to be unsatisfactory.

These crises demonstrate a pattern: an economy that has been the recipient of large scale capital inflows stops receiving such flows and suddenly faces large outflows and demands for repayment of outstanding loans which have fallen into default or are on the brink of default. This requires a rescheduling of debt payments or a rescue by a new lender whose loan comes with stringent conditionalities. Such crises have also been characterized by sudden shifts in financial flows reflecting a collapse of international confidence. They provoke deep economic contractions within debtor countries, losses to foreign investors and the collapse of domestic currencies.

Current Issues in Capital Controls and Capital Account Convertibility

It thus began to be recognized, even by economists of a neoliberal persuasion, that financial markets do not behave in the perfect manner posited by the EMH, but inherently possess characteristics that make speculative behaviour part of their functioning. A vast body of literature emerged to substantiate this framework.[7] At the same time, Keynesians and radical economists came up with alternative formulations that built on the necessity for controls on free international capital flows. The main strands of thought that have analyzed the recent crisis episodes are discussed below.

The 'hard-line' neoliberal position

Represented by the IMF, this position persists with the basic framework of the earlier generation of mainstream models, wherein market supremacy is assumed and problems that have emerged are associated with misguided domestic policies and incomplete liberalization in particular markets prior to the establishment of CAC. Capital controls as a short-term or long-term solution are treated with serious disfavour in this framework. Chilean-style capital controls, that stipulate minimum lock-in periods for short-term flows and so on, are accepted, although grudgingly.

The 'pragmatic' neoliberal position

Those who hold this position argue that in empirical terms the benefits of removing capital controls are yet to be demonstrated and that financial markets, by their very nature, are not perfect, thereby questioning market automaticity. This view has been articulated in a large volume of literature; its theoretical underpinnings lie in work done by Joseph Stiglitz, (former) Chief Economist and Vice-President at the World Bank, and others.

The broad Keynesian position

This position characterizes financial markets as driven essentially by speculative behaviour and likely to impose constraints on national policy autonomy; it therefore argues for capital controls.

More radical structuralist-Marxist positions

This position sees the globalization of finance and the spread of footloose capital as the logical culmination of the process of unequal capitalist development in the world.

The 'hard-line' neoliberal position taken by the IMF[8] in analyzing East Asia's currency crisis is an illustration of this position. It assumed that the fundamental problem lay in the weak financial systems of these countries. These financial systems, it was argued, were characterized by insider trading, corruption and weak corporate governance; this led to the inefficient investment spending of the large capital inflows and over-investment in excessively risky projects and asset bubbles that these countries experienced. This left such economies vulnerable to speculative attacks on their currencies. In all these countries, it was argued, the weak financial system was a result of incomplete financial liberalization. Furthermore, CAC was undertaken before the domestic banking and financial sector was liberalized sufficiently, resulting in the economy not being able to cope with the large inflows of capital following capital account liberalization.

In line with this analysis, the standard strategy suggested by the IMF for these countries consists of lending the afflicted countries money to help them over the crisis, then demanding they reform their economies as a condition for the loan. These conditions include keeping interest rates high in order both to continue attracting capital inflows and to stabilize their currencies, so improving investor confidence.

In theoretical terms, this analysis is a logical extension of models built to devise optimal sequencing paths. This framework emphasizes that correct timing and sequencing should involve fiscal prudence and consolidation; that inflation should be brought down to single digits; the maintenance of sustainable current account deficits and reserve positions after complete trade liberalization; the construction of a sound financial system by strengthening prudential regulation and bank supervision; and complete liberalization of transactions on the capital account only after all this has taken place. As far as reforming the global financial system is concerned, the suggestions for a new international financial architecture include transparency, accountability and globally uniform standards.

Paul Krugman, in analyzing the causes for and the solution to the East Asian crises, arrives at the conclusion that temporary exchange controls can give crisis-ridden economies the breathing space needed to reform their financial systems in a truly market-friendly manner, and to rid themselves of the excesses of what he terms 'crony capitalism'. The financial system in East Asian economies, he says, was characterized by crony capitalism rather than market considerations of risk and return. According to Krugman, considerations of 'who-knows-whom' constituted the basis for the provision of loans in these domestic markets, resulting in the funding of dubious investments by the domestic banking sector and thus the misallocation of resources. His crony capitalism construct reflects a belief that if only the East Asian economies had followed textbook prescriptions and liberalized their economies through genuine arm's length transactions, the misallocation of resources would not have taken place. We argue therefore that Krugman's analysis, in terms of its ultimate theoretical viewpoint, is similar to that of the IMF's, placing its faith in optimality of free markets and arm's length transactions for all markets. Yet his solutions to the problems faced by these economies are opposite to those suggested by the IMF. They consist of lowering interest rates to stimulate the real economy (using capital controls to achieve this). Therefore, Krugman's analysis bears a closer resemblance to what we have termed the pragmatic neoliberal position, which is elaborated below.

This position is represented in Radelet and Sachs (1998) and Rodrik (1998), to cite two sources in the vast and growing literature on these issues. The argument is that while markets for goods, even if they are not textbook perfect, operate in most instances with a certain degree of efficiency and predictability, financial markets are fundamentally different. In a world of asymmetric information, markets may fail to perform efficiently, even if there are no restrictions on price movements. Market failures can also arise due to the incompleteness of contingent markets and bounded rationality.

Market failures may produce the following consequences. Asymmetric information combined with implicit insurance results in excessive lending for risky projects. Investors are unlikely to trust their private information and instead exhibit herd behaviour that results in high volatility and contagion effects, where loss of confidence in one imprudent agent sparks off a loss of confidence in the system as a whole. Financial intermediaries are vulnerable to bank runs and financial panic because of a mismatch between short-term liabilities and long-term assets.

Sachs, in analyzing East Asia's crisis in 1997, argues that the history of financial crises in the twentieth century indicates the inherent instability of international financial markets. He asserts that there is no strong empirical evidence to indicate that economic growth has depended on unfettered short-term flows of capital, and he advocates the imposition of taxes on short-term borrowing.

In a paper on the desirability of enshrining CAC in the Articles of Agreement of the IMF, Rodrik argues that the liberalization of the capital account on the balance of payments in an orderly fashion, buttressed by prudential regulations as suggested by the IMF, is something that needs to be rejected. According to Rodrik, data from a large number of countries show that the benefits of removing capital controls have yet to be demonstrated and that the judicious application of capital controls might have prevented economic volatility. Tight integration of financial markets with international ones, therefore, may not be the best policy alternative.

To summarize, while traditional mainstream literature has advocated complete liberalization, and consequently a lifting of controls on all foreign exchange transactions, country experiences from the 1970s onwards, and practical considerations such as hyperliquidity in international financial markets, have resulted in a divergence from mainstream opinion and a range of views from complete liberalization to capital controls. As a result, the IMF position and much mainstream literature continue to assert the superiority of free markets for goods as well as for capital; in a world of integrated financial markets, they seek to promote orderly liberalization of the capital accounts of developing countries. This view seeks to give the IMF the same jurisdiction over the capital accounts of its members that it currently exercises on their current accounts. Left to themselves, however, the inability of financial markets to lead to optimum solutions renders capital controls as the obvious second-best solution, according to this understanding.

The Keynesian and structuralist-Marxist strands of thought mentioned above characterize the international financial system as prone to fundamental instabilities which systematically undermine the degree of control governments have over national economic policy making and result in asymmetric burdens of adjustment to crises that adversely affect developing countries. This view is reflected in a huge amount of literature that covers a lot of ground, from analysis of financial market behaviour in particular, to the development of a comprehensive critique of economic liberalization in general.

Among the broad Keynesians, there are those who argue for taxes on short-term flows of international private capital. This is based on the Keynesian understanding that international financial markets are inherently unstable because they are driven by speculative behaviour. Players in financial markets speculate on how other investors collectively react to news about changes in fundamentals, rather than how these changes might alter equilibrium prices *per se*. Therefore bandwagon bidding for, and herd-like dumping of, financial assets result in a high degree of volatility of asset prices. Speculative behaviour constitutes rational strategy on the part of investors because expected returns from speculative positions are high. Wide swings in asset prices increase risks for long-term investors, pushing them towards investments with shorter-term maturity. Felix (1996), on the basis of an empirical examination and validation of the above framework (for the various financial asset markets, particularly the foreign exchange market over the period 1976–98), argues persuasively for levying the Tobin tax on private foreign exchange transactions of short maturity.[9]

James Tobin came up with a proposal in the 1970s for slowing down the reaction speed of financial markets by levying a tax at a uniform rate on private foreign exchange transactions; this, according to Felix, is the 'least intrusive way' of slowing the speed of international financial markets. Felix's suggestion is also placed within the framework that was put forward at the time of the original Bretton Woods accords – that is, free capital mobility is incompatible with the objectives of free trade and full employment.

A Keynesian understanding of financial market behaviour also provides the basis for arguments to restrict the degree of integration into international financial markets: thus the analyses of Bhaduri (1998) and Banuri and Schor (1992), among many others, stress the need for countries to follow economic policies that permit the development of their domestic markets. Bhaduri uses a Keynesian model to trace the macroeconomic effects of foreign capital inflows into developing countries in the present phase of globalization. He argues that this phase is characterized by control shifting away from national governments to multinational corporations and financial intermediaries, and that in most countries, with the external market acquiring overriding importance, the expansion of the internal market is being restrained. This is particularly so because the massive volume and high mobility of international capital make governments play it safe by keeping interest rates high, thus discouraging domestic private investment. They also desist from increasing public investment because, through an expansion in government spending, it can send signals of impending increases in fiscal deficits that have the potential of destabilizing capital markets and inducing capital flight. National economies have also moved away from a wage-led or consumption-led expansion of the home market that seeks to stimulate employment and growth. Given the relative importance of the external market and of short-term capital flows, the autonomy of national government policies is severely hampered.

There is a range of views in the Keynesian critique of freeing up international capital flows. While some look essentially for the best way to 'throw sand in the gears' of international financial markets in order to reduce their speed and volatility, others stress the need for pursuing autonomous national policies which promote full employment and growth in individual countries, thereby implying a selective delinking from international markets that threaten the achievement of these objectives. Keeping capital controls in place and not making currencies convertible on the capital account constitute an important part of these proposals.

Some of the most compelling arguments for checking the degree of a country's integration into the international economy, particularly financial integration, arise from the numerous critiques of Washington Consensus proposals and reforms that have been put forward as part of the structuralist-Marxist perspective over the years. These proposals look at the liberalization of capital accounts as part – but constituting a very crucial element – of a broader package of policies for macroeconomic and institutional reform.

While there is a wide range of opinions within this strand as well, this broad perspective sees the globalization of finance and the spread of footloose capital as the logical extension of the process of world capitalist development that necessitates the retardation of economies in the underdeveloped world for growth and development in the advanced capitalist countries. This view holds that throughout its history capitalism has been characterized by the domination of metropolitan capital (or capital from the advanced capitalist countries) over underdeveloped economies.

This first took place via unilateral control in underdeveloped countries during the colonial period, through their integration into world trade as primary producers, providing cheap raw materials and a market for manufactures. Domination continued, even in newly independent states in the post-colonial period, through control by a domestic 'comprador' bourgeoisie. Even where the state embarked upon development paths that asserted relative autonomy from international capital, these attempts lost steam because of the inescapable domination of metropolitan capital and of international financial markets.

The phase of liberalization dictated by the IMF and the World Bank – through policies that necessitate close linking with the international economy – again challenges the autonomy of independent nation states to pursue exclusive policies that help the growth of a native bourgeoisie and result in domestic development. Patnaik (1995) argues in response that:

> The new regime represents a tendency towards a re-establishment in a more complex form of the 19th century pattern of free trade and free capital movements which were responsible for generating underdevelopment in the first place … this liberalization will once again leave the growth of underdeveloped countries open to the vagaries of international capital.

According to this view, the problems of addressing underdevelopment cannot be left to the dictates of the market; it will require the active role of the state.

In a specific analysis of the implications of financial liberalization for developing countries, Patnaik (1999) emphasizes that an economy that liberalizes its external financial sector exposes itself to the vortex of speculative capital flows. In a bid to attract such flows, growth rates slow through high rates of interest, thereby risking the possibility of severe crisis. The alternative to this development path lies not only in delinking economies from international financial markets, but in radically restructuring economies through land reforms, larger public investment and social expenditure financed through measures such as taxing the rich and decentralized decision making, under the aegis of an interventionist state.

In today's context, this position would see capital controls as the minimum necessary condition to shield not only the underdeveloped but also the advanced countries from the vagaries of the international market. An extreme version of this framework can be found in Chossudovsky (1995), which advocates 'financial disarmament' in terms of 'freezing the entire gamut of speculative instruments, dismantling the hedge funds, reintroducing controls on the international movement of money and progressively breaking down the structures of offshore banking'. Furthermore, instituting far-reaching changes in the structure of the global economy would also entail breaking the Washington Consensus, discarding IMF policies, reversing the 'mechanics of macroeconomic reform by the establishment of an expansionary economic agenda geared towards restoring wages and alleviating global poverty.'[10]

Conclusion

It is evident from the broad survey of issues presented above that there appears to be an emerging consensus in theoretical formulations from a wide range of ideological positions, that capital controls are essential in today's world of integrated financial markets. This reflects the practice of many Asian governments, who are imposing capital controls and cutting interest rates in promoting Keynesian fiscal expansion – what the IMF and the US Treasury now term the 'policy backlash' from Asian countries. The IMF persists, however, in its determination to impose the agenda of capital account liberalization on developing countries.

In attempting an explanation for this persistence, Wade and Veneroso (1998) argue that it is a defence of the interests of the owners and managers of international capital. Jagdish Bhagwati, whose work on the desirability of pursuing free trade policies for countries is well known, takes the argument further in stressing that the Wall Street–US Treasury nexus has a vested interest in ensuring the free mobility of capital across national boundaries. He observes, 'In my judgement it is a lot of ideological humbug to say that without free portfolio capital mobility, somehow the world cannot function and growth rates will collapse.'[11]

In our view, questioning the validity of free market outcomes in the case of financial markets and proposing controls over speculative flows of capital is not enough. In as much as there is sufficient evidence that free capital mobility has not necessarily been associated with high rates of growth, there is also ample evidence that neither trade openness nor outward orientation has necessarily been associated with higher growth rates or reduced vulnerability.

The discussion on free capital mobility therefore has to be placed within the larger discussion on the positive and normative aspects of economic liberalization. This involves not only a questioning of whether free markets allocate resources in the best possible manner, but also the crucial question of the relevance of static allocative efficiency in the context of the dynamics of development paths in developing countries. In fact, the discussion needs to go further. Should developing countries follow some unilateral approach to development or strive to retain relative autonomy in the development paradigm? Or should they pursue specific policies to tackle the stagnation and retrogression that they are currently faced with in the mainstream paradigm?

Notes

1 The proposed revisions are to amend Article I which, in stating the purposes of the fund, seeks to promote orderly liberalization of the capital account as one of its main purposes; and Article VIII, which describes the jurisdiction of the Fund and states that the Fund shall have the same jurisdiction over the capital account of its members as it has over their current accounts.

2 IMF occasional paper No. 131.

3 Reserve Bank of India, Report of the Committee on Capital Account Convertibility, 1997.
4 For a representative statement of this viewpoint, see Krueger (1990).
5 Edwards, S. (1996) 'Liberalization of the Goods Market and of the Capital Market', in Choksi (1996).
6 For a review of the literature on optimum sequencing paths that look at the problem in terms of the speed and timing of liberalization of different markets, see Edwards (1989).
7 The work of Grossman and Stiglitz was seminal in this regard. Rodrik (1998) summarizes the arguments succinctly.
8 IMF (1998).
9 Felix, D. (1996) 'Asia and the Crisis of Financial Globalization versus Free Trade; the Case for the Tobin Tax', in UNCTAD Review.
10 See Chossudovsky (1995).
11 Bhagwati (1997).

References

Banuri, Tariq and Juliet Schor, eds (1992): *Financial Openness and National Autonomy*, Clarendon Press, Oxford.

Bhaduri, Amit (1998) 'Implications of Globalization for Macroeconomic Theory and Policy in Developing Countries' in Blecker *et al.*, *Globalization and Progressive Economic Policy*.

Bhagwati, Jagdish (1978) *Anatomy and Consequences of Exchange Control Regimes*, Ballinger, Cambridge, Mass.

Bhagwati, Jagdish (1997), interview in *Times of India*, 31 December.

Choksi, Armeane, M. and Demetris Papageorgia, ed. (1996) *Economic Liberalization in Developing Countries,* Blackwell, Oxford.

Chossudovsky, Michel (1995) 'G7 'Solution' to Global Financial Crisis: a Marshall Plan for Creditors and Speculators', in *Economic and Political Weekly*, 26 December.

Crotty, James R. (1983) 'On Keynes and Capital Flight', in *Journal of Economic Literature*, Vol. 21, March.

Edwards, Sebastian (1989) 'The Order of Liberalisation of the External Sector in Developing Countries', Princeton Essays in *International Finance*, No. 156.

Felix, David (1996) 'Asia and the Crisis of Financial Globalization versus Free Trade: the Case for the Tobin Tax' in *UNCTAD Review*.

International Monetary Fund (1996) 'Capital Account Convertibility, Review of Experience and Implications for Policies', Occasional Paper No. 131.

International Monetary Fund (1998), *World Economic Outlook.*

Krugman, Paul (1998) 'Saving Asia: It's Time to get Radical' in *Fortune*, June.

Krueger, Anne (1978) *Liberalization Attempts and Consequences*, Ballinger, Cambridge, Mass.

Krueger, Anne (1990) 'Government Failures in Development', in *Journal of Economic Perspectives*, Vol. 4, No. 3.

Patnaik, Prabhat (1995) *Whatever Happened to Imperialism and Other Essays*, Tulika, New Delhi.

Patnaik, Prabhat (1999) 'The Real Face of Fnancial Liberalisation' in *Frontline*, 26 February.

Radelet, Steven and Jeffrey D. Sachs (1998) 'The East Asian Financial Crisis: Diagnosis, Remedies, Prospects' in *Brookings Papers on Economic Activity*, No. 1.

Sachs, Jeffrey D. (1995) 'Do We Need An International Lender of Last Resort?', *Princeton Essays in International Finance,* Princeton University Press, Princeton.

Rodrik, Dani (1998) 'Who Needs Capital Account Convertibility' in Stanley Fischer *et al.*, *Should the IMF Pursue Capital Account Convertibility*, Prnceton University Press, Princeton.

Wade, Robert and Frank Veneroso (1998) 'The Asian Crisis : The High Debt Model versus the Wall Street–Treasury–IMF complex' in *New Left Review*, May–June.

Wade, Robert and Frank Veneroso (1998) 'The Gathering World Slump and the Battle over Capital Controls' in *New Left Review*, September–October.

12

China: the Case for Capital Controls

YU YONGDING

In the wake of the debt crisis of the early 1980s, the World Bank published a report to summarize developing countries' experience in utilizing foreign capital. According to the report,

> Foreign finance can promote growth through higher investment and technology transfers. It can allow countries to adjust gradually to new circumstances in the world economy. But it can also be misused so that countries end up with more debt but no corresponding increase in their ability to service it.[1]

Since 1978, foreign capital has played a very important role in promoting China's economic growth and strengthening its international balance of payments. It has been fortunate for China to be a latecomer in opening up to foreign capital: the main lessons we learnt from the debt crisis of Latin American countries in the early 1980s are outlined below.

Caution in defining borrowing limits was required. The introduction of foreign capital in China was subject to aggregate controls applied in national economic planning. The emphasis was on raising domestic savings, and foreign capital was regarded as only complementary. As a result, although China is one of the largest 'sponges' for foreign capital in the world, it has maintained a more or less balanced current account over the past twenty years.

Foreign direct investment should be the preferable form of capital inflow. FDI provides finance as part of a package of technology and management, and host country and foreign investors share in both the risks and rewards of each project. When China began to open up to foreign capital in earnest, the memory of the debt crisis of Latin American countries was still fresh, and China was still feeling the acute pain of foreign exchange shortages. Therefore, the Chinese government was able to appreciate the fact that FDI would not cause the problem of debt service. Ever since, China's policy has shown a strong bias in favour of introducing FDI. Consequently, up to now, more than 90 per cent of foreign capital is FDI.

Short-term borrowing should be kept to the minimum. China also paid great attention to the stability of capital inflow, and accordingly is extremely reluctant to borrow short-term capital. As a result, about 80 per cent of China's debts are long-term.

Maintaining capital controls is necessary. Another important characteristic of China's policy toward foreign capital flows is strict capital controls. The Chinese government knew that the Chinese economy was too vulnerable to maintain a stable financial situation without strict capital control. The government did not want to abandon either its fixed exchange rate or its independent monetary policy.

For many years, observers have criticized China's slowness in developing financial markets and liberalizing its capital account. The Chinese government itself was worried by the slow progress. Rather theatrically, the disadvantage has turned into an advantage. Owing to capital controls, the underdevelopment of financial markets and the lack of sophisticated financial instruments (such as stock futures and foreign exchange forwards), the renminbi (RMB) escaped attack by international speculators. Although the Chinese economy has also been through difficult times since 1998, compared with neighbouring countries China has not too fared too badly and its external balance is particularly strong (Table 12.1).

Table 12.1. China's Balance of Payments, 1994–7 (in US \$million)

Year	1994	1995	1996	1997
Current account	7,658	1,618	7,242	29,717
Trade balance	7,290	18,050	19,535	46,222
Service, net	−969	−17,867	−14,422	−21,647
Transfers, net	1,337	1,435	2,129	5,143
Capital account	32,644	38,674	39,967	22,959
Long-term	35,756	38,249	41,554	23,877*
% of capital account	109.5	98.9	104.0	104.0*
Short-term	−3,112	425	1,587	918*
% of capital account	−9.5	1.1	−4.0	−4.0*
Errors and omissions	−9,775	−17,810	15,558	−16,952
Overall balance	30,527	22,481	31,651	35,723

Source: People's Bank of China, *China Financial Outlook*, 1998, p. 95, Qian Xiao
*Estimates

Capital Controls in China

The good health of China's economy is attributable to its success in controlling capital flows. The key elements are registration as a universal requirement, strict criteria of approval, tight control over the use of foreign exchange and severe penalties for breaching regulations. I will give a brief introduction to the rules and regulations of capital controls applied to different categories of capital flows.

Foreign Direct Investment

APPROVAL

* Relevant planning departments and foreign trade departments must approve all inward FDI.
* Chinese enterprises must obtain approval from the Ministry of Foreign Trade and Economic Cooperation and the administrations of relevant industries before investing abroad. The State Administration of Foreign Exchange is in charge of scrutinizing the foreign exchange risk of the investment and the sources of foreign exchange for the investment.

REGISTRATION

* All inward FDI must be registered.
* As for outward FDI, after obtaining approval, the investors must register their investment with foreign exchange authorities, and then proceed to remit foreign exchange to the host country of investment. In order to get registered, the investors must present the documents for approval by the Ministry of Foreign Trade and Economic Cooperation or departments authorized by the Ministry. Documents on foreign exchange risk and the sources of foreign exchange produced by foreign exchange authorities, and many other documents produced by different governmental and legal authorities, must also be presented.

REPATRIATION

* Once they are registered and approved, investors may open special accounts: foreign exchange capital accounts at designated banks that are authorized to engage in foreign exchange activities. There are no restrictions on the remitting of foreign exchange into China by approved investors of FDI.
* The conversion of foreign exchange into RMB, however, must obtain advance approval from the State Administration of Foreign Exchange or its provincial branches.
* All investment incomes from outward FDI must be repatriated to China within six months of the end of the fiscal year of the host country. Foreign exchange needed for business operations can be kept in the host country, subject to the approval of the foreign exchange authorities.

International equities

PROHIBITION

* Foreign investors are prohibited from using RMB to invest in the stock

exchanges inside China. Foreign investors are only allowed to use foreign exchange to invest inside the mainland in certain authorized shares that are called B shares. Any flotation of B shares of more than US $30 million must be subject to the approval of the China Securities Regulatory Commission of the State Council. The total amount of B shares floated each year must be within the quotas set by the government. Only a small number of Chinese companies are allowed to be listed in New York and Hong Kong. The shares they sell are called N shares and H shares, respectively.

REPATRIATION
- Except in special cases, money raised by selling shares abroad must be repatriated to China. Approval must be obtained from the State Administration of Foreign Exchange for opening foreign exchange accounts, and foreign exchange raised must be deposited at authorized banks.

International bonds

ELIGIBILITY
- The issuers of bonds abroad are limited to ten authorized window institutions for international commercial loans, in addition to the Ministry of Finance and state policy banks. The window institutions are approved by the State Council after consulting with the State Development Planning Commission and the People's Bank of China (China's central bank). Generally speaking, other borrowers can ask those ten window institutions to issue bonds on their behalf. If they wish to issue bonds themselves, they must obtain special approval from the State Administration of Foreign Exchange. The issuing of bonds by the Ministry of Finance must be approved by the State Council, and be included in the state plan for utilization of international commercial loans. Except for authorized financial institutions engaging in foreign borrowing and large enterprise groups, Chinese residents are not allowed to buy foreign securities of any kind, including derivatives for hedging.

APPROVAL
- Issuers of bonds denominated in foreign currency must hand in applications for approval to the local branches of the State Administration of Foreign Exchange. The issue must be part of the government's plan for the utilization of foreign capital. To obtain the approval, a lot of paper work needs to be done. The issuers must provide documents on their business performance over the last three years, including income statements and financial reports. Detailed information about the issue – such as the bonds markets, the method of issue, denomination of currency,

value of the issue, maturity, interest rates, issuing cost, risk management, the conditions of leading banks of issue and trustee banks, the arrangements for repayments, and so on – must be provided. Issuers must also provide additional documents according to different expected uses of the funds raised (for example, capital formation, relending, acting as agents).

- The purchase of foreign securities by authorized Chinese financial institutions must have the prior approval of the State Administration of Foreign Exchange. Relevant rules and regulations restrict the amount of purchase.

REPATRIATION

- Except in special cases, money raised by issuing bonds abroad must be repatriated to China. Approval must be obtained from the State Administration of Foreign Exchange for opening foreign exchange accounts, and the foreign exchange must be deposited at authorized banks. The breach of this regulation is a criminal offence.

International Loans

APPROVAL

- The Ministry of Foreign Trade and Economic Cooperation is the only window for loans from foreign governments. Local governments can apply for loans from foreign governments. If their applications are accepted, the Ministry of Foreign Trade and Economic Cooperation will negotiate with foreign governments on behalf of these local governments. The Ministry will entrust some authorized financial institutions to arrange the borrowing for these local governments.
- The Ministry of Finance is the window for loans from the World Bank. The People's Bank of China is the window for loans from the IMF and the Asian Development Bank. The borrowing procedure is strictly in line with the rules and regulations of those international financial institutions. The State Council must give final approval.
- Entities eligible for borrowing from foreign banks and other foreign financial institutions are financial institutions authorized by the State Administration of Foreign Exchange and industrial and commercial enterprises, or groups of enterprises, approved by the State Administration of Foreign Exchange.
- Chinese residents are not allowed to borrow from foreign banks and other foreign financial institutions without the prior approval of the government. The State Development Planning Commission is in charge of compiling annual plans of foreign borrowing. It is authorized to determine the total amount of and the allocation of the borrowing after reconciling the

borrowing applications from different departments and provincial governments. The State Council must approve the plan. The State Council must approve borrowing of more than US$100 million. Authorized departments and local governments must approve borrowing of under US$100 million. The approval procedure involves interdepartmental work by the State Development Planning Commission, the People's Bank of China and the State Administration of Foreign Exchange. All borrowing and lending agreements without prior approval of the authorized government organizations are not legally binding. The State Administration of Foreign Exchange will refuse to recognize the agreements and to register the loans as foreign debt.

- Chinese banks' extended loans denominated in foreign currency to foreign borrowers must obtain prior approval from the State Administration of Foreign Exchange. The foreign lending activities of non-bank financial institutions are subject to harsher restriction.

REPAYMENT

- The local government must provide guarantees of repayment. Unless the borrowing has been included in the central government's budget, the borrowers must repay the debt themselves.
- Only after obtaining approval from the State Administration of Foreign Exchange can the borrowers repay the principal through their designated foreign exchange banks.

REGISTRATION

- Only authorized borrowers can have foreign exchange accounts at financial institutions that are authorized to engage in foreign exchange business. Short-term borrowing by authorized institutions may proceed without prior approval. But the borrowing should be reported to and registered by the State Administration of Foreign Exchange or its local branches.
- Foreign companies can borrow directly from abroad. The borrowing must be reported and registered.

Trade Credit

- Trade credit of more than three months must be reported to and registered by foreign exchange authorities. The foreign exchange authorities must approve the servicing of debt.

Foreign Currency Deposits

- Chinese residents are not allowed to open personal foreign exchange accounts abroad. Chinese institutions must obtain approval from the State

Administration of Foreign Exchange before opening foreign exchange accounts abroad.

• Foreign ventures in China must obtain approval from the State Administration of Foreign Exchange before opening foreign exchange accounts abroad.

Collateral

• Collateral may not be provided by residents without prior approval from the foreign exchange authorities, and can only be provided by authorized financial institutions that are engaged in foreign exchange business and large enterprise groups that have foreign exchange earnings. Detailed rules and regulations cap the value of collateral.

The Evasion of Capital Controls

Capital controls have helped China during the turbulence of the financial upheaval, which began on 2 July 1997. China registered a US$40 billion trade surplus and a US$40 billion capital account surplus in 1998. By the end of 1998, China's foreign exchange reserves had reached a new high of US$150 billion, as against a current total debt obligation of US$137 billion, only 20 per cent of which is short-term debt. With its strong external position and tight capital controls, the RMB's stability, and hence the stability of the Chinese economy, should be secure. Predictions of China's imminent economic crisis that appeared in internationally renowned Western journals are either rubbish or wishful thinking.

Yet in China all is not well. Any complacency can easily lead to disaster. The litany of loopholes and points of vulnerability is long. The greatly weakened effectiveness of capital controls in China is one of the most important threats to the country's economic stability. The clearest indication of this is the fact that in 1998, while China's international balance of payments was several hundred billion in surplus, China's official foreign exchange reserves increased by only US$5 billion. Where has the rest of this money gone? Precise information is not available. According to some estimates, US$20–40 billion has left the country. How could this happen? The government recently sent a number of investigating teams around the country to find out what was going on out there. The main results of one of those investigation teams are given in Table 12.2.[2]

China's Efforts to Maintain the Balance of International Payments

Despite the fact that China's international position remains very strong, so that there is still no cause for alarm, the Chinese government has adopted

Table 12.2. Major forms of evading capital controls

Inflow	FDI	• Fixed high return without participating in management • Selling the rights of using infrastructure and fixed assets
	International borrowing	• Borrowing without government approval • Borrowing with high interest rates • Using domestic collateral to borrow by foreign ventures or joint ventures • Forging documents to disguise borrowing as export earning so as to get tax rebate
	Trade credit	• Forging import documents to get trade credit though T/T and L/C
	Equity investment	• Using residents as agents to buy shares prohibited to non-residents
Outflow		• Early remittances of profits by foreign ventures • Unauthorized investment abroad by Chinese enterprises • Moving debt repayments forward in time by Chinese borrowers • Delaying the remittance of dividends and profits by Chinese foreign investors • Delaying the repatriation of export earnings • Capital flight under the disguise of payment for patents, commissions, travel expenses, transportation insurance • Invoicing imports with higher than actual value and remitting the difference abroad • Multinational transfer price • Forging documents to obtain foreign exchange to pay for faked imported intangible assets • Forging documents to obtain foreign exchange as advances for faked imports

Source: Zhao Linghua, 'An Analysis of the Forms of Irregular Capital Flows in China', *International Economic Review*, Nos 3–4, 1999.

more draconian measures to deal with irregularities in capital flows.

In October 1998 China's Supreme Court called for a major crackdown on illegal foreign exchange activities. According to the Supreme Court, some businesses and individuals have falsified certificates or commercial documents to purchase foreign exchange, and illegally engaged in foreign exchange trading. These illegal activities have seriously damaged the nation's adminis-tration of the financial sector and foreign exchange activities, and posed a threat to the nation's economic security. The Supreme Court has ordered courts at all levels to investigate and deal with related criminal cases without delay. With the incentive of a deadline set by the State Administration of Foreign Exchange for offenders to turn themselves in so as to get more benevolent treatment, hundreds of cases have been brought to the courts. A large number of defendants who refused to surrender were punished severely according to the law. At the same time, an equally large number of defen-dants who confessed were given amnesty.

In addition to economic and administrative methods, the state has used its full weight to crack down on the illegal activities facilitating capital flight, and its measures against corrupt businessmen have gained the strong support of the public. In summary, China's current situation with regard to capital controls has the following major features:

- The Chinese government has shelved capital liberalization for the time being.

- The government sends tens of thousands of auditors to enterprises and financial institutions. Those auditors have exposed tens of thousands of cases of irregularity, and tracked down and recovered more than US$100 million in capital during the second half of 1998. Consequently, China's official foreign exchange reserves have increased quite significantly since the fourth quarter of 1998.

- The Chinese government is fully aware of the limitations of administra-tive measures for containing capital flight. A more important aspect is to formulate a comprehensive and consistent programme of macroeconomic policy. Because of the policy of capital controls, international capital flows cannot move freely across China's border. As a result, China has been able to lower the interest rate to stimulate the economy, while maintaining the stability of the RMB. Owing to the weakening of the effectiveness of capital controls, however, it has become increasingly difficult to pursue the dual objectives of high growth and currency stability. Faced with this dilemma, the Chinese government has lowered the target for economic growth from last year's 8 per cent to this year's 7 per cent, and changed the status of the target from a mandatory aim to just an indicator. Some

Chinese economists are arguing for tightening monetary policy, including interest policy and credit policy. Otherwise, they argue, the fight against capital flight is difficult to win. For example, many enterprises delay the repatriation of the foreign exchange earnings without fearing that lack of liquidity will jeopardize their operations. This is because it is very easy for them to obtain cheap credit inside China.

• Faced with the currency uncertainty, it is legitimate for enterprises and financial institutions to design ways to hedge assets denominated by the RMB. Despite the fact that the absence of developed financial markets has been of some benefit to China under the current circumstances, the legitimate demand of enterprises for hedging should be met. But how can this be done? This is an urgent issue. Otherwise, international speculators may take advantage of the situation and China's defence line may be cracked. Currently the activities in the so-called non-deliverable forward markets have been thriving. Non-deliverable forward contracts are offshore contracts for currencies with capital controls restricting forward market activity, or for which an onshore forward market does not exist. In the presence of capital controls, non-deliverable forwards may contribute to evasion to the extent that by offering a way to hedge against exchange risk, they increase the appeal of foreign credit obtained through delayed, anticipated or misinvoiced trade payments.[3] I suspect that the activities of evading capital controls by Chinese enterprises and financial institutions may have something to do with those developments. The Chinese government must guard against it.

Final Observations

Confidence is the key to financial stability. Chinese leaders have shown that they are competent in tackling difficult economic situations; hence they still enjoy the public's trust.

Public ownership is always a plus in a crisis. The public believes that the government will act as lender of last resort, that there will be no major banking crisis and that their deposits are safe as long as the political situation is stable. (And the political situation is stable.)

Capital controls are still in place. Effectiveness aside, the capital controls have greatly increased the transaction cost of evasion. However, a much better coordination of macroeconomic policies is needed. The Chinese government is moving in this direction.

Finally, further financial reform must be carried out in line with China's specific situation. While the government should continue to boost the public's confidence, more work should be done to provide covers for enterprises and financial institutions. Of course, before taking action, this should be thought through very carefully so as to minimize the inevitable destabilizing effects.

Notes

1 World Bank (1985: 6) *World Development Report*, World Bank, Washington, DC.
2 Zhao Linghua (1999), 'An Analysis of the Forms of Irregular Capital Flows in China', *International Economic Review*, Nos 3–4.
3 International Monetary Fund, *Capital Account Liberalization*, Occasional Paper No. 172.

13

An International Chapter 11:
Bankruptcy and Special Drawing Rights
ZHIYUAN CUI

There is no American legislation against fraudulent bankruptcies. Is that because there are no bankrupts? No, on the contrary, it is because there are many. (Alexis de Tocqueville, 1835)[1]

The modern legislator has been able to erect a structure of bankruptcy law wholly undreamed of by its Tudor architects. Discharge from debts, voluntary bankruptcy enforcement of majority-determined composition, moratoria, reorganization facilities – all these are now to be found in a law that began with a brief statute at the pursuit and punishment of a narrow class of fraudulent debtors. (Israel Treiman, 1938)[2]

It is instructive to compare the treatment received by Russia and the treatment received by Macy's Department Stores, which by coincidence filed for Chapter 11 relief in January 1992, the same month that Russia fell into default on its obligations. By law, Macy's was afforded a complete and automatic standstill on debt serving on the day it filed its Chapter 11, 27 January 1992. Two weeks later, Macy's obtained a $600 million debtor-in-possession loan in order to secure working capital for continued operations. By contrast, it took Russia eighteen months to receive a partial standstill on debt serving and the same period of time to receive a $600 million working capital loan from the World Bank. (Jeffery Sachs, 1994)[3]

This last observation is important and insightful. However, Professor Sachs has not worked out fully the implications of his observation. It is the purpose of this chapter to do so.

The First Implication

The very existence of the domestic Chapter 11 in the United States refutes the conventional wisdom about the market economy as a natural selection mechanism by which only the 'fittest' will survive. The idea of Chapter 11 starts, historically and logically, from the premise that financial markets are

188

not efficient (in the technical sense of the term). If financial markets were efficient there would be no need for even the domestic Chapter 11, since in an efficient market the 'good' enterprises in temporary trouble could always signal their 'goodness' by getting higher interest loans from financial markets. The very fact that a good firm could go bankrupt in a market economy requires a new understanding of the nature of market economy.

We need to remember that the proof of the 'Pareto efficiency' of a market economy (the first theorem of welfare economics) requires the following condition: aggregation of budget constraints of firms in different states of nature into a single budget constraint. In other words, in the first theorem of welfare economics, 'flow constraint' (in different states of nature) is reduced to 'stock constraint'. This reduction is only valid, however, if all assets are liquid (that is, easy to convert into cash) and the firm can borrow freely against its future income in a perfect capital market. When markets are incomplete, even good firms may be unable to borrow money from banks and equity markets. So, the reduction of 'flow constraint' into 'stock constraint' is impossible, and good firms may go bankrupt due to 'flow constraint'. Let me explain why this is so in some detail, by specifying three mechanisms operating in an incomplete set of markets.

Credit Rationing

At first sight, one might think that 'good' firms could borrow money by offering a higher interest rate to the bank, since they can produce at lower cost than their competitors. One of the main causes of the 'incompleteness' of markets, however, is incomplete information among borrowers and lenders; for this reason, the interest rate borrowers are willing to offer may signal their 'type' (risk-lover or risk-averse). The very fact that they are willing to offer a higher interest rate may signal to the lender that they are over-optimistic about their investment project. From the point of view of the bank, this leads, first, to the 'adverse selection' effect of a higher interest rate (that is, a high interest rate attracts risk-loving applicants, and thus increases default rate); and second, to the 'adverse incentive' effect (that is, a high interest rate induces former prudent borrowers to take on riskier projects). Considering the effects of adverse selection and adverse incentive, Stiglitz and Weiss argued that the expected return to the bank may well rise less rapidly than the interest rate and, beyond some critical point 'x', may actually decline. So, the bank would not lend to a borrower who offered to pay more than the critical point 'x'. As a result, even so-called 'good' firms may not be able to borrow money: 'There are no competitive forces leading supply to equal demand, and credit is rationed'.[4] This incompleteness of loan markets is one of the mechanisms which could lead 'good' firms into trouble.

Equity Rationing

At first sight, one might also think that 'good' firms can raise money in the stock market by offering a higher dividend. However, similar adverse incentive and adverse selection effects cause rationing in the equity market. As Greenwald, Stiglitz and Weiss argued:

> First, incentive problems may intensify when a firm is equity financed. Managers, who receive only a small fraction of any additional profit, are likely to put forth less-than-optimal effort.... Second, signaling effects may restrict a firm's access to equity markets ... [because] attempting to sell equity may convey a strong negative signal about a firm's quality and reduce its market value accordingly.[5]

Therefore, firms have very limited access to the equity market, even if they are 'good'. In fact, in all major Western economies new equity issues raise only a very small fraction of new capital.

Multiplier Effect and Recession

Credit and equity rationing are two mechanisms that may prevent 'good' firms from being able to borrow, even in normal times. These are individual shocks to the 'good' firms. However, there is also aggregate shock: more 'good' firms go bankrupt in times of macroeconomic recession. It is difficult for believers of the 'invisible hand' paradigm to explain the existence of recession, because, according to this paradigm, flexible price reactions tend to smooth out initial disturbance, thereby ensuring that individual shocks will not multiply into aggregate recession. But, from the perspective of incomplete markets, credit and equity rationing can have a multiplier effect which leads initial disturbance to recession. Once again, as Stiglitz points out, an economic disturbance (regardless of its origins) 'results in higher than anticipated defaults, lowering banks' net worth. This, combined with the greater uncertainty associated with lending, reduces their lending activity, amplifying the economic downturn'.[6]

We have seen, therefore, that at least three mechanisms – credit rationing, equity rationing and their multiplier effect on recession – are responsible for 'good' firms going bankrupt. This explanation is based on the logic of the incomplete markets theory and is consistent with the historical facts about the development of bankruptcy law.

The crucial historical stage in the development of bankruptcy law was the introduction of 'reorganization' provisions in the 1898 Act. This reorganization stage began with the Wabash Railway receivership of 1884. On 28 May 1884 Jay Gould, president of the Wabash Railway, requested the federal district court in St Louis to appoint his representatives to be receivers of the still solvent Wabash Railway. This was a completely unprecedented request.

As Gerald Berk puts it, at that time 'nowhere in the available theories of the corporation or in receivership practice could a justification be found for putting a corporation into receivership prior to default, or for appointing its managers to job of receiver'.

The court agreed with this unprecedented request, which marked the beginning of 'reorganization' practice. By reorganizing Wabash Railway, Jay Gould 'was able to wring enormous concessions from his creditors: both principal and interest were slashed substantially in the final settlement'.[8]

From my perspective, what is significant about this story of the Wabash Railway receivership is the argument used by Jay Gould and his supporters in court. Basically, they argued that liquidation could put society at large in jeopardy:

> If the lines of road are broken up and fragments thereof placed in the hands of various receivers (creditors), and the rolling stock, materials, and supplies seized and scattered about, the result would be irreparable injury to all persons having any interest in said line of the road.[9]

The inherent validity of this argument is beyond the scope of this chapter. My point here is to note that the very justification for 'reorganization' was, as a matter of historical fact, the interest of society at large.

Influenced by the 1884 Wabash Railway management receivership (rather than traditional creditor receivership), and pushed by the financial depressions in 1885 and 1893–7, the 1898 Bankruptcy Act explicitly included reorganization provisions. The 1938 Chandler Act (amending the 1898 Act) was also the result of the concern for saving 'good' firms that were in a bad general financial situation. It is well known that the first legislation sent by President Roosevelt to the Congress was the Emergency Banking Act of 1933, legalizing a nationwide 'banking holiday' which he declared two days after his inauguration. Obviously, saving 'good' firms in this general financial distress was the motive of the Chandler Act of 1938, which made it easier for firms to file for reorganization, because, as James Olson pointed out, 'a national holiday without a sound reorganization plan would be foolish'.[10]

The Second Implication

The international counterpart to the domestic Chapter 11 should also be based on an understanding of the inefficiency of the foreign exchange market and the eurodollar markets as means of providing international reserve assets and financing balance of payments, especially for developing countries. There are several reasons for this: despite the rhetoric of the new age of global economy, there are plenty of signs today which indicate that we are repeating the dangerous game of 'competitive devaluation' of the inter-war period. The worldwide currency chaos in mid-September 1992 and the US effort to undercut the competitive advantage of foreign producers through exchange rate manipulation (such as advocating a rise in the yen to reduce Japan's competitiveness) are just two recent, startling examples of this sort.

First, many developing countries are too small to be optimal currency areas: the cost of floating the exchange rate exceeds the benefits. Second, the European Monetary System (EMS) is not available for developing countries, and this makes the international Chapter 11 even more necessary for them. Finally, the eurocurrency market is too costly a way for developing countries to create their international reserve asset, owing to similar problems of 'credit rationing' and 'equity rationing' discussed above in the domestic context.

SDR as a Crucial Device in International Chapter 11

What are the technical devices for the international Chapter 11? Let us look first at the domestic Chapter 11. Only minor differences separate Chapter 11 under the 1978 Bankruptcy Reform Act from the 1938 Chandler Act version. As before, the firm can choose to file for liquidation under Chapter 7 or for reorganization under Chapter 11. According to Chapter 7, the bankruptcy court appoints a trustee who shuts down the firm, sells its assets and turns the proceeds over to the court for payment to creditors. According to Chapter 11, by contrast, the existing managers of the firm usually remain in control and the firm continues to operate. During the first six months after the bankruptcy filing (and length extensions are often granted), only a plan proposed by management can be adopted. More importantly, firms reorganizing under Chapter 11 have the right to terminate underfunded pension plans, and the government picks up the uncovered pension costs. Also, their obligation to pay interest to pre-bankruptcy creditors ceases.

The trouble is that there is no counterpart at international level to this unconditional tax relief of domestic Chapter 11. This observation leads me to the Special Drawing Right (SDR) as a crucial device for the international Chapter 11, because the allocation of SDR is unconditional. SDR was created in the 1968 Rio de Janeiro agreement as a form of international liquidity to supplement a nation's official reserve holdings of gold, dollars and IMF quotas. Later, the IMF stipulated SDR as the principal reserve asset. It is not backed by any specific reserve held by an issuing authority, but only by the mutual commitment and confidence of IMF member countries. In this respect, SDR represents the first triumph of 'world money' –the denaturalization of the medium of exchange in human societies.

In order to understand the nature of SDR better let us trace the history of the idea and practice of 'world money' and a 'world central bank'. Keynes required his 'clearing union' to operate on the basis of a world money which he named Bancor. It was not in conflict with Keynes's concern for national economic sovereignty. Why this is the case is illustrated by the design of his clearing union. Each country would denominate its national currency in terms of the international clearing union's unit of account (that is, Bancor), which could be expressed in terms of gold. Gold would only be convertible into Bancor in one direction, however – a national central bank could increase the balance on its account with the international clearing union by selling gold, but it could not reverse the process. This made Bancor the ultimate reserve asset in the world. Then Keynes gave each country a quota (equal to half of the average sum of the country's exports and imports over the previous five years) and allowed countries overdrafts against this quota. This overdraft facility, in contrast to the subsequent IMF conditionality (which was not in the original Articles of Agreement in 1944), leaves a large space for national economic experimentation.

In national contexts, the clearing house was historically the prototype of the central bank. In fact, today's IMF already possesses some limited functions of a world central bank. First, the IMF can create international money in two ways: its lending operations at the initiative of a borrowing country can in turn create a 'reserve position' for the country whose currency has been drawn; this reserve position can then be drawn by that country; and it can issue new SDRs.

Second, the IMF can perform the lender-of-last-resort function when it waives the quota for a particular country in extreme balance of payments trouble. However, the potential of the IMF as a world central bank (based on SDR as a major international reserve asset) has not been realized fully. Instead, this potential has been blocked by the developed countries. Since 1970, SDR has been issued only twice. As mentioned earlier, the developed countries have more resources (such as the EMS and eurodollar markets) to maintain equilibrium in the balance of payments. They are not desperately in need of SDR as an international reserve and as international liquidity. But for most developing countries, SDR represents the hope of an international reserve and of international liquidity, because it is much better than other sources of international financing.

Theoretically SDR is better than gold or dollars as an international reserve asset. This can be seen as an implication of the 'Triffin Dilemma': keeping the US dollar as the global liquidity device required continuous US balance of payments deficits, but the long-term stability of the dollar depended on America's ability to return to surplus. A corollary of the 'Triffin Dilemma' is that when the dollar is backed by gold the growing worldwide dollar holdings mean that the ratio of US gold reserves to US external liabilities is declining. Also, when any particular country's currency is used as an international reserve that country's domestic policy will unduly influence the fate of other countries.

This is part of the reason for the debt crisis of the Third World. Therefore, in order to lay secure foundations for an international Chapter 11, the necessity of which was implied by Jeffrey Sachs's criticism of the IMF, we must use SDR as a crucial device of international liquidity and international reserve. In a recent speech, Michel Camdessus, the outgoing Managing Director of the IMF, argued strongly for a new allocation of SDR.[11] He asked only, however, for a 'voluntary' reallocation of SDR from developed to developing countries. It is the belief of this author that we must go further, so as to make SDR a vital component of the international monetary system, especially in the creation of an international Chapter 11.

Notes

I thank Roberto Unger for many useful discussions, although we reach different conclusions from the same premise.

1 Tocqueville, A. de (1835) *Democracy in America*, Anchor Books edition, New York, 1969.
2 Treiman, I. (1938) 'Acts of Bankruptcy: a Medieval Concept in Modern Bankruptcy', *Harvard Law Review*, Vol. 2, No. 2.
3 Sachs, J. (1994: 40) 'Russia's Struggle with Stabilization: Conceptual Issues and Evidence', working paper, April.
4 Stiglitz, J. and Weiss, A. (1981: 397) 'Credit Rationing in Markets With Imperfect Information', *American Economic Review*, Vol. 71, No. 3.
5 Greenwald, B.C., Stiglitz, J.E. and A. Weiss (1984: 195) 'Information Imperfections in the Capital Markets and Macro-Economic Fluctuations', *American Economic Review*, Vol. 1.
6 Stiglitz, J. (1993: 292) 'Capital Markets and Economic Fluctuations in capitalist economies', *European Economic Review*, Vol. 36.
7 Berk, G. (1990: 141) 'Constituting Corporations and Markets: Railroads in Gilded Age Politics', *Studies in American Political Development*, 4, Yale University Press, New Haven.
8 *Ibid.*, p. 144
9 *Ibid.*, p. 144.
10 Olson, J. (1990: 37) *Saving Capitalism*, Princeton University Press, Princeton.
11 International Monetary Fund Survey, 3 May 1993.

14

The Tobin Tax and the Regulation
Of Capital Movements*

BRUNO JETIN AND SUZANNE DE BRUNHOFF

The instability of the international monetary and financial systems during the 1997–8 financial crisis was a cause for great concern. Neoliberal (free market) economists and Western governments were perplexed by the chain of events. The IMF was severely criticized for the way in which it intervened in those 'emerging'[1] countries which had asked for its help – its analyses were often erroneous and, in the end, it was incapable of lessening the extent, length, or contagiousness of the crisis. This impotence was noted. As a result, above and beyond the usual wishful thinking and calls for a reduction in international instability, a few systemic reforms were mooted.

Amongst these proposals, a place of honour should be given to an idea which James Tobin had first developed during the 1970s – that of a tax on foreign exchange transactions. When Tobin first came up with this line of thought, the dollar was in a state of crisis, and had been since the end of the 1960s. Tobin's objective was to 'throw some sand on the fire of [currency] speculation' in an effort to reduce exchange rate volatility. In and of themselves these ideas were not revolutionary – but, for several reasons, they have taken on a great importance.

Critically, Tobin's ideas involve the major capitalist currencies: the dollar, the euro (as the successor to the deutschmark) and the yen, all of which are linked in a floating rate system. These currencies are at the core of the international foreign exchange market, which is a cornerstone of the international capital market. Hence, a reduction in exchange rate volatility is first and foremost of interest to the industrialized capitalist states and regions, which issue dollars, euros, and yens. Unlike local measures such as the foreign exchange controls which 'emerging' nations can impose, the Tobin tax has a universal calling – as such, it has a non-hierarchical character.

The adoption of the Tobin tax would be an important political act, a break both with the neoliberal practices that accompany economic globalization,

* Translated from French by Transalver.

and with the fatalism which goes along with them. This idea assumes that the level of cooperation that exists between the nations of the world goes well beyond the narrow framework of G3 or G7 summit meetings. The Tobin tax implies that all governments would have to act within their own financial spheres so as to help control the short-term movement of capital. This would ease the pressure on emerging countries, whose own currencies depend on the major currencies. Moreover, there would be an easing in the level of commercial and financial competition between the industrialized capitalist countries, as such conflicts often include disagreements over current exchange rates.

In general, most governments have adopted a policy of benign neglect towards the exchange rates of the major currencies, abdicating most of their decision-making capacity to the market and, above all, to the United States government, since the dollar is at the apex in the hierarchy of world currencies. Since 1985, however, this *laissez-faire* attitude has been accompanied increasingly closely by crisis (for example, in Japan, a country that has been forced to sell or buy dollars periodically on a massive scale to support or weaken the yen). In addition, the Bundesbank's discount rate policy has been increasingly independent from that of the US Federal Reserve Bank. The advent of the euro in 1999, replacing the deutschmark in its role as a key currency, cannot but increase the tensions born of the current rivalry between the world's major currencies.

Promoting the Tobin tax would lead to greater stability, as it would increase the level of cooperation between the powerful countries or regions which issue the world's major currencies. Taxing foreign exchange trading so as to reduce the role of speculators would also be a clear political warning to the various actors on the world's economic stage. Deregulation and restructuring have been at work since the 1970s and have contributed everywhere to an imbalance of power and the abetting of capitalist forces to the detriment of the forces of labour. In the areas of salaries, jobs, social benefits or taxation, the pressure on employees has been rising continuously in an attempt to achieve the increased company profits which shareholders have been demanding. This pressure has been presented as if it were inevitable, an unstoppable force which everyone must accept. Taxing currency speculation would have an important symbolic impact, as it would create a breach in this wall of fatalism, which is so detrimental to the forces of labour.

We shall be undertaking a further analysis of the Tobin tax and rebutting the usual criticisms of this idea by so-called experts. First, however, it would be useful to recount briefly a few other reforms which have been proposed in recent times. Some of these don't mention the Tobin tax and others reject it explicitly. We are not claiming that the Tobin tax is a panacea. It doesn't involve any reform of the international monetary system, nor a tax on all financial trading. On these questions, and on many others, necessity, political will and public opinion will lead the way to new avenues for discussion and action. Still, the Tobin tax implies greater control over short-term capital movements and as this can serve to reduce the instability of the international monetary and financial systems, it is a necessary measure – albeit an incomplete one. The currency market cannot be stabilized unless the financial speculators who destabilize it are confronted politically.

A few of the reforms which have been proposed purport to improve the management of public and private financial institutions: increased transparency in dealings by banks and by the IMF; supervision of banks' balance sheets to bring them into line with their Cooke ratios;[2] and other measures of this ilk. Everyone agrees with these steps – but they have brought about few real changes.

Other proposals have been more innovative. There is the example of the neoliberal J. Sachs, who envisages the creation of an international organization other than the IMF. This new institution would be expected to issue liquidities so as to help countries affected by sudden financial panics such as those which devastated Asian currencies in 1997. One objection to this idea involves the issue of which currency would be used in these interventions, given that there is no officially acknowledged international money of reference.

Several economists have criticized the IMF, which was acting in accordance with its neoliberal orientation for having pressured 'emerging' countries into opening up their capital accounts. Some consider this to be premature, while others deem the very principle to be questionable since the countries involved become exposed to an inflow and outflow of foreign capital over which they have no control. On this point, it is essential to reform the methods which the IMF uses to lend funds.

There have been many declarations in favour of a reform of the IMF, including one that was made in an official French document[3] that discussed the issue of international financial stability. This paper envisaged the establishment of a new 'Bretton Woods', that is, a new agreement covering international monetary cooperation. It did not advocate the adoption of a new exchange rate system, nor did it seek a shake-up of the current international hierarchy, which is based on the domination of a few key currencies. Rather, the statement described how the IMF, itself born of the 1944 Bretton Woods agreements, could be changed. It called for the creation of a 'veritable governmental policy for the IMF, to be achieved through a transformation of the Council's current interim committee'. The current interim committee has 24 members, all of whom are at least finance ministers or central bank governors. It meets twice per year to study the IMF's main orientations. The industrialized capitalist nations dominate its proceedings.

The type of reform which the French paper proposes does not constitute any real break with the current situation, involving, as it does, the domination of the global monetary system by the major capitalist powers. In fact, the document doesn't even indicate the areas in which the new IMF would intervene. It simply repeats the habitual exhortations for a wider and more transparent dissemination of information, as well as for the implementation of measures leading to greater cooperation between the public and the private sectors – but only once a financial crisis has actually broken out.

The validity of these official French proposals is particularly compromised by the fact that the Tobin tax had been explicitly rejected in a preceding policy paper which had not seen fit to accord this measure any real analysis. It is true that, since December 1998, French and German finance ministers have been calling for lesser volatility in the euro–dollar exchange rate through the creation of a band of tolerance, beyond which monetary authorities would intervene. The Japanese government was also very interested by this proposal, for it too has been seeking to create a yen zone – despite the opposition of the United States. In any event, if it is politically necessary to restrict the free circulation of capital before one can implement a reform which effectively lessens monetary and financial instability, a stopgap measure of the type included in this French proposal does not amount to a credible alternative to the Tobin tax.

Objective, Usefulness and Limitations

Exchange rates are subject to the double influence of the productive and the financial economies. It is difficult to assess the weighting of each of these, nor can one identify readily the way in which the productive economy affects the financial economy, or vice versa – especially since the process of globalization has made all of these interactions even more complex. As a result, economists are forever debating these issues.[4] Nevertheless, most people acknowledge that financial activity can sometimes provoke excessive currency volatility, fluctuations that have no direct or immediate connection with the realities of the productive economy.

According to its author,[5] the aim of the Tobin tax is to fight against excessive exchange rate volatility. In the current floating rate system, prices move all the time. Now, it is true that minor fluctuations in a rate of exchange do not, as such, pose any major problems to companies. On the other hand, if there is a discontinuous jump in an exchange rate, and if the magnitude of its move is great,[6] companies may have to postpone or even cancel their investment programmes. For instance, building a factory, or exporting, are decisions which require a certain long-term commitment; it is difficult to resell or close a factory without damaging a company's profits –

and managers who are under pressure to satisfy their shareholders' ever increasing demands are loathe to suffer losses of this type.[7]

When seen in this perspective, exchange rate volatility engenders the spectre of reduced profitability, thereby causing a drop in productive investment, and thus lower economic growth. In addition, it can cause governments to formulate economic policies which are more concerned with the way in which the financial markets are going to react than with the issues of growth and full employment. At the same time, some governments, particularly in Europe, have decided to grant independence to their central banks. These are institutions which are so obsessed by their fear of inflation that they fail to notice the threat of deflation, and in the name of protecting their currency on the domestic and external fronts, refuse to lower interest rates.[8]

It is estimated, these days, that 80 per cent of all transactions on the currency markets will be unravelled within a week or less. Day traders have a decision-making horizon of a few hours. In this environment, the Tobin tax would have immediate impact. It would reduce the profits which speculators are hoping to make out of the currency markets. Yet it would not penalize the long-term financial transactions which are a necessary attribute of international trade and overseas productive investment.

The Tobin tax would achieve its purpose through an extremely simple 'filtering' of currency trading. Let's assume that a trader wants to convert francs into dollars. He or she would have to pay, for instance, a tax of 0.1 per cent on this deal. If later the trader were to convert the dollars back into francs, the same tax of 0.1 per cent would again have to be paid. If such 'in and out' trades were undertaken once a day, at the end of the year the trader would have paid up to 48 per cent of the trade's face value in taxes. If such a trade occurred on a weekly basis, the annualized tax receipt would be ten per cent, while if it were to occur once a month, the figure would be 2.4 per cent.[9]

Thanks to this 'filtering' the tax would reinforce the influence exerted by long-term exchange rate expectations, those which guide companies' investment decisions, to the detriment of short-term expectations, which only reflect speculative profit strategies.

Three Additional Benefits

First, national monetary policies would regain part of the autonomy which they have lost in the current situation. The tax would, to a certain extent, free national interest rate policy from the task of defending the country's currency. It would no longer be necessary to implement hikes in the interest rate as a proportion of the desired rise in the currency – and this would make it easier to make monetary policy serve the interests of investment. These findings have been based on the following calculation.[10]

Let's assume that domestic investments have an annual yield of i per cent. The yield required on overseas investments, i^*, depends on the Tobin tax t, and on the duration of investment y, measured by the number of years, or fractions thereof.

Imagine the case of a financial trader who first invests funds overseas and then repatriates the entire investment after a period y. In such circumstances, the trader would be paying taxes twice – both on the way out, and on the way back in. For the overseas investment to be justified it would have to yield at least as much as a domestic investment – and we can therefore calculate its breakeven point:

$$(1 + i^*y)\ (1{-}t) - t = 1 + iy$$

We can rearrange this equation so as to express i* :

$$i^* = \frac{iy + 2t}{y(1 - t)}$$

$$i^* = \frac{i + \frac{2t}{y}}{1 - t}$$

Let's assume now that the interest income is repatriated whilst the principal remains overseas. The trader would still have to pay the tax twice. In order for the overseas yield at least to match the domestic yield, the following equation would have to hold:

$$i^* y(1 - t) - t = iy$$

Or: $$i^* = \frac{iy + t}{y(1 - t)}$$

Or again:
$$i^* = \frac{i + \frac{t}{y}}{1 - t}$$

This final equation clearly shows that the Tobin tax will above all affect short-term trades. Let's take a situation in which the domestic yield is 10 per cent, and the Tobin tax rate is a very low 0.1 per cent per annum. On a twelve-month investment, the overseas yield i^* must at least be equal to 10.1 per cent so as to match the domestic yield. If the trade has a one-month horizon (1/12th of a year), i^* would have to exceed a yearly rate of 11.3 per cent; 15.35 per cent for a one-week trade; or 46.5 per cent for a one-day trade.[11]

Thus, the tax allows for an interest differential of 1.3 per cent over a one-month period; 5.35 per cent over a one-week period; and 36.5 per cent for a day trade.

The second benefit of the Tobin tax, one which the author himself often evokes, is rather limited in scope as it only has short-term effects and is closely tied to the tax rate itself. If the Tobin tax rate is too high, it would engender tax evasion. Most of the economists who are in favour of the Tobin tax propose a range of 0.1 per cent to 0.25per cent, as they feel that these rates are suited to the levels of commission currently being paid on foreign exchange transactions. With such a low rate, potential tax revenues are reduced; but the stabilizing effect on the exchange rate remains whole.[12]

Thirdly, the tax revenues would make it possible to fund the fight against domestic poverty, as well as to subsidize global projects of mutual interest. This latter benefit of the Tobin tax, which Tobin himself only sees as a by-product of the idea and not its main justification, is nevertheless of great significance. The magnitude of the tax revenues at stake would be difficult to estimate, since the tax would lead to a reduction in the volume of specula-tive trading.

J. Frankel offers the following calculation:[13] in 1995, on the London and New York currency markets, the ratio between the total volume of trading compared to the volume of trading involving at least one non-financial agent was five to one.[14] Now, in a somewhat extreme scenario, this ratio could fall to two to one, representing a drop of 60 per cent in annual trading volumes. As in 1995 the daily volumes on the global currency markets reached US$1230 billion,[15] an annual volume of US$295.2 trillion (over 240 working days), a drop of 60 per cent would mean a new annual volume of US$118.1 trillion. A Tobin tax rate of 1 per cent would create additional tax revenues of US$1.118 trillion. A Tobin tax rate of 0.1 per cent, the most commonly proposed level, would bring in US$118.1 billion.

In April 1998 daily volumes on the global currency markets reached US$1587 billion,[16] that is, an annual volume of US$380.9 trillion. By doing the previous calculation, and using a Tobin rate of 0.1 per cent, tax revenues could reach US$152.4 billion.

Limitations

There are two clear limitations to the Tobin tax: first, it does not stop major speculative attacks on a given currency. And second, it does not solve the problems caused by the disappearance of the previous international monetary system, and by the fact that it has not yet been replaced.

The Tobin tax only represents a 'few grains of sand thrown on the roaring fire of international finance'.[17]

The two limitations noted above intimate that the Tobin tax must be supplemented by other measures aimed at reducing the power of the international financial markets – and that these markets must again be placed under the tutelage of political authorities with the responsibility of defining national economic policies.

All the same, the Tobin tax, in and of itself, can greatly enhance the supervision of financial markets. We shall defend this point of view whilst analyzing the common objections to the Tobin tax. These objections can be divided into two categories. First, there are fundamental objections which attack the tax's very existence. Will this tax paralyze the currency markets to the extent that they are no longer able to function? Second, there are objections concerning the tax's feasibility.

Fundamental Objections

The currency markets fulfil an essential function in the global economic system. They facilitate international transactions (overseas trading, direct foreign investment, portfolio investment) by making it possible to convert units of money. They enable the transmission and dissemination of risk between those who wish to protect themselves against the consequences of exchange risk, and those who assume this risk in the hope of making money out of it.

These two functions are closely related. Since exchange rates are continuously changing, it is impossible to complete an international transaction without taking on some currency risk. Given the conditions under which economies function at present, it is impossible to imagine the end of speculators – if this were to occur, there would be no other economic agent ready to accept the risks which everyone else refuses to take. Speculation is an integral part of markets – without it, they can neither exist nor function. Does this mean that the Tobin tax should be rejected, in that it may penalize indiscriminately both the speculative trading which is indispensable if commercial transactions are to take place, and 'purely' speculative dealings? For the reasons discussed below, we are not of this opinion.

Excessive trading volumes on the currency markets

Trading volumes on the currency markets are 60 times higher than the level required for international commerce to take place.[18] This was not the case in the 1970s when the financial markets were more strictly regulated than they are now. We can reasonably estimate that the Tobin tax, even though it would cause a substantial drop in trading volumes,[19] would allow a sufficient volume of financial trading to continue – enough, in any event, to enable speculators to offset the risks which are caused by international commerce and by direct foreign investment. Still, those who criticize the Tobin tax will object that any hindrance to the free circulation of capital reduces market liquidity and increases exchange rate volatility – the exact opposite of what the tax seeks to obtain.

This criticism is based on the supposedly obvious link between market liquidity and market stability. Yet this link has never been proven – far from it. Empirical investigations do not confirm the existence of any correlation between an increase in market volumes and an increase in market stability.[20] Over the last two decades, it has even been possible to observe a parallel increase in the volumes traded on the currency markets and a rise in foreign exchange instability.

Above and beyond this absence of empirical proof, the arguments in favour of unfettered market liquidity, as a supposed guarantee of exchange rate stability, are also empirically weak.

Speculation and stabilization

Starting with Milton Friedman and the monetarists, and continuing with the School of Rational Expectations, many people's view of the financial markets has been dominated by the idea that speculation is a factor of stabilization. Financial markets supposedly function like Walrasian markets. Speculators determine equilibrium prices. They sell when the existing price is higher than the equilibrium price, and by so doing, they precipitate the return to equilibrium. Conversely, they buy when the existing price is lower than the equilibrium price. In this conception, there is little difference between speculation and arbitrage – and both participate in the convergence of financial markets towards a state of stability.

Years later, monetarist theory has been completely contradicted by the facts. The advent of a floating rate system in the early 1970s has had a magnifying effect. Speculative bubbles have been created in the currency markets, yet this exchange rate volatility has not even come close to rebalancing the endemic current account deficits of some nations, nor has it made it possible for their economic policies to become more autonomous.

From a theoretical point of view, the idea that speculation is always a factor of stability is tantamount to an act of faith. One must believe that an equilibrium exchange rate exists, that speculators know what it is, and that their actions are always taken in reference to it, thus spurring the return of prices to their one, single equilibrium. The hypotheses which make it possible to demonstrate the existence, uniqueness, and stability of an equilibrium price are so radical, however, as to be hardly credible. If there were a multiplicity of equilibrium prices, speculative attacks against exchange rates could be successfully unleashed, even in the absence of the macroeconomic imbalances to which speculators are supposedly so sensitive.[21] As for inflation and the level of interest rates, two other factors of which speculators are also supposed to be aware, we should note the example of the French franc, which in 1993 was not even close to being overvalued with respect to the deutschmark, and yet became the object of a speculative attack which led to an abandonment of the franc's margin of fluctuation of 2.25 per cent against the ecu.

Thus speculation is not always a factor of stability, and should not be given the role of controlling exchange rate management. As Keynes noted, the currency markets will alternate periods of stability and instability. Using a Keynesian approach to finance, we would say that periods of stability can be explained by the existence of a convention, that is, an average point of view, the opinion of the majority of traders, concerning the state of the economy at some future date.[22] This convention serves as a benchmark, and it creates a stable environment, a state of confidence, allowing traders to decrypt the information that they receive on a regular basis. Decoding new bits of information, traders develop their own expectations of short-term exchange rates through the use of probability calculations.[23] These short-term expectations are heterogeneous, and they lead to temporary fluctuations in the exchange rate. Arbitragists with open positions, for example, speculate by betting on a weak currency whose future price is in a state of backwardation, unlike speculators who are seeking capital gains by betting on a strong currency which is usually in contango.[24] These two types of operations have inverse effects on the currency market – they offset one another partially, and cause short-term fluctuations, which are compatible with the existence of a convention – as long as the volatility is temporary and non-systematic. In sum, these periods of stability are characterized by the fact that the elasticity of expectations is less than one,[25] meaning that a rise in the exchange rate at any one time does not lead to the expectation of a higher rate over the long term.[26]

In this Keynesian vision, periods of instability prevail in the currency markets when traders start to lose their trust in the conventions which govern long-term expectations. During these periods of a crisis in confidence, the traders who remain active in the markets have no other choice but to imitate one another. The generalization of this imitative behaviour creates a herd mentality that facilitates the creation of speculative bubbles, be it on strengthening or on weakening currencies, at a time when the currency markets are in a state of uproar. A drop in the current exchange rate can provoke an expectation of a greater drop in the future exchange rate. The ambient instability stems from the fact that the drop in the current exchange rate leads to a drop in current demand, as a result of the expected drop in the currency's future exchange rate. The lower current demand ensures that these expectations become self-fulfilling. In such circumstances, the elasticity of expectations is greater than one.

According to P. Arestis and M. Sawyer,[27] the main use of the Tobin tax would be to intervene upstream from the markets – that is, before a speculative bubble is created. A rise in the current exchange rate above its normal value would not lead traders to expect a further rise, since the cost of the tax would discourage them from buying enough of this rising currency to magnify its strength. It would therefore be easier for the monetary authorities to intervene and to maintain exchange rate stability; and, in the end, the volume of transactions to be taxed would not be enormous. The Tobin tax would make a positive contribution to the stabilization of exchange rates by acting as an 'uncertainty reducing institution' through the influence which it would exert in the creation of expectations. Thanks to the tax, the elasticity of expectations would remain less than one.

The empirical investigations undertaken by J. Frankel in 1996 go along with this analysis.[28] His findings show that exchange rate expectations with a maturity of less than three months are by nature extrapolative, and that they only become adaptive, regressive, or based on a notion of mean reversion after this three-month mark. Thus, an increase over one week of 1 per cent in the spot exchange rate would lead traders to expect an additional increase of 0.13 per cent the following week.

As a result, the Tobin tax, by its disproportionate impact on short-term transactions, would contribute to a reinforcement of those long-term expectations which by nature create greater stability, based as they are on convention, and on the fundamental variables of macroeconomics. Traders would have to take the Tobin tax into account, and include it in their assessments of a situation – that is, in their convention. The tax would make it more difficult for a minor and temporary speculative attack to generate a speculative bubble, which could then be transformed into a major speculative attack. On this point, one can acknowledge the argument employed by P. Arestis and M. Sawyer concerning those periods during which the currency markets function 'normally'.

It may well be, however, that the tax is not sufficiently dissuasive against a speculative attack of the type that can result in a major currency crisis. With a Tobin tax rate set at 0.1 per cent, a position which is taken on a currency only to be taken off within one week would be hit by a tax which is equivalent to an annual interest rate of 10 per cent.

Now, during the periods of a currency crisis, speculators bet on a devaluation of at least 10 per cent, within a period of a few days or at most a few weeks. Complementary measures are therefore necessary to help the Tobin tax in its fight against speculation. A first possibility would be to authorize those countries which have been victimized by a major attack to increase their Tobin tax rate temporarily until it reaches a prohibitive level.[29] Other measures can be envisaged as a complement to the Tobin tax.

Malaysia, for example, adopted a set of strict currency controls in September 1998 in an effort to stave off the flight of capital, and to force companies and financial traders based in Malaysia to repatriate their capital. These measures – aimed at stemming the collapse of the exchange rate without having to raise interest rates to an excessive level, thus worsening the recession – unleashed a barrage of criticism from the international financial community, which removed Malaysia from its list of acceptable countries, whilst hypocritically keeping silent about Taiwan's existing currency controls.[30]

These other measures are often contrasted to the Tobin tax, or described as an alternative to it. They are systematically presented as being relevant for Third World countries – yet no one has ever explained why they could not be used by the wealthy nations. The measures adopted by Latin American countries, such as Chile, are often cited as an example. Many lessons can be learned from these countries' experiences, as long as they are interpreted correctly. In the early 1990s the countries of Latin America were again faced with a massive inflow of foreign capital. Many then pegged their currency to the dollar, at a fixed or a quasi-fixed rate,[31] with the aim of eradicating the hyperinflation from which they were suffering. They committed themselves to a strategy of opening up their commercial and financial markets, and tried to restructure their economies to increase exports.

This excessive inflow of capital caused the currencies of these countries to become overvalued, thereby worsening their trade deficits – and when this deficit reached a critical level, the international financial community would become frightened. A massive withdrawal of capital would follow, causing currency collapse and a major economic crisis.

To counteract this phenomenon, in June 1991 Chile adopted a series of measures aimed at restricting the inflow of capital. Foreign banks which lent to Chilean companies and banks had to make a non-remunerated deposit of one year at the central bank, equal to 30 per cent of the face value of the loan. Compared to the Tobin tax, this measure was especially expensive for those who were investing on a short-term basis. As M. Agosin and R. French-Davis demonstrated in 1996,[32] this system allowed Chile to enjoy a rate of growth that was higher and more stable than Argentina's or Mexico's.[33] Above all, it allowed Chile to avoid the crises from which these other countries have suffered recently.

One particularity of these measures is that a state can impose them unilaterally – a definite advantage with respect to the Tobin tax. This does not necessarily mean, however, that these steps comprise an alternative to the Tobin tax – rather, they could be used to complement it. The Tobin tax applies to all foreign exchange trading, to both capital inflows and outflows, whilst the Chilean system only covers inflows. The Tobin tax rate is much lower than the explicit and implicit rates which were applied by the Latin

American countries.[34] Finally, the tax constitutes a first step towards the reform of the international monetary system, whilst the Chilean system is a set of defensive measures which does not help to solve the fundamental problem of exchange rate instability. Moreover, it concerns an emerging country, one that is dominated by the major capitalist nations, who are continuing to define the rules of international economics in a festival of self-interest.

As long as the dollar continues to dominate all the other currencies, together with its rivals the yen and the euro, a floating rate system will continue to engender exchange rate instability. We are not going to delve into this at the present point, however, as it is an issue that goes far beyond the present chapter, which is devoted to the Tobin tax.

Is the Tobin Tax Feasible?

We may be convinced of the Tobin tax's usefulness, but the question remains as to whether it can actually be implemented. We will explore the two aspects of this question: the tax's political and economic feasibility.

With the rise in power of the neoliberal ideology throughout the world, it is clear that, unlike the 1960s and 1970s when governments considered it legitimate to regulate markets, the present era is not very favourable to the taxation of financial transactions. Yet, the financial markets are already subject to certain taxes, even though most people don't realize it.[35] S. Griffith Jones[36] gives the example of the City of London, where stamp duties on deals involving financial assets brought in tax revenues of £830 million in 1993 (about US$1300 million).[37] She adds that the British tax authorities have also demonstrated their ability to counteract fiscal evasion by adapting the conditions in which they apply their tax policies.

In addition, we can hope that the financial crisis, which started in South East Asia in July 1997 after the Mexican crisis of 1994–5, will cause people to modify their attitudes towards this topic, and to be more objective when analyzing the usefulness of a reregulation of the financial markets – a policy of which the Tobin tax could be a component.

Finally, political feasibility seems less problematic once an analysis of the tax's economic feasibility, and of the issues that it raises, has been conducted. The first objection concerning the economic feasibility of the Tobin tax is that it supposedly cannot be implemented unless every country adopts it simultaneously. According to this viewpoint, financial capital's great mobility would cause a massive inflow of capital towards those countries that did not adopt the tax. Even worse, it would make sense for certain countries not to adopt the tax in order to attract the lion's share of those capital flows, which are specifically undertaken in an attempt to avoid taxation.

P. Kennen has come up with an appropriate rebuttal of this objection.[38] Even if it is preferable that all the nations of the world adopt the Tobin tax, this is not a prerequisite for its implementation[39] – although the tax would have to be accepted by all of the world's major financial centres. This list includes the G7 countries, all other European Union countries that are not members of the G7,[40] plus Singapore, Switzerland, Hong Kong and Australia. The political problems would indeed be considerable, but it would be unduly pessimistic to believe that tax havens such as the Bahamas or the Cayman Islands could hold off the Tobin tax all by themselves. As Tobin himself has commented (1996), if these tax havens are all that attractive, why is it that the international financial community has not already massively migrated towards them, given the taxes which are already being levied in the main financial centres?

The question still remains whether the Tobin tax would be the last straw – that is, the measure that finally provokes a massive flight of capital. There are at least two arguments, however, which counteract this concern. First, as P. Kennen notes, the currency markets currently function in such a way as to distinguish between the site where the order is given to buy or sell a currency (the trading site), the place where the deal is booked (the booking site), and the place where the transaction actually occurs (the settlement site). If currency trades are taxed at their trading site rather than at their booking site,[41] then the fixed costs which would result from a displacement of trading rooms[42] would discourage traders from trying to escape the Tobin tax by migrating towards countries which refuse to apply it. It is only when the banks are planning the renovation of a trading room, or the building of a new one, that they will want to consider the alternative of getting themselves established in a tax haven.

Second, to staunch the phenomenon of progressive migration, P. Kennen suggests that a punitive tax[43] be levied on any transaction involving a country that refuses to apply the Tobin tax. The only deals that would escape this type of tax would be those between two tax havens. A very large number of banks and other financial agents would have to decide to migrate before it would become worthwhile to eschew the advantages of the main financial centres (their great liquidity and economies of scales). Unless everyone migrated at once, the first institutions to move their operations to these tax havens would have to pay a very high price.

A second objection involves the possibility that certain players could escape the Tobin tax by substituting derivative products for spot foreign exchange trading. The answer to this is that, in principle, the tax should be extended to all derivative trading. For instance, a three-day forward contract is a close relative of a two-day spot deal. For this reason, the tax would have to be levied on forward transactions as well.[44]

A forex swap[45] is also a close relative of a spot deal. Banks usually use these trades for their limited risk interest rate arbitrage plays, or to cover their currency positions. As such, forex swaps are very sensitive to transactional costs, and P. Kennen suggests that they be construed as one and the same transaction, and therefore taxed just the once. On the other hand, since the purchase and the resale of a futures contract follows the same logic as a sale and resale in the spot market, a currency future could be taxed both on the way in and on the way out.[46] The tax would cover the notional value of the contract, and would be collected by the clearing centre.

The situation with currency options is somewhat more complex.[47] There is no justification for not taxing them, since they are a close relative of a futures contract, yet their taxation creates certain problems. The first one has to do with the fact that a large percentage of options are dealt over the counter and this would make it difficult to collect the Tobin tax. The second problem has to do with the fact that some options are never exercised. This could make it all the more delicate to justify levying the full tax rate on the option's face value.

Finally, other problems arise concerning the level of tax receipts, depending on whether the market is dominated by economic agents who are seeking to cover themselves against a real exchange risk, or by speculators who are trying to profit from market volatility. A company that needs a certain quantity of yen in three months to settle an invoice might buy either a forward contract, futures, or a currency option. If the Tobin tax were only to be levied on forward contracts, the company would choose futures or call options. This would reduce the volumes traded on the forward markets and the taxes which could be collected on them. Still, if the firm really needs yen three months down the track, it will buy yen anyway – albeit at the rate and on the future or the option's maturity. Hence, a spot trade will take place and will be taxed, thereby compensating the loss of fiscal revenues from the forward markets.

Nonetheless, if the firm is simply seeking to speculate on a rise in the yen, having no real need of this currency, and if the yen does not rise, the company will abandon its option (not exercise it). In this case, the loss of tax revenues from the forwards or futures markets will not be compensated. If one of the main goals of the Tobin tax is to increase fiscal revenues, a solution to the taxation of currency options has to be found. However, if the goal is simply to stabilize exchange rates, the fact that the option has not been exercised is not a problem as such, since the priority is to levy taxation on currency deals.[48]

P. Garber raises a final issue, one which involves the effects of substitution.[49] Treasury bills of the same maturity can be exchanged instead of currencies. These securities are then sold immediately. This type of substitution is not without risk, since different markets do not share the same level of liquidity. Each party must purchase Treasury bills, exchange them, and then sell them – and each transaction carries with it frictional costs. Since these deals would not be perfectly synchronized, the two parties could be exposed to interest rate risks in two separate countries. This risk could be covered if the two banks agreed to repurchase the securities at the market price just before the swap took place. The authorities could argue in this situation, however, that the real objective of the swap was to avoid paying the Tobin tax. People would dream up increasingly complex and opaque derivative products, but by doing so, they would be running the risk of illiquidity. As J. Tobin and P. Kennen note, it is hard to imagine that the banks would consider it worthwhile to go through all these steps just to avoid a small tax on the spot foreign exchange market!

We can add to this that any tax generates some evasive behaviour with some economic agents (though not with all) who do not want to pay. Yet no one has ever seriously advocated the abolition of income tax simply because of the existence of a certain amount of tax evasion. In addition, we know that a lower tax rate does not lead to an increase in tax receipts – this has been demonstrated by certain economists' unsuccessful attempts at empirically substantiating the Laffer curve. So why should we demand that there be zero tax evasion before we deem the Tobin tax to be legitimate?

Conclusion

We can now summarize the main arguments made in this chapter concerning the usefulness and the limitations of adopting a measure such as the Tobin tax within a framework of reforms aimed at reducing a level of financial instability which has become unacceptable. First of all, this is a tax, proposing a type of relationship between the public and private sector that leaves no room for collusion between these two spheres. Moreover, it is a preventative measure aimed at stemming currency crises before they break out. Most other reforms involve an *ex post facto* crisis management – they try to save market systems that have failed. Markets and traders have been rescued too many times in the past. One example was the intervention of the US Federal Bank in September 1998, when it lowered its discount rate three times to shore up Wall Street. All the while, it was putting pressure on the large international banks, creditors of the big US hedge funds, which were considered 'too big to fail'. Neoliberals tolerated these measures – and yet they consider the Tobin tax to be intolerable, because of the control over short-term capital movements which it would introduce.[50]

Second, the Tobin tax is a cooperative measure which is universal in nature – and yet, at the same time, each country would be responsible for its implementation. It would not be run by a council dominated by the countries that issue the world's main currencies. All units of money, from King Dollar to the dependent currencies, are concerned. This would also have the benefit of dissuading countries that feel they have been given a raw deal from resorting to nationalism. Moreover, reducing the competition between the key currencies is one of the main issues which a reform seeking to stabilize international financial relationships has to address.

Third, the Tobin tax designates those who are responsible for the instability of the international financial system – the major players of the world's currency markets. The aforementioned argument, wherein speculation is deemed to be a factor of stability, does not explain the dynamics of financial behaviour, nor does it account for its internal logic. By criticizing this logic, the Tobin tax is an attack on the current political consensus, with its neo-liberal characteristics, and it is a counter-attack against the idea that the free circulation of capital is advantageous because of the standards of profitability which it imposes.

This is not to say that the Tobin tax is a panacea against financial deregulation, which itself is an intrinsic part of the capitalist mode of accumulation. It is important to study this tax, however, and to analyze the way in which it has been attacked, as these criticisms in and of themselves express a political conflict. Hence the priority given in this chapter to a discussion of the political dimension of the debate over the Tobin tax.

Since late 1997, a number of ideas have been mooted involving a new regulation of the global monetary and financial systems – yet they have all been nothing more than a symptom of the excesses of a capitalist financial system which has been sanctioned by its recent crisis. Economists have started to discuss seriously the idea of taxing currency trading. This concept has gained popularity, especially in Europe, because of its aim, which is to establish control over short-term capital movements. An ever-growing number of people are in favour of financially punishing the speculators whose actions in the markets were behind the 1997–8 financial crises. Public opinion wants to prevent further speculative bubbles and crashes. This is important, especially if one feels that political reforms should not only be the affair of financial specialists, or even of governments alone, but that they should be debated and approved by the people who will be affected by them.

Notes

1 The 'emerging' nations, in today's economic and financial literature, are those newly capitalist countries which are participating in the international financial markets. For the last few
years, the *Economist* has been giving a list of these nations, including Portugal (despite the
fact that it is part of Western Europe), Russia and the Czech Republic. South Korea and
Mexico are also included, even though they are already members of the OECD.

2   This denotes a proposal made in 1988 by the Cooke Committee to the Bank of International Settlements. It is an attempt to determine the optimum ratio between a bank's capital and its assets. The goal is to reduce systemic credit risks.

3   An annex to the 1999 French draft legislation entitled 'Towards a New Architecture for the Global Monetary and Financial Systems'.

4   On this topic, see F. Chesnais (1994), the volume edited by F. Chesnais (1996) – especially S. de Brunhoff's contribution – and the 1997 'Proclamation of Economists Against Unitary Thinking'.

5   See J. Tobin's interview with *Le Monde*, 17 November 1998.

6   The term 'volatility' is used here to designate the excessive fluctuation of the rates of foreign exchange.

7   Such is the attitude of the Confederation of British Industry (CBI), which has expressed its wish that the UK quickly adopt the euro so that British companies are not placed in a position of competitive disadvantage in case the pound strengthens. Japanese companies, such as Toyota and Nissan, who have used their British factories as a platform from which they export to the rest of Europe, have publicly threatened to postpone their investment programmes and to reconsider their presence in the UK if the English government does not declare its support for a rapid entry into the euro zone.

8   The 'franc fort' (strong franc) policy which France followed throughout the 1980s is an example of this attitude. The policy was supposed to restore the competitiveness of French business, and then lead to a drop in joblessness. It was successful on the first point – but not yet on the second. Will the 'strong franc' mutate into a 'strong euro'?

9   Tobin J. (1996: xi), Prologue. In ul Haq, M., Kaul, I. and I. Grunberg eds, *The Tobin Tax. Coping with Financial Volatility*, Oxford University Press, Oxford and New York.

10 Frankel, J. (1996: 57–58) 'How Well Do Markets Work? Might a Tobin Tax Help?", in ul Haq, M., Kaul, I. and I. Grunberg eds.

11 Frankel, J. (1996: 58) implicitly calculates on the basis of a 360-day year. If we were to use the more plausible hypothesis of 240 working days in the year, i^* becomes 34.5per cent.

12 Frankel, J. (1996) has put together a small model which allows him to reach the following conclusions: with a tax of 0.001 per cent, a one-year investment in a foreign asset would have to yield at least 10.1 per cent to be preferred to an investment in a domestic asset which yields 10 per cent. For a one day trade, however, the overseas asset would have to yield 46.5 per cent to remain attractive. This cannot but discourage the vast majority of speculators – even the most audacious.

13 Frankel, J. (1996: 62).

14 In April 1998 the foreign exchange markets located in Great Britain and in the United States represented 50 per cent of all worldwide currency trading, against 46 per cent in April 1995 (BIS, 1998: 8).

15 This figure includes spot deals, forwards and FX swaps as well as other currency derivatives (currency swaps, options, and miscellaneous.) These are net figures, which have swapped out double accounting (BIS, 1998).

16 US$1490 billion for the traditional instruments and US$97 billion on derivative currency products (BIS, 1998).

17 Tobin, J., (1978: 153–9) 'A Proposal for International Monetary Reform', *The Eastern Economic Journal* Vol. 4, Nos 3–4.

18 Arestis, P. and M. Sawyer (1997: 760) 'How Many Cheers for the Tobin Transactions Tax?', *Cambridge Journal of Economics*, No. 2. The authors arrived at this figure by simply comparing the yearly volumes on the global currency markets (300 trillion dollars in 1995) with the volume of international commerce in that year (5 trillion dollars).

19 See the example given on p. 201.

20 ul Haq, M., Kaul, I. and I. Grunberg, eds (1996: 5).

21 Dooley, M. (1996) 'The Tobin Tax: Good Theory, Weak Evidence, Questionable Policy',

and Eichengreen, B., and C. Wyplosz, (1996: 89–91) 'Taxing International Financial Trans-actions to Enhance the Operation of the International Monetary System', in ul Haq, M., Kaul, I. and I. Grunberg, eds.

22 On the notion of convention, see Chapter 12 of Keynes's *General Theory* (1936).

23 According to Keynes, 'if conventions do exist, an investor can legitimately gain some confidence from the idea that he is *not running any other risk* than that of a real change in the information concerning the near future – and he can try to develop his own opinion on *this probability risk*, which, in any event, will not be very large' (1936: 164–5, our italics).

24 Plihon, D. (1991: 38) *Les Taux de change*. Collections 'Repères', La Découverte, Paris. Backwardation is where the future price (the forward price) of a currency is lower than the current price (the spot price) – where it is at a discount. Contango is the opposite situation where the future price (the forward price) of a good, of a commodity, an exchange rate etc. is higher than the current price (the spot price) – where it is at a premium.

25 Hicks, J. (1946: 254–5) *Value and Capital: an Inquiry into Some Fundamental Principles of Economic Theory* (second edition), Oxford University Press, Oxford.

26 Hicks (205) defines the elasticity of an individual's expectations concerning the price of a good X as the ratio between the expected future rise in X's price over the present rise in X's price.

27 Arestis, P., Sawyer, M. (1997: 760).

28 Frankel, J. (1996: 54).

29 Spahn, P.B. (1995) 'International Financial Flows and Transactions Taxes: Survey and Options', International Monetary Fund, Washington, DC.

30 On this point, see the *Economist*, 22–28 August 1998, pp.59–60.

31 Chile was not part of this group, as it had abandoned fixed parities in 1982, following a major economic crisis which had caused its GDP to drop by 15 per cent.

32 Agosin, M. and French-Davis, R. (1996: 181–2) 'Managing Capital Inflows in Latin America', in ul Haq, M., Kaul, I. and I. Grünberg, eds.

33 The reader should also study the example of Colombia, which adopted comparable measures. For a detailed analysis of this country's actions, see Agosin, M., French-Davis, R. (1996: 181–2).

34 *Ibid.*

35 Frankel, J. (1996: 70, appendix B).

36 Griffith Jones, S. (1996:146) 'Institutional Arrangements for a Tobin Tax on International Currency Transactions', in ul Haq, M., Kaul, I. and I. Grunberg, eds.

37 Stamp Duty on Security Transactions.

38 Kennen P. B. (1996) 'The Feasibility of Taxing Foreign Exchange Transactions', in ul Haq, M., Kaul, I. and I. Grunberg, eds.

39 See an interview with J. Tobin in *Le Monde*, 17 November 1998.

40 Tax havens such as Luxembourg, the Channel Islands, and the Isle of Man.

41 For a detailed analysis of the respective advantages and disadvantages of taxing at the trading or the booking site, see P. Kennen, 1996: 112–15.

42 It is very expensive for a bank to run a trading room. Costs include human resources, capital costs, and financial costs such as the capital which serves as trading collateral.

43 P. Kennen (1996) envisages, for example, 500 basis points (5 per cent) instead of 10 or 2.5.

44 A currency forward is a forward deal in which traders commit themselves to buying or selling a certain quantity of a currency, at a given rate and for a fixed maturity. These contracts are traded over the counter against spot deals. D. Plihon, 1991, 20.

45 A forex swap is a financial trade in which two parties commit themselves to an exchange of currencies today, for example, French francs against dollars at the spot rate, and to the exchange of the same currencies at the contract's maturity (3 months, 1 year, etc.) at a forward rate which will be determined now. See also D. Plihon, 1991.

46 Currency futures are forward contracts in which traders commit themselves to buy or sell a

certain amount of currency, at a rate and at a maturity which is established in advance. See also D. Plihon, 1991: 25. Unlike a forward contract, futures are negotiated on a specific market, located at a certain site.

47 A currency option gives its owner, the purchaser of the option, the right but not the obligation to buy (a call option) or to sell (a put option) a given amount of currency at a rate which is determined in advance, the strike price, and at a maturity which is also determined in advance. For this right, the purchaser pays a premium. See also D. Plihon, 1991: 28.

48 On this question, see J. Tobin (1996: xv), in ul Haq, M., Kaul, I. and I. Grunberg, eds.

49 Garber P. (1996) 'Issues of Enforcement and Evasion in a Tax on Foreign Exchange Transactions', in ul Haq, M., Kaul, I. and I. Grunberg, eds.

50 Although the *Financial Times* did criticize the rescue of the hedge fund LTCM as an unwanted collusion between the public and the private sectors.

15

A Feasible Foreign Exchange Transactions Tax

RODNEY SCHMIDT

A tax on foreign exchange transactions was proposed twenty years ago by Nobel laureate James Tobin.[1] Tobin intended it to increase monetary policy independence and reduce nominal exchange rate volatility when capital flows freely across international borders. Recently Tobin's tax has also been promoted to defend exchange rates from speculative attacks, manage transitions between exchange rate regimes, and finance international public projects.[2]

Tobin's tax is thought to be impracticable, however, both by those who object to it as an interference in an efficient market and by those who support it in principle.[3] Some think it impracticable because it would have to be applied globally. For the critics

> enforcement is a big problem. Certainly if some countries adopted the Tobin tax but others did not, the foreign-exchange trading would simply move to where it was not taxed. For this reason, everyone agrees that it would have to be imposed in virtually all countries, large and small. This would require more widespread support than seems possible politically.[4]

Even if Tobin's tax were internationally legislated, for example by making it a condition of membership in the IMF,[5] some think it still impracticable because foreign exchange trades are hard to monitor.[6] The international foreign exchange market is decentralized and does not have a systematic, comprehensive system for recording individual trades. Instead, to regulate private banks and financial institutions and measure capital flows, central banks and supervisory bodies require them to register overnight balance sheet positions. In today's 24-hour global marketplace, however, foreign exchange traders can hide positions by shifting them between branches in different time zones and so always remain within working hours, or they can use derivative financial instruments that do not show on balance sheets.[7] Finally, traders can avoid the foreign exchange market altogether by buying and exchanging securities, such as bonds or treasury bills, denominated in different currencies.[8]

Every foreign exchange trade, however, has to be settled with an exchange of assets – usually bank balances – denominated in different currencies. Compared with the market for trading foreign exchange, the international infrastructure in place to settle foreign exchange trades is increasingly formal, centralized and regulated. Can Tobin's tax be applied to foreign exchange trades as they are settled? The answer depends on whether the settlement infrastructure permits a one-to-one correspondence between foreign exchange payments and their originating trades, and on whether the tax can be applied to payments made offshore and to foreign exchange derivatives.

This paper contends that a transaction tax applied to foreign exchange payments is feasible. The contention is based on an analysis of recently established settlement technology and institutions designed to reduce and eliminate settlement risk. 'Settlement risk' exists when one party to a transaction makes an irrevocable payment of a currency, or delivery of a security denominated in that currency, before his or her counterpart makes the opposing payment to complete the exchange of assets and settle the transaction. The risk is that the counterpart will default on the payment. Settlement risk is eliminated when the two payment obligations are matched and traced to the original foreign exchange trade, and then the two payments are made simultaneously. In exchanges of bank balances, this is known as 'payment-versus-payment' (PVP) settlement; if securities are exchanged, it is known as 'delivery-versus-payment' (DVP) settlement. The technology and enforcement mechanisms that make this possible in various settlement institutions also make Tobin's tax feasible.

Overview of the Argument

We evaluate the feasibility of a tax on foreign exchange payments made to settle interbank foreign exchange transactions. We believe that such a tax is now feasible as a result of the recent formalization and centralization of the international infrastructure for making interbank foreign exchange payments. This organization of the interbank foreign exchange settlement system is due to rising foreign exchange trading volume, new payment processing and communications technology, and coordinated efforts between central and major trading banks to reduce settlement risk.

There are three ways for major trading banks and other financial institutions ('banks') to make interbank foreign exchange payments. One way is for banks to make payments to each other in domestic large-scale payment systems, which are overseen by the central bank that issues the currency being paid. Another way is for banks to cancel mutually offsetting amounts owed among banks in offshore netting systems or securities clearing houses. Finally, banks can use derivative foreign exchange instruments to define the terms of a transaction. If the derivative is of the 'contract for differences' (CFD) variety, it does not require payments of principal to settle the trade, but only of earnings from movements in the exchange rate.

There is no other way for major trading banks to make foreign exchange payments, unless they drop out of the interbank market and into the retail market for foreign exchange. There, settlement procedures are informal and decentralized, and transaction costs are correspondingly higher, so much so that retail banks cannot compete with wholesale banks (those that settle in the interbank market) in foreign exchange trading. A tax on interbank foreign exchange payments is feasible if one can (1) identify gross payments made to settle individual foreign exchange transactions; (2) enforce the tax in offshore payment netting systems; and (3) tax implicit payments underlying foreign exchange derivatives.

Three corresponding features of the current payment or settlement infrastructure in the interbank foreign exchange market satisfy these requirements. *First*, most modern domestic payment systems are Real Time Gross Settlement (RTGS) systems, meaning that they process payments individually. RTGS systems support PVP settlement of domestic financial transactions (where both payments made to settle a transaction are denominated in the domestic currency). That is, domestic payments are matched and traced to the original financial trade, then processed simultaneously.

Domestic payment systems with RTGS capability currently do not support PVP settlement of foreign exchange transactions. This is because settling a foreign exchange trade requires payments to be made in different domestic payment systems, often in different time zones. If the working hours of the two payment systems do not continuously overlap, the payments cannot be matched and processed simultaneously. By mid-2000, however, a central global settlement bank – the Continuous Linked Settlement (CLS) Bank – will open. This bank will operate around the clock throughout the week and, with direct links to numerous domestic payment systems, will support PVP settlement for foreign exchange transactions. In effect, the CLS Bank will be an extension of domestic payment systems.

When the CLS Bank opens, it will support PVP settlement of foreign exchange payments. Then, participating domestic payment systems will be able to directly identify and tax individual foreign exchange payments, by matching them and determining if they are denominated in different currencies. In the meantime, since domestic payment systems already support PVP settlement of domestic financial transactions, if a payment in the domestic currency is not matched with another payment in the domestic currency, it can be treated as a foreign exchange payment and taxed.

Foreign exchange netting systems and securities exchange clearing houses also operate PVP or DVP settlement by netting. Foreign exchange payments or securities submitted for netting are matched and traced to the original trade before netting proceeds for both payments or securities simultaneously. This is needed to maintain the integrity of the netting system since, when payments or securities are accepted for netting, the original foreign exchange obligations between the two parties to the trade are replaced by obligations between each party and the netting system. PVP or DVP netting ensures that the netting system does not take a net creditor, debtor, or open foreign exchange position. Thus, gross foreign exchange payments can be identified and taxed as part of the netting process.

Second, central banks or their supervisory bodies regulate offshore foreign exchange netting systems and enforce those regulations. The same mechanisms can be used to enforce a foreign exchange payments tax offshore. The right of central banks individually and collectively to regulate offshore netting systems was codified in 1990 as the 'Lamfalussy Minimum Standards' by the Bank of International Settlements Committee on Interbank Netting Schemes of the Central Banks of the Group of Ten Countries. This prerogative of central banks was reaffirmed by the same Committee in 1998. The Standards provide for measures to reduce settlement risk and otherwise promote domestic and international financial stability. Central banks enforce the regulations by refusing non-cooperating netting systems access to the domestic payment system, and by sanctioning banks that are members of both the domestic payment system and the offshore netting system. This is effective because offshore netting systems cannot process a currency payment unless they have access to the domestic payment system. Furthermore, banks are not accepted as members of the netting system unless they trade in the interbank market for foreign exchange, which is to say they participate in a domestic payment system.

Offshore netting systems and offshore netting activity are easy to identify because the technology is subject to economies of scale and therefore requires many participants to be viable. Also, most netting services, whether in formal systems or informally between pairs of banks, are provided by a single third party, the Society for Worldwide Interbank Financial Telecommunications (SWIFT). Nearly all electronic netting activity can be accessed via SWIFT, which also provides the standard automated communications network for individual banks and for netting and domestic payment systems, effectively integrating worldwide netting and communications systems.

Third, implicit principal payments underlying foreign exchange derivatives of the CFD variety can be taxed via the derivative contract, wherein the currency principal implicitly traded is specified. The derivative contract is transferred between parties when it is bought and when it is executed. The price of the contract, reflecting expected net profits and risk, would be taxed directly via the payment made to purchase the contract. The implicitly traded principal would be taxed when the contract is executed. Since a derivative is a contract to trade, rather than an immediate trade, it leaves an 'audit trail' which can be accessed to enforce the tax. The contract is therefore treated as a virtual payment of principal. Like actual payments, derivative contracts can also be netted periodically, through 'netting by novation' (maintaining a running balance of net amounts due) in clearing houses and 'master agreements' for 'over-the-counter' (OTC) derivatives. Both methods also leave a record of transactions.

Currently there is little use of foreign exchange derivatives other than simple outright forwards and swaps. Other foreign exchange derivatives, such as options, are now normally settled with a transfer of a paper contract. However, should the market for CFD foreign exchange derivatives grow significantly, it is almost certain that the contracts will be prepared and exchanged electronically. SWIFT already offers an electronic confirmation and matching service for OTC derivatives. This means that implicit exchanges of foreign exchange principal, entailed by the purchase of a relevant CFD derivative contract, could be taxed just as explicit exchanges to settle spot market trades would be taxed.

A Tax on Interbank Foreign Exchange Transactions

In the retail market for foreign exchange, foreign exchange transactions occur between end users or between major trading banks and their customers. In the interbank market for foreign exchange they occur among major trading banks. We consider a tax on interbank foreign exchange transactions exclusively for two reasons. First, they are the natural target for a tax that aims to modify exchange rate behaviour; and second, since they have a well-defined and regulated settlement infrastructure, there is little scope to avoid the tax by shifting trading outside the interbank market. The Appendix and its accompanying Figures 15.1 to 15.4 outline the settlement infrastructure of the interbank foreign exchange market.

Participants in the interbank market for foreign exchange are called 'tier one' banks, while banks in the retail market may be 'tier two' or 'tier three' banks. Banks achieve tier one status on the basis of their financial and trading importance and their reputation for creditworthiness. This status provides them with direct access to the domestic payment system, which usually means having an account with the central bank. Selection of tier one banks requires the explicit or implicit agreement of the central bank as the ultimate guarantor of domestic financial stability. Like market makers on securities exchanges, tier one banks routinely make and accept offers to trade with other such banks, as well as with retail banks. They locate in major financial centres to take advantage of the liquidity available to facilitate domestic currency payments. This is also why banks trading in a foreign currency maintain foreign exchange trading balances in correspondent banks located in a financial centre of the foreign country (see Appendix, page 231).

Tier two and lower banks operating in the retail market for foreign exchange do not have direct access to the domestic payment system. They incur substantially higher transaction costs than tier one banks because of lost economies of scale and greater exposure to settlement, credit, liquidity and operating risks. To minimize these additional costs, retail banks keep domestic currency trading balances in correspondent banks with access to the domestic payment system. Retail foreign exchange transactions thus are also eventually settled in the interbank market.

We do not address a tax on open currency positions on overnight bank balance sheets,[9] from which international capital flows are measured. Overnight balance sheets reflect neither within-the-day and after-hours deals nor off-balance sheet trades, such as those using derivatives. These omissions are important because banks tend to avoid taking open overnight balance sheet positions, regarding them as too risky because of the high volume of trading that continues abroad.[10] They do take open currency positions during the day and off balance sheets.[11]

Overnight positions are taken primarily by non-bank financial institutions, such as hedge funds (private, closed-end investment funds) and institutional investors (mutual and pension funds, and insurance companies).[12] These are retail transactions processed in the interbank market via correspondent banks. The information gleaned from them and other transactions made by banks in the interbank market determines the daily exchange rate. For these reasons, an effective Tobin tax must be assessed on individual interbank foreign exchange transactions.

Settling Interbank Foreign Exchange Transactions

The settlement infrastructure in both foreign exchange and securities markets is evolving in response to rising trading volume, new technology and heightened awareness of settlement risk. The trend is to formalize and centralize settlement systems in order to exploit economies of scale and reduce or eliminate settlement risk. As a result, settlement systems in the interbank foreign exchange market look much like those of organized securities exchanges, which themselves are becoming more centralized through the sharing of clearing houses.

There are three ways to settle foreign exchange transactions in the interbank market. Each way is becoming more organized and the links between them are strengthening – a tendency that will be close to fulfilment with the achievement of full PVP foreign exchange settlement, expected with the creation of the CLS Bank, as described below.[13]

To settle interbank foreign exchange transactions one can:

- make a payment in the domestic payment system of the country that issues the currency being sold;

- cancel offsetting payments between traders in an offshore netting system; or

- use a foreign exchange CFD, where available. CFDs, like domestic financial derivatives, only require payment of profits or losses realized as a result of movements in the exchange rate relative to the notional principal amounts traded.

In practice these settlement methods are used sequentially, in reverse order. For example, a CFD could be used to define a trade, although currently this is very rare.[14] Payments arising from numerous trades involving all kinds of financial instruments, CFDs and others, are then netted, typically in an offshore netting system or securities clearing system. Finally, net amounts due are paid in domestic payment systems (Figure 15.3 illustrates the connection between netting and domestic payment systems for foreign exchange cash transactions; Figure 15.4 does the same for foreign exchange securities transactions).

Because the various ways to settle interbank foreign exchange transactions are used together, participants in netting systems are typically also members of the relevant domestic payment system, or keep foreign currency trading balances with a correspondent bank that is a member of the domestic payment system. This is also why both PVP foreign exchange settlement and Tobin's tax must be coordinated across settlement institutions to be effective.

Domestic Payment Systems

The most direct way to settle an interbank foreign exchange transaction is for each party to make a gross payment, consisting of a transfer of bank balances for the full sale of the currency, in the domestic payment system of the country that issues the currency (Figure 15.1). This means that the two or more payments needed to settle the transaction are made in different systems, possibly located in different time zones. Unless the payments are coordinated and the operating hours of the payment systems overlap, the payments occur at different times, creating settlement risk. In the case of domestic financial transactions where all payments are denominated in the domestic currency, however, there is no settlement risk if the linked payments are made simultaneously in the domestic payment system.

When PVP foreign exchange settlement is available in domestic payment systems, it will also be possible for gross payments from a single foreign exchange transaction to be matched and processed simultaneously. There are two ways to achieve this in domestic payment systems. One is to have all payment systems operate around the clock, so that operating hours continuously overlap. The other is to create a global settlement institution to process payments continuously, 24 hours a day, with direct links to domestic payment systems. This is the objective of the new CLS Bank, headquartered in New York with operations in New York and London. It is expected to open in mid-2000 (Figure 15.2).[15]

The CLS Bank concept was developed at the urging of the G10 central banks by a group of major foreign exchange trading banks. These banks organized in 1995 and created CLS Services Ltd (CLSS) in 1997. The CLS Bank is designed to settle worldwide trading in all major currencies.[16] It will eliminate settlement risk by simultaneously making the two or more payments of a foreign exchange transaction on its own accounts. Payments will be final by legal dispensation of the countries whose currencies are being settled. In most cases, the CLS Bank will be operationalized by giving it settlement accounts directly with central banks. In other cases, the CLS Bank will access domestic payment systems through correspondent banks. Effectively, the CLS Bank will be an extension of participating domestic payment systems.

Netting Systems

A complementary way to settle interbank foreign exchange transactions is to cancel periodically offsetting payments due among banks (Figure 15.3). Traditionally, this was done informally between pairs of banks, an activity that is hard to monitor systematically. Since the late 1980s, however, netting has increasingly occurred in formal systems exploiting new technology and economies of scale and using standard processes.[17] These systems are easy to identify and access.

New technology now permits continuous multilateral netting of payments in the various currencies of members located around the world. The greater the number of participants and currencies, the more effective the netting in terms of the volume and value of payments that can be offset against each other. For this reason, the leading multilateral and multicurrency netting systems – Exchange Clearing House Organization (ECHO) and Multinet International Bank (MIB) – are merging, with each other and with the CLS Bank, to create a global, one-stop, foreign exchange settlement institution. Netting systems are now able to settle up to 90 per cent of foreign exchange payments submitted to the system, compared to about 25 per cent for bilateral netting.[18]

Netting software and interfaces are also becoming standardized and automated in both formal systems and informal bilateral activity. Netting for both is now done by a common third party, SWIFT – a non-profit cooperative owned by banks – through its Accord service.[19] Accord is, in effect, a virtual central netting system encompassing both physically centralized netting institutions (including the new ECHO in London) and physically dispersed netting between pairs of banks. Hence, virtually all netting activity is now done through formal, centralized services.

Contracts for Differences

A relatively unexploited way to settle foreign exchange transactions is through CFDs. Like some domestic financial derivative instruments, CFDs allow parties to a trade to settle foreign exchange transactions by making a payment equal to the profit or loss due to movements in the exchange rate, without having to exchange principal amounts. This would be suited especially to trades made for speculative or hedging reasons, which involve round-trip flows in the foreign currency.

An early example of a CFD-like foreign exchange derivative is the Rolling Spot currency futures contract introduced by the Chicago Mercantile Exchange in 1993.[20] The contract is designed to replicate the net gain or loss from an overnight spot currency position, without requiring payments of the principal amount invested. When the Rolling Spot contract is not used, principal payments are made to purchase, and then sell, the foreign currency. This typically is achieved with a spot/next currency swap (a spot foreign exchange transaction coupled with an opposing one-day forward transaction). By contrast, when a Rolling Spot contract is purchased, one pays only the price of the contract, reflecting the overnight movement in the exchange rate, and the difference between overnight interest rates in the money markets of the two currencies, as specified by the contract. The sum of these two obligations, made in a single payment, is equal to the net gain or loss from an overnight spot currency position.

CFDs or similar derivative instruments are not yet important in the foreign exchange market.[21] Whether they can be introduced on a wide scale depends on their suitability to foreign exchange trading conventions. For example, the Rolling Spot contract was created to reduce the transactions costs of an oft-used means of taking a low-risk foreign exchange position.

It also depends on the adaptability of the means of settling foreign exchange derivative contracts so as to realize reductions in transactions costs.[22] Currently most foreign exchange derivatives are traded with a transfer of paper contracts. This is an unwieldy practice that results in frequent and risky confirmation and settlement delays.[23] Significant use of foreign exchange derivatives will almost certainly entail a systemic move to electronic contracts, at least for all but the most complex derivatives. Similarly, the rapid growth of offshore money markets and the global foreign exchange market was largely due to significant reductions in transactions costs following electronic automation and standardization of communications protocols.[24] Use of electronic derivative contracts is already beginning, encouraged by the BIS.[25] SWIFT's Accord service now offers automated confirmation and matching of electronic OTC derivative contracts.[26]

Requirements of a Feasible Transactions Tax

A tax on foreign exchange transactions is feasible if the settlement infrastructure permits one to identify and access gross foreign exchange payments in domestic payment and offshore netting systems and securities exchanges, and to identify and access the notionally traded currency specified in derivative contracts. In the light of this and the preceding discussion, necessary and sufficient conditions for achieving these capabilities are threefold:

- domestic payment and offshore netting systems must process gross foreign exchange payments or payment obligations, and match them to the originating individual foreign exchange transactions;

- central banks or their delegates must enforce Tobin's tax in offshore netting systems and securities exchanges; and

- CFD-type derivatives contracts must be accessible.

Three features of foreign exchange settlement systems satisfy these conditions. First, both domestic payment and offshore netting systems and securities clearing houses have technological capability for PVP settlement. Second, central banks regulate offshore netting systems, and have the means to identify such systems and enforce the regulations in them. Third, CFD derivative contracts specifying the notionally traded principal are exchanged when purchased or executed, and can be treated as explicit payments of principal for tax purposes.

Identifying Foreign Exchange Transactions

For tax feasibility, domestic payment systems must process gross payments individually for two reasons. The first is to match linked domestic financial payments, equivalent to PVP financial settlement, so as to distinguish them from foreign exchange payments. The second is to tax gross foreign exchange payments submitted directly to the payment system. Modern systems that simultaneously process linked gross payments are RTGS systems. The desire to achieve domestic financial PVP settlement is the reason why nearly all G10 countries – and many others, including Thailand, Hong Kong, Korea, the Czech Republic, and, soon, China – have RTGS payment systems.

RTGS domestic payment systems do not currently support PVP settlement of foreign exchange transactions, for institutional reasons outlined earlier that are unrelated to technological capacity. Thus, it is not currently possible directly to identify payments made to settle a foreign exchange transaction. Only the domestic currency payment passes through the domestic payment system and it is not matched to its counterpart in another payment system. With PVP domestic financial settlement one can, however, indirectly identify and tax foreign exchange payments as those that cannot be matched with a counterpart payment in the same currency. When PVP foreign exchange settlement is available in domestic payment systems, via the CLS Bank, it will be possible to identify directly, and tax, gross foreign exchange payments.

In RTGS systems, small processing or user fees are already routinely imposed on payments.[27] User fees are equivalent in application and effect to Tobin's tax except that they are applied to all payments rather than only to foreign exchange payments. Most foreign exchange payments are netted before being submitted to domestic payment systems. Hence, Tobin's tax must also be applied to gross payments submitted for netting at the point or during the process of netting. For this, netting systems must process gross payments individually, just as RTGS domestic payment systems do, and must be able to identify payments deriving from foreign exchange transactions. Netting systems can do this because, as a result of settlement risk controls imposed by central banks and their regulatory bodies, they operate PVP settlement in the netting process. This means that netting systems match multiple payments originating in a common transaction and then net them simultaneously, or not at all.

When a netting system accepts payments for netting, the original foreign exchange payment obligations between the two parties to a foreign exchange trade are replaced legally by payment obligations between each party and the netting system. That is, the netting system itself incurs payment obligations to confer payment finality, just as when payments are made in domestic payment systems. To eliminate the settlement risk exposure of the netting system, and ensure that the system does not make net loans to or receive net loans from its member trading banks (beyond certain limits allowed to enhance settlement liquidity in the netting system), it processes payments associated with a common foreign exchange trade simultaneously, according to the PVP principle. The netting system therefore does not take open foreign exchange positions. The transfer of the payment obligation from the traders to the netting system occurs when the gross payments have been successfully matched.[28] In the process it would be easy to identify foreign exchange payments automatically and systematically, and apply Tobin's tax.

Securities exchanges around the world also operate DVP netting and settlement in their clearing houses, for the same reasons as foreign exchange netting systems.[29] It is therefore also technologically easy to apply Tobin's tax to foreign exchange transactions intermediated by an exchange of securities (Figure 15.4).

Enforcing Tobin's Tax in Offshore Netting Systems

Although it is technologically possible to apply Tobin's tax in both domestic payment and netting systems, it remains to be shown that the tax can be enforced in offshore netting systems (the following discussion refers to foreign exchange netting systems, but is equally relevant to securities exchange clearing houses). There are two dimensions to this problem. One is the ability of central banks or their delegates to regulate recognized offshore netting systems. The other is their ability to identify netting systems or less formal netting activity.

Regulating offshore netting systems

The interest and ability of central banks and supervisory bodies to regulate offshore netting systems, and the willingness of netting systems to comply with such regulations, stem from the institutional links between the two systems. Net amounts owed by netting systems to their member banks, and vice versa, are paid in the domestic payment system of the relevant currency. This requires formal and legally defined links between netting and domestic payment systems. Netting systems are often offshore and process multiple currencies, so they maintain such links with numerous domestic payment systems.

Netting systems and their members maintain close ties to domestic payment systems for several reasons. First, net payments made in domestic payment systems have legal status, and the regulator of the domestic payment system can also confer legality on the gross payments that were settled by previous netting. This is important in the event of a default, when losses need to be distributed among members of the netting system. Legal status also renders payments made in the netting and domestic system irrevocable. Second, domestic money markets are integrated into the domestic payment system, and the central bank is ready to 'lend as a last resort' to safeguard the integrity of the system. Thus, credit and liquidity to support netting and payments are to hand. Third, the domestic financial and payment system is supervised and regulated to ensure the creditworthiness of member banks and control systemic risk. Only members of domestic payment systems have access to formal netting systems.[30]

Central banks or their delegated regulatory bodies are also interested in maintaining ties with netting systems. If a netting system were to fail, the viability of participants who are members of the domestic payment system would be at risk, as would the domestic financial system. The right of central banks individually and collectively to supervise netting procedures and risk control measures in offshore netting systems, for the purposes of controlling settlement risk specifically and financial stability generally, is codified in the Lamfalussy Minimum Standards and was recently reaffirmed.[31] The Standards establish three principles governing offshore supervision, which apply irrespective of the type of financial instrument or the payment netted.

First, their application should ensure that cross-border systems are subject to review 'as systems' by a single authority with responsibility to consider the system's impact in different countries. Second, they should provide a cooperative approach to ensure that the interests of different central banks and supervisory authorities are reflected in the oversight of any one system. Third, cooperation between central banks should help preserve the discretion of individual central banks with respect to interbank settlements in their domestic currency.[32]

These principles support both effective coordinated supervision of netting systems and the prerogative of individual central banks to maintain their own interpretation of measures necessary to preserve domestic financial stability. For example, ECHO, based in London, is regulated by the Bank of England in consultation with other interested central banks under the terms of the Lamfalussy Report.[33] To process a new currency, ECHO needs the permission of the central bank that issues the currency. This is granted depending on ECHOs settlement risk management safeguards and the legal enforceability of the netting process in the domestic payment system of the currency.

> We [ECHO] therefore need to work very closely with the local regulators on understanding how the local payment system works and to know the law on netting.... The central banks have agreed that trades in their respective currencies may be settled within the system and that the rules, operational structures and systems of ECHO are appropriate to their national markets.[34]

Similarly, the CLS Bank will be formed under US Federal law and supervised by the Federal Reserve: 'The [CLS] consortium's plan is in response to a demand by central banks that the private sector find a solution to the problems of settlement risk in foreign exchange markets....'[35]

Individual central banks reserve the right unilaterally to regulate any offshore netting system that processes its currency in order to control settlement risk. In accordance with the Lamfalussy Minimum Standards, the US Federal Reserve now requires systems that net obligations denominated in

US dollars to monitor and limit net amounts owed by each participant. The Federal Reserve also requires such systems to have procedures to prevent contagion effects in the event that the participant with the largest net amount owing is unable to make the payment. These procedures may include reversing the netting operation yielding the payment due and using collateral or the system's capital to cover the original gross amounts due.[36]

Central banks enforce regulations in offshore netting systems by exploiting the institutional links between them and the domestic payment system.

> To enforce these regulations, the Federal Reserve reserves the right to prohibit the use of Federal Reserve payment services to support fund transfers that are used to settle, directly or indirectly, obligations on large-dollar multilateral netting systems that do not meet the Lamfalussy Minimum Standards.... Moreover, in order for Federal Reserve Banks to monitor the use of intraday credit, no future or existing privately operated large-dollar multilateral netting system will be permitted to settle on the books of a Federal Reserve Bank unless its participants authorize the system to provide position data to the Reserve Bank on order.[37]

Hence, by refusing to process or settle net payments from non-cooperating systems, central banks can unilaterally enforce a netting tax in offshore systems netting payments of the domestic currency. They can also impose less onerous sanctions on members of the domestic payments system that participate in non-cooperating offshore netting systems.

Identifying offshore netting activity

It is easy to identify and regulate organized offshore netting systems that process a particular currency. For example, the preceding Federal Reserve requirements apply to all systems with three or more participants that net payments or foreign exchange contracts involving US dollars, and have on any given day net payments in any currency or currencies combined of more than US$500 million, or routinely process individual payments or foreign currency contracts with a daily average value larger than US$100,000. Further, netting systems that meet these threshold criteria are subject to the requirements if they or any of their participants are members of the Federal Reserve System, or if participants' net payments are settled through a Federal Reserve settlement account (one that is on the books of the Federal Reserve), which account belongs either to the netting system, the participants in the netting system, or their agents individually.

It is now also relatively easy to identify less formal netting activity between pairs of banks. This is because most such activity is done by SWIFT, which also provides the netting services of many formal netting systems such as ECHO. In addition, SWIFT provides the standard communications and messaging network among banks, as well as between banks and netting and domestic payment systems.[38] SWIFT is ubiquitous because it is cost-effective to have such sophisticated services provided by a central third party, and to standardize the services to achieve an automated and seamless interface between all participants in the foreign exchange settlement system. SWIFT's dual function as a virtual netting and interbank communications system enables automatic and electronic recording of the transit, matching, netting and final settlement history of foreign exchange payments. This would also facilitate coordination of Tobin's tax among netting and settlement systems.

SWIFT's main service is continuously to confirm, store, and deliver payments of bank balances, securities and OTC derivatives. Payments identify the sending and receiving banks and generate automatic status reports. SWIFT's Accord service also does continuous payment and OTC derivative contract monitoring, matching, and netting for individual banks and netting systems.[39] Accord provides both parties in a foreign exchange trade with accurate information about the progress of both payments from the time the trade is made through the netting process and the final payments in domestic payment systems.[40] Many domestic payment systems either use SWIFT's technology directly or allow payments sent between two or more banks via SWIFT to be reformatted electronically and channeled through the domestic payment system without further intervention. SWIFT also automatically copies payment information to the operator of the domestic payment system so as to reduce errors or delays. SWIFT is therefore an integral part of domestic payment systems.

Taxing Foreign Exchange Derivatives

Most foreign exchange derivatives in use today, such as outright forward and swap contracts, do not challenge the feasibility of Tobin's tax, since they have no purchase price and require payments upon execution of the principal amounts of the currencies traded.[41] Foreign exchange options, which have a price and may never be executed, and CFDs, which do not require payment of principal, need closer examination.

The price of a foreign exchange option reflects the expected profit from an open position or the value of the reduction in risk when an open position is hedged. The price or value of the option can be taxed when payment is made to purchase the contract, just as payments to settle spot or forward foreign exchange transactions would be taxed. If the option is executed, the resulting payments of principal would be taxed in the same way.

Principal payments underlying foreign exchange derivatives that are purchased but not executed, such as foreign exchange options, would also be reached effectively by Tobin's tax, via the arbitrage relationship with the synthetic equivalent of the derivative contract. The value of a derivative contract depends on its underlying financial instrument. In the case of a foreign exchange derivative, the underlying instruments are the relevant currencies. Hence, a derivative contract can always be duplicated synthetically by spot or forward foreign exchange transactions, in combination with parallel domestic money market transactions in each of the two currencies. Arbitrage by major foreign exchange trading banks, entailing purchases of both derivative contracts and execution of their synthetic equivalents (but not necessarily in a one-to-one ratio), ensures that both methods of achieving a given foreign exchange position are equally valued, after accounting for differences in transactions costs. Indeed, the more complex derivatives are priced on the basis of this arbitrage relationship.

CFD-type foreign exchange derivatives are specifically designed to obviate the need to make principal payments. Just as in the case of OTC domestic financial derivatives, however, standard CFD contracts must specify the face value or notional principal currency amounts traded, on which profits or losses resulting from movements in exchange rates are calculated. Tobin's tax could then be assessed on the principal implicitly traded, as coded into the CFD contract or electronic template. This treats the CFD contract itself as a foreign currency payment, and will be easier to do as contracts are increasingly made and exchanged electronically, just like explicit payments.

How to Implement a Foreign Exchange Transactions Tax

Unlike foreign exchange trading, the global infrastructure for making payments to settle interbank foreign exchange transactions is formal, organized and regulated. This development is due to new technology, rising trading volume and efforts to eliminate settlement risk. Thus, while there are serious doubts about the feasibility of imposing a foreign exchange transactions tax on foreign exchange trades, it seems feasible to collect the same tax on the payments made to settle foreign exchange trades.

It is now possible to match gross payments automatically, electronically and seamlessly to the originating individual foreign exchange transactions, and tax them both onshore and offshore, regardless of the financial instrument used to define the terms of the transaction or the location of the parties to the transaction. This can be done by coordinating a payments tax across domestic payment systems and offshore netting systems, and treating CFD-type foreign exchange derivative contracts as actual payments of the notional principal amounts traded. The technological means for doing this are available in the RTGS domestic payment and PVP offshore netting systems, linked by the standard interbank and netting communications systems and protocols implemented by SWIFT. The enforcement mechanisms are the same as those now used to ensure PVP netting offshore.

Appendix

Figures 15.1–15.4

Figures 15.1 to 15.4 illustrate various features of the foreign exchange inter-bank settlement infrastructure referred to in the text.

Foreign exchange trades are made among banks in financial centres around the world and between banks in different centres. The figures identify financial centres by the currency of the country in which they are located and by the name of the domestic payment system. Fedwire processes dollars in New York; Clearing House Automated Payment System (CHAPS) processes pounds sterling in London; and the Bank of Japan (BOJ-NET) processes yen in Tokyo. Banks within centres are so labelled: 'N' denotes banks and other financial institutions in New York; 'L' banks in London; and 'T' banks in Tokyo.

Since there will not be any global payment system until mid-2000, and each foreign exchange transaction involves payments in two currencies, trading banks make payments in the domestic payment systems of the currencies involved in the trade (Figure 15.1). To do so they use 'correspondent' banks located in the countries that issue the traded currencies. Correspondents are banks or other financial institutions with access to the domestic payment system for a currency (tier one banks). This means that they have an account with the central bank that issues the currency, because payments are ultimately made by entries debiting the sender's account and crediting the recipient's account on the books of the central bank. Domestic banks which do not have an account with the central bank (so-called second or third tier banks) use domestic correspondent banks to make payments.

In the figures, correspondent relationships between banks are indicated by bank identifiers having the same whole number digit (to the left of the decimal point). For example, N3 and L3 in Figure 15.1 have a correspondent banking relationship, as do N1.1 and N1 in Figure 15.3. There are two second tier banks in Figure 15.3, both in New York, identified by a digit to the right of the decimal point (N1.1 and N2.1). The others are first tier banks.

In Figure 15.1 an agreement to exchange bank balances denominated in US dollars and pounds sterling, respectively, is made between traders located in the two associated centres (New York and London). Settling the agreement requires two payments, one of dollars and the other of sterling. In this case, since only one trade is pictured, there are no opportunities to net payments. The transaction is completed when the two payments are made in the associated payment systems, not necessarily simultaneously.

Figure 15.2 illustrates a similar foreign exchange transaction, this time involving yen and pounds sterling. However, in this case there is PVP settlement of the transaction, whereby the payments of yen and sterling are matched and made simultaneously in the CLS Bank. The CLS Bank is a central payment system with direct links to offshore netting systems (ECHO) and domestic payment systems.

Foreign exchange payments may also be made by cancelling offsetting payments in offshore systems. In Figure 15.3 the netting system is ECHO, the most ambitious of the multilateral netting systems. The figure illustrates ECHO's netting of payment obligations created by two foreign exchange transactions. One is a retail trade between tier two banks in New York. This trade is settled for the tier two banks by their tier one correspondent banks, also in New York. The other trade is an interbank trade between tier one banks in New York. The two trades require four payments, three of which are denominated in foreign currency and are sent to ECHO for processing. The payment denominated in domestic currency (dollars) is sent directly to Fedwire in New York. At ECHO there is an opportunity to net payments, since the yen payment by N2 is partially offset by the yen payment from N1. After netting, ECHO makes payments of the remaining amounts due in yen and sterling in Tokyo and London, respectively. Netting results in a volume reduction of one payment and a value reduction of 540 yen in domestic payment systems.

In general, payments of net amounts due from offshore netting systems such as ECHO are made in domestic payment systems (Figure 15.3) or in the CLS Bank (Figure 15.2). ECHO may have access to domestic payment systems via correspondent banks (Figure 15.3) or may have direct access, as in the CLS Bank (Figure 15.2).

For the purposes of Tobin's tax, securities clearing houses operate much like foreign exchange netting systems. Figure 15.4 illustrates a foreign exchange transaction settled by an exchange of securities denominated in different currencies. Net payments from securities clearing houses are also made in domestic payment systems.

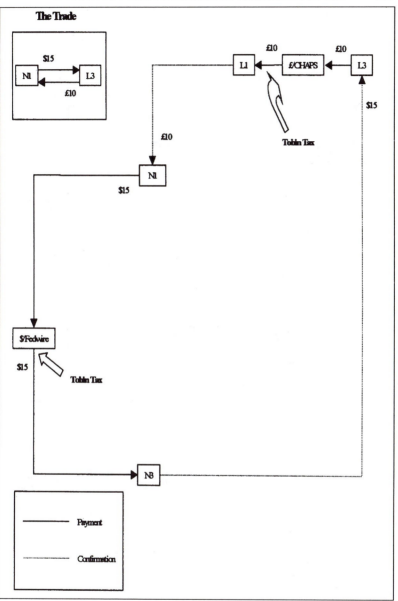

Figure 15.1 Settling a Foreign Exchange Trade in Domestic Payments Systems

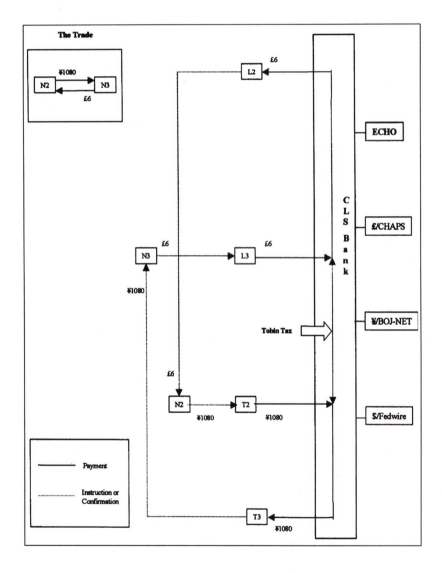

Figure 15.2 PVP Foreign Exchange Settlement

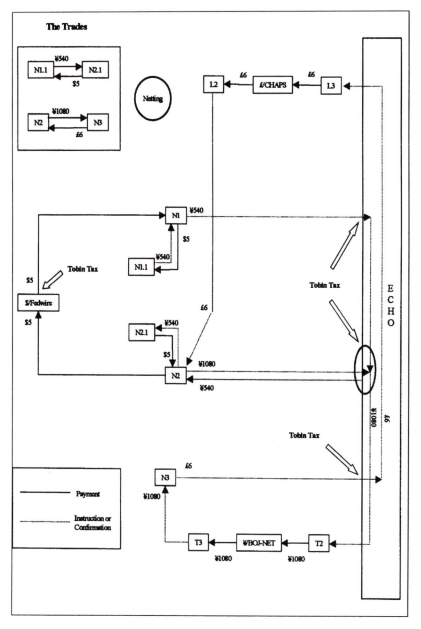

Figure 15.3 Offshore Netting of Foreign Exchange Trades

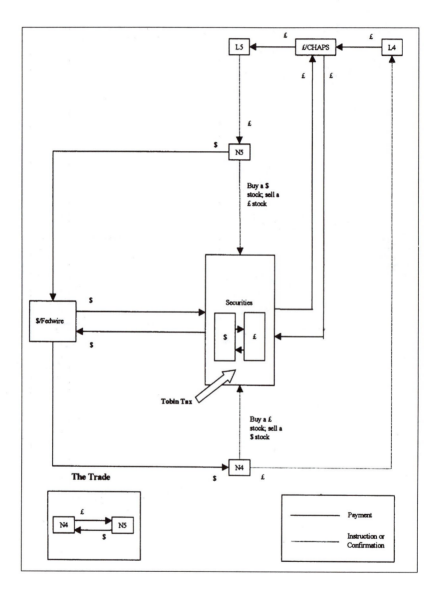

Figure 15.4 A Foreign Exchange Trade intermediated by a Securities Trade

Notes

The paper on which this chapter is based was written for the North–South Institute. I would like to thank Roy Culpeper, President, the participants in a North–South seminar and, especially, Patrick Georges for helpful comments on earlier drafts, without implicating them in the views expressed in this paper or in any remaining flaws.

1 Tobin, J. (1978: 153–9) 'A Proposal for International Monetary Reform', *The Eastern Economic Journal*, Vol. 4.
2 See ul Haq, M., I. Kaul, and I. Grunberg, eds (1996) *The Tobin Tax: Coping with Financial Volatility*, Oxford University Press, New York; Eichengreen, B., Tobin, J. and Wyplosz, C. (1995) 'Two Cases for Sand in the Wheels of International Finance', *Economic Journal*, 105; and Felix, D. (1995) 'Financial Globalization vs. Free Trade: The Case for the Tobin Tax', Discussion Paper 108, UNCTAD, Geneva.
3 See ul Haq, M., I. Kaul, and I. Grunberg, eds (1996), *The Tobin Tax: Coping with Financial Volatility*, Oxford University Press, New York; Frankel, J. (1996) 'Recent Exchange-Rate Experience and Proposals for Reform', *AEA Papers and Proceedings*, Vol. 86, No. 2; and Garber, P. and Taylor, M. (1995) 'Sand in the wheels of foreign exchange markets: a Skeptical Note', *Economic Journal*, 105.
4 Frankel, J. (1996: 156).
5 See Eichengreen, B., Tobin, J. and C. Wyplosz (1995).
6 Garber, P. and M. Taylor (1995).
7 Garber, P. (1998) 'Derivatives in International Capital Flow', *Working Paper 6623*, National Bureau of Economic Research.
8 Garber, P. and M. Taylor (1995).
9 Kennen, P. (1996: 109–28) 'The Feasibility of Taxing Foreign Exchange Transactions', in ul Haq, M., Kaul, I. and I. Grunberg, eds.
10 Ul Haq, M., Kaul, I. and I. Grunberg, eds (1996).
11 See Garber, P. (1998); Lyons, R. (1991) 'Private Beliefs and Information Externalities in the Foreign Exchange Market', *Working Paper 3889*, National Bureau of Economic Research; Lyons, R. (1995) 'Tests of Microstructural Hypotheses in the Foreign Exchange Market', *Journal of Financial Economics* 39: 321–51; and Lyons, R. and A. Rose (1995) 'Explaining Forward Exchange Bias … Within-the-Day', *Working Paper 4982*, National Bureau of Economic Research.
12 IMF (1993) 'Exchange Rate Management and International Capital Flows', Part I of *International Capital Markets*, International Monetary Fund, Washington, DC.
13 CLS Services Ltd (1998) *An Introduction to Continuous Linked Settlement*, brochure.
14 See Garber, P. (1998).
15 CLS Services Ltd (1998).
16 *Financial Times*, 27 June 1997.
17 See Summers, B. (1991) 'Clearing and Payment Systems: the Role of the Central Bank', *Federal Reserve Bulletin* Vol. 77, No. 2: 81–91; and IMF (1996) 'Developments, Prospects and Key Policy Issues', Part I of *International Capital Markets*, International Monetary Fund, Washington, DC.
18 Perold, A. (1995: 33–80) 'The Payment System and Derivative Instruments', in Crane, D., Froot, K., Mason, S., Perold, A., Merton, R., Bodie, Z., Sirri E., and P. Tufano. (eds), *The Global Financial System: A Functional Perspective*, Harvard Business School Press, Boston.
19 See BIS (1993) *Payment Systems in the Group of Ten Countries*, Bank for International Settlements, Basle; and BIS (1998a) 'OTC Derivatives: Settlement Procedure and Counterparty Risk Management', *Technical Report*, Bank for International Settlements, Basle.
20 Perold, A. (1995: 74) in *The Global Financial System: A Functional Perspective*.
21 See Garber, P. (1998).

22 Bank for International Settlements (BIS) (1998b) 'Reducing Foreign Exchange Settlement Risk: a Progress Report', Technical Report, Bank for International Settlements, Basle.

23 BIS (1998a).

24 Perold, A. (1995) in *The Global Financial System: A Functional Perspective*.

25 BIS (1998a).

26 BIS (1998a).

27 Summers, B. (1991: 81–91) 'Clearing and Payment Systems: The Role of the Central Bank', *Federal Reserve Bulletin*, Vol. 77, No. 2.

28 See BIS (1998b) and ECHO (1998), Exchange Clearing House Organization, 10 October 1998, <http://www.exchangeclearinghouse.co.uk/>.

29 BIS (1992) 'Delivery versus Payment in Securities Settlement Systems', *Technical Report*, Bank for International Settlements, Basle; Borio, C. and P. Van den Bergh. (1993) 'The Nature and Management of Payment System Risks: an International Perspective', *BIS Economic Papers 36*, Bank for International Settlements; and *Economist*, 9 May 1998.

30 BIS (1990) Report of the Committee on Interbank Netting Schemes of the Central Banks of the Group of Ten Countries (Lamfalussy Report), *Technical Report*, Bank for International Settlements, Basle.

31 BIS, 1998b; BIS, 1990.

32 BIS, 1990, p. 7.

33 CLS Services Ltd, 1998.

34 ECHO, 1998.

35 *Financial Times*, 27 June 1997.

36 Federal Reserve (1994) Policy Statement on Privately Operated Large-dollar Multilateral Netting Systems, U.S. Federal Register 59/249 Part IV, US Federal Reserve.

37 *Ibid.*

38 Perold (1995); BIS (1993).

39 BIS (1998a); BIS (1993).

40 ECHO (1998).

41 BIS (1998a).

Index